Base Ball 10

Base Ball 10

New Research on the Early Game

Edited by
Don Jensen

McFarland & Company, Inc., Publishers
Jefferson, North Carolina

ISSN 1934-2802

ISBN (print) 978-1-4766-6385-2
ISBN (ebook) 978-1-4766-2332-0

softcover : acid free paper ∞

Back issue requests to McFarland by mail
at Box 611, Jefferson NC 28640, by phone at 800-253-2187,
by fax at 336-246-5018, or online at www.mcfarlandpub.com.

© 2018 McFarland & Company, Inc., Publishers. All rights reserved

*No part of this book may be reproduced or transmitted in any form
or by any means, electronic or mechanical, including photocopying
or recording, or by any information storage and retrieval system,
without permission in writing from the publisher.*

Front cover: "The American national game of base ball,"
Currier & Ives lithograph, 1866

Printed in the United States of America

McFarland & Company, Inc., Publishers
Box 611, Jefferson, North Carolina 28640
www.mcfarlandpub.com

Table of Contents

Editor's Note   vii

Articles

Addie Joss and the Benefit Game
    JOHN MCMURRAY   1

Unraveling a Baseball Mystery
    JOHN THORN   21

Better Than Creighton
    ERIC MIKLICH   31

Ballplayer for Hire: The Life and Times of Charles "Famous" Krause
    JUSTIN MCKINNEY   46

Mother Watson: A Look Back at One of 19th Century Baseball's Most Obscure Players
    BILL LAMB   59

Doctoring the Ball: The Underrated Role of Physicians in the Rise of Early Baseball
    THOMAS W. GILBERT   70

Baseball's Financial Revolution of 1866 and the Rise of Professionalism
    RICHARD HERSHBERGER   84

Early Baseball and Journalism in the Midwest: Illinois College and Illinois Baseball
    STEVE HOCHSTADT *and* JAMES BRANDON TERRY   99

Table of Contents

Binding the (Baseball) Nation: The National Base Ball Club's Tour of 1867
    BOB THOLKES 120

The Catch Heard Around the World
    GARY SARNOFF 131

Baseball and the Yellow Peril: Waseda University's 1905 American Tour
    ROBERT K. FITTS 141

A Closer Look at the Pennsylvania Base Ball Club
    PETER MORRIS 160

"The American Ideal of Manly Beauty": Isaac Broome's *Base Ball Vase*, 1875–76
    JAMES E. BRUNSON III 167

Never on a Sunday: Baseball's Battles with the Blue Laws in Rochester
    ALAN COHEN 190

Book Reviews 203

Contributors 222

Index 225

Editor's Note

Welcome to the new incarnation of *Base Ball: A Journal of the Early Game*. A journal since its launch in 2007, *Base Ball* here begins its run as an annual book. The change is intended primarily to harness each volume to McFarland's strengths—namely, the publisher's book-oriented production, sales, and marketing activities—and expose contributors' research to a broader audience. The goal, however, remains the same: publication of the highest possible scholarly work on baseball before 1920.

As the new editor, I firmly intend to maintain the high standards established by my predecessor, founding editor John Thorn. *Base Ball* will continue to feature groundbreaking research, good writing, and fascinating illustrations on a variety of topics. But I also hope to explore some new areas (both thematic and geographical), even as we continue to examine longstanding subjects of interest to the baseball community—the game's origins, new looks at old controversies, long-ignored players and teams, and the game off the diamond, especially its social history. The book review section reappears here after an absence of some years. In the years ahead, we will also introduce new departments.

This tenth volume offers a varied menu for your consideration. John McMurray paints a memorable picture of the Addie Joss benefit game in 1911, an event better remembered today than the career of the tragic Hall of Fame pitcher himself, who died at age 31. The contest was unremarkable but represented the greatest collection of talent assembled on a baseball field prior to the first official All-Star Game in 1933. John Thorn and Eric Miklich examine the short career and long legacy of Jim Creighton, the game's most famous early star. Although Creighton has appeared often on these pages, both authors tackle the man and the legend from new perspectives. Thorn reexamines one of the game's most celebrated and valuable images, the 1866 Currier & Ives lithograph "American National Game of Base Ball: Grand Match for the Championship at the Elysian Fields, Hobo-

Editor's Note

ken, N.J." He concludes that it depicts a fantasy game with a rare image of Creighton. Miklich compares Creighton's brief career with that of a contemporary, Joe Sprague of the Eckford Club of Brooklyn, and argues that Sprague may have been even better than the legendary hurler.

Justin Mckinney and Bill Lamb remind us of the far more numerous 19th-century ballplayers who fell well short of legend status. Mckinney's profile of the nomadic Charles "Famous" Krause shows how one player parlayed the gift of self-promotion and entrepreneurship into a career, making stops with 16 clubs—if also wearing out his welcome quickly with most of them. Lamb does a skillful job of making the career of the only player in major league history ever nicknamed "Mother" less obscure.

Topics focusing on baseball off the field range widely. Thomas W. Gilbert shows us that a surprising number of individuals who held leadership positions in the first clubs and associations in New York were physicians. Lacking a scientific understanding of infection, reformist physicians believed that cleanliness, fresh air and physical fitness were keys to fighting disease and improving public health. These doctors saw the potential of adult participant sports to popularize exercise nationally and eventually succeeded with baseball. *Base Ball* stalwart Richard Hershberger, meanwhile, examines the game's financial revolution in 1866, when clubs started charging 25 cents to attend games rather than the established price of 10 cents, and describes how that change contributed to the rise of fully professional teams.

Several articles in this volume deepen our understanding of the game's geographical spread. Steve Hochstadt and James Brandon Terry show how baseball and sports journalism developed in a particular college in Illinois and throughout the Midwest. The 1867 western tour of the National Base Ball Club of Washington, D.C., is Bob Tholkes' topic. He chronicles the club's startling defeat in Chicago following several one-sided matches and discusses the effect of the tour on the remainder of the club's season and on subsequent tours. Record crowds, Bob notes, were attracted everywhere. Gary Sarnoff likewise looks to the Nation's Capital for his subject, the day in August 1908 when catcher Gabby Street caught a ball dropped from the top of the Washington monument.

As always, we highlight the social context of the early game. The racial prejudice that greeted the tour of the Waseda University baseball team in California in 1905 is the focus of Robert K. Fitts' contribution. The visit, he points out, also sparked the creation of Japanese American baseball and inspired the eventual development of a truly international game. Historian

Editor's Note

Peter Morris challenges the existing scholarship on the social class of antebellum baseball clubs. In his article he disagrees with David Voigt's description of the pre–Civil War Pennsylvania Club of Philadelphia as one of the era's rare blue-collar clubs. Morris calls for a review of earlier assumptions on this subject in light of the growing amount of digitized nineteenth-century demographic source material. We return to the subject of baseball and art in James E. Brunson III's study of *Base Ball Vase*, an art object portraying a white ballplayer, designed by Trenton, New Jersey's Etruria Pottery for the Philadelphia Centennial Exhibition of 1876. Brunson emphasizes the work's darker side, noting that it belongs to a class of art that reinforced notions of class, gender, and race, especially as it contributed to a cultural discourse of white racial masculinity. The battle over ball playing on Sunday is taken up by Alan Cohen, who focuses on the struggle in Rochester, New York. He vividly chronicles the interrupted games, arrests, legal maneuvering, lawsuits, and trials over the issue, which eventually forced the Rochester Brownies to move to Montreal in July 1897.

Finally, our revived book review section takes up three recent works and a golden oldie. (It would be wrong to say there is a canon of work on the early game, but from time to time we hope to include articles of possible interest to readers seeking to build a library of essentials.) In this department Richard Hershberger evaluates Robert B. Ross's recent book on the Great Player Revolt. Steve West looks at Richard Bressler's volume on 1910, which saw the end of one dynasty (Cubs) and the beginning of another (A's). Bill Scheeren examines Jim Leeke's award-winning account of baseball during World War I. Not least, Peter Mancuso reappraises Voigt's work on the game in the 1890s and pronounces it a keeper.

I welcome your comments and suggestions.

Don Jensen

Addie Joss and the Benefit Game
John McMurray

Most baseball fans are aware of the celebrated Addie Joss benefit game, but how the game came to be played and the details of the game itself are seldom discussed in any depth. No other game in the early 20th century came close to rivaling this one for its star power, as Ty Cobb, Walter Johnson, and Cy Young were among the participants. It was Joss' esteemed place in the game of baseball, both as a player and as a person, which inspired this groundbreaking event. Even if the game itself often included lackluster play, the Joss benefit game laid the groundwork for the first All-Star Game, held twenty-two years later. That Addie Joss is most recalled for the benefit game held in his honor rather than for his Hall of Fame playing career speaks to the game's remarkable place in baseball lore.

For all of its name recognition, most baseball followers know little about the Addie Joss benefit game, played in Cleveland on July 24, 1911, and held to honor Joss' memory in order to provide monetary support to the family of the Cleveland Naps' recently-deceased star pitcher.[1] Indeed, the contest is remembered mostly for its participants rather than for anything that happened on the field. Still, not only was it the precursor of the modern All-Star Game, but the game's resonance more than a century later also speaks to Joss' oft-unappreciated impact on baseball in the early 20th century.

The tale of the game is usually told through a photograph of what were called "The All-Stars," a team of prominent American League players set to play the Cleveland Naps for the benefit of Joss' widow, Lillian, and their two young children. In it are two rows of essential figures from the early century: Bobby Wallace, Frank Baker, Joe Wood, Walter Johnson, Hal Chase, Clyde Milan, Russ Ford, and Eddie Collins in the back. Germany

Addie Joss and the Benefit Game

Schaefer, Tris Speaker, Sam Crawford, Jimmy McAleer, Ty Cobb, Gabby Street, and Paddy Livingston were in the front.[2]

With the All-Stars having seven eventual Hall of Famers on their roster and the Naps having two (Napoleon Lajoie and Cy Young), the *New York Tribune* may have been understated in its appraisal the day after the game that "rarely has such a luminous gathering appeared on the same diamond."[3] Another contemporary account was more robust: "Galaxy of diamond luminaries is all the humble scribe can attempt but that is very tame. It is safe to say that never before in the history of the national game have so many real ball players appeared on one lot for a single game of the pastime."[4]

In spite of the game's perceived novelty, another benefit game had been held slightly more than one year earlier to support the family of Philadelphia Athletics catcher Mike "Doc" Powers, who died at age 39 in 1909. That event at Shibe Park drew more than 12,000 fans and approximately $8,000, a hefty sum at the time. Because they were the only teams with no games scheduled for that day, only the four eastern American League teams (Boston, Philadelphia, New York, and Washington) participated. Hence, the Doc Powers benefit necessarily lacked the star power of the Joss game, which fielded an All-Star team from across the American League.[5] A game to benefit Boston catcher, Charlie Bennett, who lost both legs in a train accident, also had been held in August 1894 between the Beaneaters and a team of local college players.

Today, the Addie Joss benefit game is perhaps second only to the Fred Merkle game among well-remembered events from the Deadball Era. Whereas the Merkle game is scrutinized for specific on-field events, the Joss benefit game is recalled largely because of the occasion rather than for its specific details. In the game itself, Joe Birmingham's outfield assists in three consecutive innings and Hal Chase's 17 chances accepted at first base remain perhaps the most noteworthy on-field achievements from that day.[6] Few summaries of the benefit game itself exist, and it remains the least known of baseball's widely celebrated games. To understand how the Joss benefit game came to be and how it unfolded as it did, it is important to examine Joss' impact on contemporary baseball and the events following his death.

Joss' Stature in the Game

By any standard, Joss was one of the most dominant pitchers in baseball history. His biographer, Scott H. Longert, wrote that, on many days,

Joss was "absolutely King of the Pitchers."[7] His career exemplified both great achievement and remarkable consistency: Joss won twenty games four times, led the American League in earned run average twice, never had a losing season, walked more than 50 batters in a single season only once, and shut out the opposition in 45 of his 160 victories. Had there been an award for the top pitcher in baseball, Joss likely would have received it in both 1907 and 1908. Joss was efficient and never accumulated strikeouts with much frequency, resembling, in those respects, Deacon Phillippe and Sam Leever rather than Walter Johnson and Ed Walsh.[8]

Even with his sterling 160–97 overall record, however, Joss' nine-year Cleveland career was short.[9] His peak years of pitching brilliance were between 1905 and 1908, during which he won at least twenty games each season and did not have an ERA above 2.01 during that span. Since Joss pitched in only 13 games in the 1910 season, his last in the major leagues due to ligament problems in his pitching elbow, it is unclear whether the second half of his career would have been equal to the first.[10]

His pitching style was distinctive: Joss was known as the "Human Hairpin" for the way he twisted around and hid the ball in his delivery. "Joss had not only great speed and a fast-breaking curve, but a very effective pitching motion, bringing the ball from behind him with a complete body swing and having it on the batter almost before the latter got sight of it."[11]

Joss is best recalled for his perfect game against Chicago's Walsh on October 2, 1908, delivered near the peak of a hotly-contested pennant race with the Naps one-half game out of first place and only five games to play. Joss, under enormous situational pressure, pitched a perfect game with only 74 pitches.[12] The 1–0 victory, during which Walsh gave up only four hits himself, was recounted by Frederick G. Lieb in 1924 as "what is generally classed as the greatest pitching duel of the ages."[13] A retrospective published nearly 80 years later noted that "many reporters have called it the greatest game ever pitched."[14] That Joss would no-hit the White Sox again, on April 20, 1910, thus becoming the first pitcher to hold the same team hitless twice, only enhanced his reputation.

Yet while many of his contemporaries are well-recalled today, Joss remains a shadowy figure. "He lives for us in the mists of baseball's mythological past in posed pitching images and stiff portraits and vague recollections of distant tragedy," wrote Longert.[15] Joss' on-field image is that of workmanlike efficiency with a taciturn, if almost forlorn, approach. In contrast to many ballplayers of the period, there are neither jarring out-of-character anecdotes about Joss to report nor controversial quotes to explain.

Addie Joss and the Benefit Game

While Joss is admired, there is no sense that his personality is known or understood in any depth, the way there might be with, say, Ty Cobb or Honus Wagner. These accumulated factors may be why Longert noted in 1998 that "Addie Joss is a nearly forgotten name as we approach the 100th anniversary of his rookie season."[16] Even in *The Glory of Their Times*, the definitive oral history of the Deadball Era, Joss is mentioned only once, in passing.[17]

What is missing from the calculation is the reverence with which Joss was held by his contemporaries. In a rough-and-tumble era, Joss was a unifying and well-loved figure who was a model teammate and who took no part in the many rivalries and rumbles which often characterized early-century baseball. "Never before had a player of such stature, and one so respected, died while still in the game," wrote baseball historian John Husman.[18]

That Ty Cobb and Napoleon Lajoie, bitter rivals in the famously acrimonious 1910 batting race from only a year before, could put their differences aside to be part of the Joss benefit game speaks to the high regard in which Joss was held around baseball.[19] It is fair to say that few contemporary players would have inspired such a reaction at his death, which led to such an extraordinary outpouring of grief and support. Joss' stature in baseball was the motivating force.

The Death of Addie Joss

Joss pitched his final game in the major leagues on July 25, 1910, during which he was ineffective in five innings against the Philadelphia Athletics. An "ailing elbow," which had curtailed Joss' effectiveness since June 5, proved too much for him to endure.[20] Joss did not pitch during the remainder of the 1910 regular season but did head to Hot Springs, Arkansas, for spring training with the team in 1911. Though Joss initially experienced no pain in his arm, his symptoms began to recur when he made use of all of his pitches.[21]

On April 3, 1911, before the Naps were to play an exhibition game against the Chattanooga Lookouts in Tennessee, Joss collapsed into the arms of Rudy Hulswitt, the onetime St. Louis Cardinals shortstop now playing for the Lookouts, in the middle of a friendly conversation. The initial consensus was that Joss had suffered heatstroke on a hot day. In spite of an ambulance being called, Joss rallied and rejoined the team the next day.[22]

Soon thereafter, when the team was on the train, Joss experienced pain in his chest. His personal physician, Dr. George W. Chapman, believed Joss' affliction to be either "nervous indigestion or maybe ptomaine poisoning," according to Longert. Joss lost weight rapidly, suffered from a diminished appetite, and had sunken cheeks. His poor health was evident to those who saw him. A further examination by Chapman on April 9 resulted in a diagnosis of pleurisy, a respiratory infection. According to Longert, though, while Chapman noted Joss' breathing difficulties in making the diagnosis of a severe attack of pleurisy, Chapman neglected to pay sufficient attention to Joss' loss of appetite and abrupt weight loss—both of which were potential symptoms of tuberculosis.[23] Joss soon experienced a quick physical decline, highlighted by intense coughing and a relentless headache. He was in excruciating pain. Dr. Morrison Castle, the Naps' team physician, performed a lumbar puncture, draining fluid from Joss' spine for analysis.[24] "There was no way to sugarcoat the findings," wrote Longert. "Addie had contracted tubercular meningitis."[25] Longert suggests that Joss, a pool devotee, may have inhaled the bacteria at a pool hall which he owned and frequented.[26]

Few photographs of Joss's delivery exist. This posed shot bears a 1911 copyright. The great pitcher died that April. (Bain News Service, Library of Congress).

Joss' physical descent from the illness was steep. He died in the early morning hours on April 14, 1911, two days into the baseball season at his family home in Toledo. "[I]n his fight with the grim destroyer he was confident of recovery until almost the last. He remained conscious until a short time before death, a contemporary *Plain Dealer* (Cleveland, OH) account said.[27] "The final struggle" against the illness was "hopelessly one-sided."[28] Joss' mother, Theresa Joss, came to the house from her home in Wisconsin, inquiring how her son was doing. When she saw the wreath of flowers on the door just after entering the house, she fainted, realizing then that her son had died. She then had to be carried into the house. Regarding Joss'

Addie Joss and the Benefit Game

wife, the *Plain Dealer* reported: "Mrs. Joss, jr. [sic], although a very much griefstricken [sic] woman, is bearing up wonderfully under the strain."[29]

Beyond being a preeminent baseball star, Joss had a unique celebrity in his hometown of Toledo. Recognized for owning a popular billiard hall, Joss in 1906 also had begun writing baseball columns for *The Toledo News-Bee*, becoming a charter member of the Baseball Writers Association of America. In his popular column "Winter Base Ball by Addie Joss," which always included a large photo of the pitcher alongside his byline, Joss offered both general commentary and opinions about the modern game.[30]

Beyond the human impact of Joss' death, his passing would have a notable impact on the 1911 baseball season. The Naps, buoyed by the remarkable rookie season of pitcher Vean Gregg and outfielder Joe Jackson posting the highest batting average of his career (.408), rose to the first division in 1911, finishing in third place in the American League. While it is a stretch to say that Cleveland could have made up a 22-game margin with the Philadelphia Athletics if Joss had been healthy, Cleveland might have been at least in pennant contention were it not for Joss' extraordinary misfortune.

Joss' death, therefore, had such a strong local resonance because he was known across the community for his several endeavors and was held in especially high esteem both as an athlete and as a person. In that sense, he bore some similarity to Christy Mathewson. The shock of Joss' abrupt passing was a compounding factor: "The particular sad feature of Joss' death was the total unpreparedness of the public for the news, for it was only a week ago Wednesday that Joss was running his billiard parlor on St. Clair-st [sic] looking apparently as well as ever."[31]

Praise for Joss following his death was widespread. In its depth and breadth, the outpouring of grief was similar to that which Lou Gehrig would receive upon his death in 1941. Lajoie said: "Having admired [Joss] so deeply the mere thought of never again being associated with him is appalling." Said Cy Young: "You can't say anything too good for Addie Joss. My baseball experience has thrown me with practically every man in the big leagues for more than twenty years, but I never met a fairer or squarer man than Addie."[32]

Given these emotional attachments, Joss' funeral on April 17 became a place for collective grief. "The baseball world was stunned. Joss' funeral, at Toledo, Ohio, where he made his home, was a major event," wrote Husman. "Hundreds attended, from the whole spectrum of society."[33] Even several players from the Tigers team, which was originally scheduled to play

Cleveland in Detroit that day, attended his funeral, which "showed how high Joss' character was perceived around the league."[34]

Still, whether to postpone that day's Naps-Tigers game had been a point of contention. Ban Johnson, the American League president, originally insisted that the game be played as scheduled, relenting only when the Cleveland team vowed not to participate. The situation had grown so heated that Naps players signed a petition protesting Johnson's initial decision to force them to play and threatened to strike.[35] Lajoie and first baseman George Stovall, the team's captain, were particularly insistent that the game be postponed in order to allow Cleveland players to attend their teammate's funeral.[36]

The sentiments of Jim "Deacon" McGuire, manager of the Naps for the first seventeen games of the 1911 season, were perhaps the most effusive and underscored the widespread admiration which Joss inspired: "He was a man in all that term implies. No ball player ever was as thoroughly loved by players and fans. No man ever was more worthy of a deep, sincere love and admiration of his fellow men. There was never a greater pitcher, there never was a finer gentleman." Added Stovall: "His kindness to and thoughtfulness toward other players always won their undying friendship."[37] No faint praise of Joss is to be found.

It was against this backdrop of mourning and affection that Joss' funeral procession took place. One contemporary account said that 5,000 people observed Joss' body lie in state from approximately 10 a.m. that day until 2 p.m. at the local Masonic Temple, where Joss had served as an active Mason himself, and that "not since the death of 'Golden Rule' Jones has there been such an impressive burial scene."[38]

Joss' hearse was drawn by horse through the city streets, with "thousands of mourners lining the curbs," and a "mountain of flowers and wreaths" were waiting at the Masonic Temple, where the funeral service took place.[39] The many rivals who also sent flowers included Mr. and Mrs. Ty Cobb.[40] At the service, "the entire Cleveland ball team, especially Cy Young and Napoleon Lajoie, wept unashamed."[41]

The sermon from Billy Sunday, a former ballplayer who was "a warm personal friend and admirer" of Joss and the most noted evangelist of his day, spoke first to Joss' stature as a player.[42] "Joss was one of the great athletes of the world because he was a king of the game of baseball, and that is acknowledged as the star game everywhere," said Sunday. Sunday also proclaimed: "The name of Joss has always brought terror to the opposing nine."[43]

Addie Joss and the Benefit Game

Sunday's praise for Joss on a personal level was even more grand: "He was one of the men who, by his gentlemanly manner, sterling manhood, and unimpeachable honesty, was an honor to the profession. He was one of those men who, by their character and manhood have helped the game to maintain its hold upon the American people, from the president in the White House to the newsboy of the streets; from the staid and dignified members of the supreme court [sic] to the huckster selling his wares from a wagon."[44]

The procession to the cemetery was similarly wrenching. The *Toledo News-Bee* reported: "On almost every corner, diminutive newsboys wept as the cortege went by."[45]

The Benefit Game

The grief for Joss in the days after his death was so substantial that it inspired Charles "C.W." Somers, the owner of the Cleveland Naps, to organize a game benefiting Joss' wife and children akin to the one held in 1910 for the family of Mike Powers.[46] Somers, no doubt, was motivated partially by his strong relationship with Joss. According to one contemporary account, Somers "always considered Joss more in the light of a colleague and partner rather than an employee."[47]

In April 1911, the redoubtable Somers was concurrently serving as vice-president of the American League and as Cleveland's owner. With the local goodwill that Somers had engendered by helping to bring baseball back to Cleveland ten years prior, Somers was well-positioned to recruit superior talent for Joss' benefit game.[48] In keeping with his always outsized aspirations, Somers "wanted to host the greatest benefit ever seen."[49] An active, if impulsive, personality, Somers quickly scheduled the event at League Park for July 24, a Monday, since every American League team other than Boston and Chicago had an off day.[50]

There is no mention that any player invited by Somers to the game declined. On the contrary, American League players appeared without exception to view offers to participate as a great honor. Jimmy McAleer, the Washington Senators manager best known for his role in introducing presidential first pitches to baseball, offered to manage the All-Star team.[51] Though the White Sox did not field any players that the game due to the scheduling conflict—making Walsh's absence at the game particularly conspicuous—Boston's Tris Speaker and Joe Wood received permission to miss that day's game and to attend the Joss benefit. The two Red Sox said they could stay for only the first three innings before having to depart for Boston.[52]

Contributions directed to Joss' family abounded, both from players and teams. Ty Cobb, notably, pledged $100, ruffling some feathers when his personal donation equaled that of Somers himself. Cy Young donated $25. American League clubs from New York, Boston, St. Louis, and Washington collectively added an additional $350. Dozens of other donors, many not well known, also contributed.[53]

With ticket prices for box seats reaching $100, prices for the game could be lofty.[54] At the same time, prices for the lower-priced seats were in line with what regular-season games cost: first tier boxes at $1.25; second tier boxes at $1.00; reserve seats at $1.00; pavilion seats at $0.50; and bleacher seats at $0.25.[55] Sales were brisk, as combined receipts for tickets were at $8,184 by noon, well before the game was to begin at 1:45 p.m.[56]

Ticket purchasers were of a wide mix. They included Billy Sunday, who bought $10 of tickets himself, and White Sox owner Charles Comiskey, who purchased $190 worth of tickets. Employees of the Ohio Gas Meter Company and members of the county auditor's office, among other local organizations, also bought tickets.[57] George Sisler, a future Hall of Famer, was in the crowd, witnessing his first major league game while visiting his uncle in Cleveland.[58] In addition, the management of *Baseball Magazine* asked that receipts from the publication's sales during the game be directed to the Joss family for "this very proper testimonial to such a worthy exponent of the national game as Addie Joss."[59] The breadth of financial support that the Addie Joss benefit game received was central to its success.

A highlight of the day was Germany Schaefer's pregame routine, which brightened the mood on a difficult occasion. Schaefer, known for his antics, took over announcing duties on that day in Cleveland from concessionaire Teddy Wanstall. As one article written before the game suggested, Schaefer was expected to "furnish continuous entertainment."[60] He seems to have delivered, as a subsequent article noted that the Washington infielder "furnished plenty of comedy before and during the game."[61] Another said: "The coaching of Germany was the biggest part of the afternoon's entertainment."[62]

Schaefer announced the game's starting batteries to the crowd, including mention of "Cy Young of Peoli, O-h-i-o." Afterwards, he jumped up shortly before the team picture was to be taken, stepping in for the team photographer and holding up the camera bulb. Schaefer said mischievously to the assembled players: "Now, boys, just one smile!" During practice,

Addie Joss and the Benefit Game

Above and facing page: **For this classic panoramic photograph of the men who played in the Addie Joss Game, it took so long for the photographer to pan that Cleveland's Jack Graney was able to run around from left to right and thus appear at each end of the finished image!**

Schaefer sat on first base, fielding ground balls hit his way from a sitting position on the bag. He continued his shenanigans as a coach, imitating Hughie Jennings, where Schaefer "'Ey-Yahed' and frothed about as naturally as the Tiger leader."[63]

Schaefer's role speaks to the celebratory nature of the Joss benefit game. No lachrymose affair, "the event was as Addie would have wished," wrote J.P. Garvey, a sportswriter for the *Plain Dealer*. "There was no mourning, save that the flag hung at half mast from the pole in center field. No drab colorings decorated the big grand stand." According to Garvey, "the crowd sat quietly applauding every applaudable play."[64] Wrote Jim Weigand: "Although the reasons for the game were solemn, the game itself was played with baseball's life-affirming zest."[65]

Joe Wood, who needed to depart for Boston later in the afternoon, and Young, the Naps' most prominent player along with Lajoie, were the starting pitchers. Cobb, in what is perhaps the most commonly repeated anecdote from the game itself, played in a Cleveland uniform, as his regular Detroit Tigers uniform was apparently lost in transit.[66]

Leading off for the All-Stars in the top of the first inning, Speaker lined a ball over second base for a single.[67] Collins, batting second, hit a triple to right field, scoring Speaker and giving the All-Stars a 1–0 lead. Cobb, the third man to come to bat, "got a wonderful ovation" before hitting a single. Cobb's hit scored Collins, but Naps centerfielder Joe Birmingham threw to George Stovall at first base, catching Cobb when he overran the base.[68]

The All-Stars' first-inning lead could have been greater, as Baker then

reached first base on Naps shortstop Ivy Olson's error. Crawford, though, flied out to Birmingham, and Baker subsequently was thrown out stealing by Cleveland catcher Syd Smith, with Olson making the tag. The bottom of the first inning, with the Naps trailing 2–0, was representative of the general inefficacy of Cleveland's performance that day, as Jack Graney grounded out to Wallace, Olson popped up to Collins, and Joe Jackson popped out to Wallace.

The first inning turned out to be the most consequential. Said Garvey:

> In inning No. 1, as the champion old gentleman of the upper ranks—Cy Young—swung over his mixture of circlers to three successive batters, it was very easy to foresee the finish. Those three young stellar movers of the circuit—Speaker, Collins, and Cobb were the first batters, and even on an off day where nothing was at stake, Young was not master enough to puzzle them. Each of the trio hit the ball and directed it to portions untrammeled by the spikes of Naps performers. The result was that the picked aggregation gained a lead of two runs.[69]

The All-Stars added to their lead in the top of the second inning. Hal Chase hit a leadoff single to left field. After Wallace lined out to Birmingham, Gabby Street singled to right, moving Chase to third base. Joe Wood's sacrifice fly scored Chase. Even with Street being thrown out at second base by Birmingham to end the inning while trying to advance on the same play, the All-Stars led 3–0, with the Naps yet to record a hit.

The bottom of the second inning provided a rare highlight for Cleveland. Stovall, who "got a big hand" when he came to bat, singled to left field. He scored quickly on account of Birmingham's single and Speaker's error fielding it in center, which allowed Birmingham to reach second base. Ball and Turner consecutively popped out to Chase, the former in foul ground, and Smith grounded out to Wallace, thus leaving the score 3–1 in favor of the All-Stars through two innings.

In the third inning the All-Stars should have added to their lead. Speaker doubled but was thrown out at third base trying to record a triple—

Addie Joss and the Benefit Game

it was Birmingham's third outfield assist of the afternoon. Collins grounded out to Turner at third, and Cobb, having singled, was thrown out trying to steal second, Smith to Ball. The All-Stars were the more aggressive team in this game, often attempting to take an extra base.

In the bottom of the third, Walter Johnson relieved Wood, while Clyde Milan replaced Speaker in center field. Wood, who gave up two hits and one run without a strikeout in the two innings he pitched, would be the game's winning pitcher.

Johnson, who had said before the game that he would "do anything they want for Addie Joss' family," was effective in the three innings he pitched.[70] He retired the first batter he faced getting Art Griggs, pinch-hitting for Young, to fly out to Cobb. The Naps then showed some promise when Jack Graney singled to center, stole second, and advanced to third base when Olson grounded out to Collins. But Joe Jackson grounded back to Walter Johnson, ending the threat.

In the top of the fourth inning, George Kahler (sometimes referenced in contemporary box scores as "Kaler") entered the game for Cleveland, replacing Cy Young. Baker and Crawford immediately singled, with both advancing one base on Birmingham's error in center. Chase's sacrifice fly brought Baker in to score and moved Crawford to third. A Street pop up to Turner and a Wallace force out ended the inning, with the All-Stars firmly in control, 4–1.

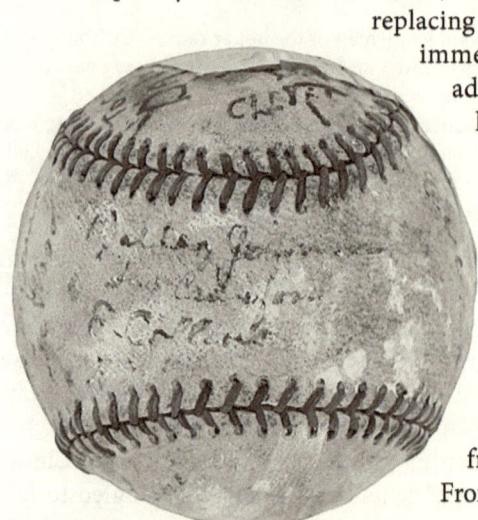

This is a ball used in the Addie Joss memorial game of July 24, 1911, the first major-league all-star game played during the regular season. Among the visible autographs are those of Walter Johnson, Sam Crawford, Eddie Collins, and Joe Wood.

The game's lackluster reputation derives particularly from the remaining 5½ innings. From the bottom of the third inning to the end of the game, a parade of ground outs, fly outs, and pop ups ensued, and only two runs were scored. The on-field engagement of the players also seems to have flagged. As

Garvey said about the benefit game in general: "Many an amateur game has been crowded with features more stirring."[71] Another contemporary account said: "It was not a great game from a playing standpoint, none of the players exerting himself to any extent."[72] Suspense, too, was absent: "The outcome was not concealed by any doubtful contingencies, and it was not necessary to resort to witchcraft to predict the victor," wrote Garvey.[73]

The bottom of the fourth inning was a case in point. Johnson retired the overmatched Naps on six pitches: Stovall flied out to Milan in center, followed by ground outs from Birmingham and Ball, respectively.[74] In the bottom of the next inning, the Naps performed similarly, as Turner grounded out, pinch-hitter Ted Easterly lined out to Collins, and Kahler struck out.

Meanwhile, the All-Stars also were unable to provide much offense. In the top of the fifth inning, as Lajoie took over for Stovall at first base and Easterly replaced Smith at catcher, Milan's single to center was followed by Collins flying out to Birmingham, Cobb popping out to Lajoie, Milan stealing second, and Baker grounding out to Lajoie. In the top of the sixth, with Hank Butcher entering the game for Joe Jackson in right field, Crawford flied out to Birmingham. Chase then got an infield single but was erased when Wallace hit into a double play—the only one of the game—Olson to Ball to Lajoie.

The Naps threatened in the bottom of the sixth. After Russ Ford had replaced Johnson and Livingston took over for Street, Graney's groundout to Collins was followed by a single to left field by Olson.[75] A single by Butcher that was "too hot" for Wallace and moved Olson to third. But Butcher was caught off of first base—the rundown going Ford to Chase to Collins to Chase—and after Milan made a running catch of Lajoie's line drive, the Naps' scoring chance was thwarted. The Cleveland offense continued its lackluster ways in the seventh inning: Wallace threw out Birmingham leading off and Ball then grounded out to Wallace, making for two quick outs. After Turner beat out an infield single, the inning ended in short order when Easterly fouled out to Chase.

In the top of the seventh inning, Fred Blanding relieved Kahler. Following Livingston's groundout to Olson and Ford's strikeout, Milan hit a long fly ball. Although he made a good effort after it, Graney dropped the ball, which fell for a double. Collins' single up the middle scored Milan, making the score 5-1. Butcher ended the inning with a catch against the wall of a long drive hit by Cobb. The top of the eighth was more quotidian, with Baker and then Crawford each flying out to Birmingham and Olson throwing out Wallace after Chase had doubled to right field.

Addie Joss and the Benefit Game

Four men who played in the Addie Joss benefit game: left to right, catcher Gabby Street, third baseman Frank Baker, and pitchers Walter Johnson and Joe Wood.

The remaining half-inning of consequence was the bottom of the eighth. There, Blanding hit a leadoff double, aided by the ball "bounding away" from Cobb in the outfield.[76] Blanding advanced to third on Graney's sacrifice fly to Milan and scored on Olson's triple over Sam Crawford's head. Butcher's groundout to Wallace scored Olson. Lajoie then also grounded out to Wallace, ending the inning with the Naps having scored two runs, making the score 5–3 in favor of the All-Stars.

The ninth inning proceeded quickly and uneventfully. In the top half, Livingston led off with a single. After Ford struck out, Livingston stole second base. Milan, however, grounded out to Olson and Collins flied out to Birmingham, ending the frame. Cleveland's half of the ninth consisted of Birmingham flying to Collins, Ball grounding to Wallace, a walk to Turner, and a strikeout by Easterly to end the game.

Eleven players—Collins, Cobb, Baker, Crawford, Chase, and Wallace for the All-Stars and Graney, Olson, Birmingham, Ball, and Turner for the Naps—played all nine innings, a feat unlikely to be repeated in any modern All-Star Game. Completed in one hour and thirty-two minutes, the final score was All-Stars 5, Naps 3.[77]

Long-Term Consequences

That interest in the Addie Joss benefit game remains high more than a century later speaks to the uniqueness of the event. The game represented the greatest collection of talent assembled on a baseball field prior to the first official All-Star Game in 1933. The cooperation that the Joss benefit game required, especially from often bitter rivals, speaks to the sense of camaraderie that existed in the game's early years and a shared respect among competitors which provides a contrast with the modern, one-dimensional caricatures of early-century players as churlish at best and bellicose at worst.

The Joss benefit game, according to an article in *Baseball Magazine* from September 1911, "was a touching and beautiful instance of the human side of the national game."[78] In an era where baseball was not known for gentlemanly behavior, the Joss game became an episode "when baseball shall not be selfish nor grasping in any sense, but kind and generous and beneficent as becomes the favorite pastime of the most generous people in the world."[79] Said Husman: "[R]ivalries flourished and conflicts grew and sometimes became bitter. The game for Joss transcended all this. The game itself was a celebration. The atmosphere was World Series–like; the only sign of mourning was the flag being set at half-mast."[80]

Moreover, the game succeeded as a tribute to Joss himself. Garvey noted the next day: "Addie Joss still lives! His body may be molding into dust under the damp earth of Woodlawn cemetery, Toledo, O., far away from the cheers of a major league crowd, but his spirit remains a potent, living thing in the sphere where his name won an honorable place."[81]

For Joss, a member of the Hall of Fame, to be better remembered for the game held in his honor than for his singular playing career speaks to the striking success of the entire endeavor. Even if the play of the game itself was undistinguished and no National League players participated, such details are easily forgotten amidst the spectacle of the only event of its kind held during the Deadball Era.

More than two decades later, when Arch Ward, sports editor of the *Chicago Tribune*, proposed a "Game of the Century" fielding the game's greatest players, it was not out of any particular fidelity to the Joss benefit game.[82] Rather, Ward was motivated by the prospect of holding an event to complement the World's Fair in Chicago, not to mention an opportunity to take advantage of Babe Ruth's popularity at the gate.[83] If the Joss benefit game was not a direct inspiration for the newer version, it at least served

Addie Joss and the Benefit Game

as a model for how an All-Star Game on a grand scale might look and proceed.

In at least two senses, that 1933 All-Star Game had the imprint of the Addie Joss benefit game, as the proceeds were donated to a charitable cause and affordable seats were available to local fans.[84] For practical purposes, the Addie Joss benefit game was half of an All-Star Game, but it is remembered in the mind's eye as a seminal baseball moment. The idea it inspired endures.

NOTES

1. The term "benefit game" is an unofficial one which has been used with increasing frequency over time. Some articles will refer to this game as the "memorial game" or as "the Addie Joss All-Star Game." While any of these terms is apt, this article makes use of the former because it readily suggests that the primary purpose of the game was to raise money for Joss' family rather than to commemorate the life and career of the star pitcher.

2. With thanks to the Giamatti Research Center at the National Baseball Hall of Fame for providing copies of articles cited in this piece. It is worthwhile to note that there is a panoramic photograph of every player from the Joss benefit game, with the Cleveland players lined up to the left and the All Stars to the right. Perhaps because the faces are less easy to see, the photograph is less renowned than the one of the smaller group of All Stars.

3. "All-Stars Defeat Naps: Big Crowd at Benefit for Addie Joss's Widow and Children," *New York Tribune*, July 25, 1911, 5. Paul Green noted that, even including the pitcher, the lifetime batting average for All Star team at the time of the game was .312. See Paul Green, "Best Team Ever?," *Sports Collectors Digest*, July 22, 1983, 81.

4. Unidentified clipping from Addie Joss' file available in the Giamatti Research Center at the Baseball Hall of Fame.

5. Robert D. Warrington, "A Ballpark Opens and a Ballplayer Dies: The Converging Fates of Shibe Park and 'Doc' Powers," *Baseball Research Journal*, Fall 2014. Available at http://sabr.org/research/ballpark-opens-and-ballplayer-dies-converging-fates-shibe-park-and-doc-powers. An article titled "Dr. Powers Day" in *Sporting Life* from July 9, 1910 called the game "another unexcelled achievement in baseball."

6. A box score citing Chase's 17 putouts can be found at J.P. Garvey, "Fans Crowd Stands in Honor of Great Pitcher," *Plain Dealer* (Cleveland, OH). Clipping from Joss' file in the Giamatti Research Center at the Baseball Hall of Fame.

7. Scott H. Longert, *Addie Joss: King of the Pitchers* (Society of American Baseball Research, 1998), 81.

8. See also Bill James, *Whatever Happened To The Hall of Fame: Baseball, Cooperstown, and the Politics of Glory* (New York: Simon & Schuster, 1995), 333–335. [Originally published as Bill James, *The Politics of Glory: How Baseball's Hall of Fame Really Works* (New York: Macmillan, 1994)]. James says that he believes that "the selection of Joss [for the Hall of Fame] was a mistake." He notes that some observers draw comparisons between the career records of Joss and Sandy Koufax, whose career was similarly short. James notes: "Joss won 20 to 27 games a year from 1905 to 1908. There were sixteen 25-win seasons in those four years; Joss had only one of them. That ain't Koufax."

9. Because Joss did not pitch in ten seasons in the Major Leagues, he was not eligible for the Hall of Fame. Due to ill health, Joss did not pitch in 1911, leaving him short of ten years of active playing time. Many have postulated that if Joss had thrown one pitch that year, he likely would have been elected much sooner than he was. An exception to the voting rules was made in the 1970s, which led to Joss' election in 1978.

10. Accounts differ whether Joss had a problem with a ligament or a tendon. In an article titled: "Joss' Arm in Plaster Cast" published in the *New York Times* on February 21, 1911, it says: "A strained tendon in the lanky pitcher's elbow had been neglected. Inflammation set in, which spread to the other tendon, causing a crook in the elbow. This was straightened out and the trainer hopes by proper treatment the arm will again be placed in fine shape in a short time."

11. "Addie Joss: The Memory of the Once Famous Pitcher Still Lingers," *Baseball Magazine*,

August 1911, 70. Clipping from Joss' file available in the Giamatti Research Center at the Baseball Hall of Fame.

12. Among extraordinary starting pitching performances thrown under such competitive duress, Joss' perfect game is rivaled only by that of Don Larsen during the 1956 World Series. It is noteworthy that Joss came close to having his perfect game broken up with two outs, as Chicago's John Anderson, among the team's best hitters that season, "slashed a line drive toward left that slowly curved and landed foul by inches." Then, Anderson hit a ground ball to third baseman Bill Bradley, who tossed it to George Stovall at first base. Stovall initially dropped the low throw but was able to pick it up in time and record the out, finishing the perfect game. See James Buckley, Jr., *Perfect: The Inside Story of Baseball's Twenty Perfect Games* (Chicago: Triumph Books, 2002), 47–48.

13. Frederick G. Lieb, "Addie Joss Was One of the Game's Greatest Pitchers: One of Five Twirlers to Turn in Perfect Game; Performed Feat Against Ed Walsh and White Sox in 1908," 1924. No publication given. Clipping from Joss' file in the Giamatti Research Center at the Baseball Hall of Fame.

14. Duane Lindstrom, "The Juneau Wonder," *Milwaukee Magazine*, April 1986, 98.

15. Longert, 81.

16. *Ibid.*, 81.

17. Lawrence S. Ritter, *The Glory of Their Times* (New York: HarperCollins, 1966), 36. The reference to Joss comes in the chapter with Davy Jones, where Jones says about a Detroit-Cleveland game: "Unfortunately, the Cleveland pitcher that day was Addie Joss, who Schaefer couldn't hit with a paddle. A corking good pitcher. Three swings, and Schaefer strikes out. Never came close to the ball." Jones adds that Schaefer went on to strike out again and then pop up, and notes that Schaefer had been so humbled in the game that the crowd was yelling to take him out in the ninth inning when he came up to bat.

18. John Husman, "Baseball's first all-star game, in 1911, honored the memory of pitching great Addie Joss, dead before his time." *Sports History*, January 1990, 8.

19. Husman notes: "These players coming together on the same field was the ultimate tribute to Joss. There was no love lost among several of the players. Many of the hard feelings revolved around the hated Cobb. He was not even on speaking terms with fellow-Tiger outfielder, Sam Crawford. Cobb had left the marks of his spikes on Baker and was in a heated chase with Collins for the stolen base leadership. Cobb had just battled in 1910 with Lajoie for the league batting championship, endearing himself to no one when he sat out the last two games of the season to protect a seemingly safe lead." See Husman, 56.

20. Longert, 67. Longert notes that Dr. Morrison Castle, the team's physician, recommended that the pitcher rest his arm for the remainder of the season. Joss found, though, that the torn ligament in his arm continued to hurt every time he tried to throw a curveball. Joss did pitch into the sixth inning in an exhibition game between Cleveland and Cincinnati following the season, giving fans hope for the future. See Longert, 67–68.

21. *Ibid.*, 68–69.

22. *Ibid.*, 70. Lindstrom notes that Joss fainted in the Chattanooga dugout. Husman notes that Joss tried to brush the fainting episode off as insignificant, calling it "a baby trick." See Husman, 8.

23. Husman, 8.

24. Longert noted in an e-mail on June 10, 2017 that: "The lumbar puncture was performed by Dr. Morrison Castle, the Naps team doctor. He consulted at Dr. Chapman's request. Dr. Castle had taken care of Addie most of his career." E-mail correspondence with author of June 10, 2017, cited with permission.

25. Longert, 71.

26. *Ibid.*, 71. Joss owned a "fashionable billiard parlor" in Toledo. See "Joss Kin Happy, Sad with His Election to Hall," *The Blade* (Toledo, OH), February 1, 1978. Other sources make reference to a billiard hall which Joss owned, as mentioned below. Longert clarified in an e-mail that "the pool hall and billiard hall are the same." E-mail correspondence with author, May 26, 2017, used with permission.

27. "Toledo Stricken by Death of Joss," *Plain Dealer* (Cleveland, OH), April 15, 1911. No page number given. Clipping from Joss' file available in the Giamatti Research Center at the Baseball Hall of Fame.

28. *Ibid.*

29. *Ibid.*

Addie Joss and the Benefit Game

30. One Joss column notes that: "Any club that plays a conventional style of a game will never win a pennant" since other teams will soon catch on and adjust, while another points out: "There is absolutely no question but that the game is faster today than it ever was and for this reason alone it is safe to presume that the players of today must necessarily play a speedier game than did their brethren of years ago." Both unidentified columns are from Joss' file available in the Giamatti Research Center at the Baseball Hall of Fame.

31. "Toledo Stricken by Death of Joss," *Plain Dealer*.

32. "Want Monday's Game Postponed So They Can Attend Joss' Funeral," *Plain Dealer*. No other publication details available. Clipping from Joss' file in the Giamatti Research Center at the Baseball Hall of Fame.

33. Husman, 8.

34. "Addie Joss All-Star Game," Baseball Almanac. Available at http://www.baseball-almanac.com/tsn/addie_joss_benefit_game.shtml. Accessed on May 25, 2017.

35. Al Howell, "Joss Is at Rest: The Great Player Highly Honored in Death," *Sporting Life*, April 29, 1911, 3. A *New York Times* article titled "Funeral of Addie Joss: Cleveland Team and Free Masons Pay Tribute to Famous Pitcher" published on April 18, 1911 notes: "It was said that the Cleveland team refused to play to-day's game, and when President Johnson was apprised of the disposition of the Cleveland man he ordered the postponement of the game."

36. Longert, 73. According to Longert, Tigers owner Frank Navin originally agreed to postpone the game, only to be swayed by Hughie Jennings, who resisted the idea. Based upon the potential for a "player revolt," Johnson eventually yielded to the pleas of Cleveland team owner Charles Somers, to whom he owed a great deal for Somers' support during the formative years of the American League. One contemporary story said: "The players of the Cleveland baseball club went on strike Sunday night and forced Ban Johnson, president of the American League, to call off Monday's game with Detroit so they could attend Addie Joss' funeral in Toledo at 2 pm on Monday. Johnson was insistent until informed by E.S. Barnard, Nap secretary, that the players refused to play. See United Press, "Cleveland Team Strikes for Sake of Dead Comrade." Unidentified clipping from Joss' file in the Giamatti Research Center at the Baseball Hall of Fame. Stovall would become Cleveland's manager beginning with the 18th game of the 1911 season.

37. "Game's Celebrities Eulogize Ad Joss." Unidentified clipping from Joss' file in the Giamatti Research Center at the Baseball Hall of Fame.

38. Tom Terrell, "Good-Bye Addie: Funeral of Late Cleveland Pitcher Largest in Toledo Since That of Mayor Jones." Unidentified clipping from Joss' file in the Giamatti Research Center at the Baseball Hall of Fame. "Golden Rule" Jones is Samuel M. Jones, mayor of Toledo from 1897 to 1904. The same article notes that Cy Young escorted Joss' mother, Theresa, to the service. Neither of Joss' children attended. Son Norman, then age 8, was "heartbroken," said Terrell. "He cannot bear to look upon the cold, marble-like features of his dead father. Little Ruth, the four-year-old daughter of the great pitcher, has not been informed of her father's death."

39. Longert, 74.

40. *Toledo News-Bee*, April 17, 1911. No further information available. Clipping from Joss' file in the Giamatti Research Center at the Baseball Hall of Fame. Cobb, as quoted in the *Cleveland Leader* as cited by Lindstrom, also had noted that "a more gentlemanly ballplayer never existed" and that Cobb had gotten only two hits in eighteen at-bats in his career against Joss. See Lindstrom, 94, 100

41. Howell, 3.

42. *Ibid.*, 3. Rev. Richard D. Hollington, a pastor from St. Paul's Methodist Church, also participated. Longert notes that Sunday spoke at the request of Mrs. Joss. E-mail correspondence with author, June 10, 2017, used with permission.

43. *Toledo News-Bee*, April 17, 1911. Unattributed clipping from Joss' file in the Giamatti Research Center at the Baseball Hall of Fame.

44. *Toledo News-Bee*, April 17, 1911.

45. *Ibid.*, April 17, 1911. Longert noted of Sunday: "His skill as an evangelist was never better. He used every bit of his ability to deliver a classic oration that would help him take his place as the foremost evangelist in the country." See Longert, 74.

46. Longert, 76.

47. Unidentified clipping from Joss' file in the Giamatti Research Center at the Baseball Hall of Fame.

48. Somers had helped to return baseball to Cleveland after the Cleveland Spiders had folded following the 1899 season. For details of Somers' often tumultuous tenure as Cleveland's owner, see his SABR biography at https://sabr.org/bioproj/person/ee856cc8.

49. Longert, 76.

50. Ibid., 76.

51. That McAleer volunteered to manage is noted at http://www.baseballalmanac.com/tsn/addie_joss_benefit_game.shtml. McAleer was also a former Cleveland manager, having managed the Cleveland Blues in 1901.

52. Longert, 77.

53. Ibid., 76.

54. "Joss Receipts Reach $2,360." Unidentified clipping from Joss' file in the Giamatti Research Center at the Baseball Hall of Fame. Cobb himself bought a $100 box.

55. Unidentified clipping from Joss' file in the Giamatti Research Center at the Baseball Hall of Fame. The clipping notes that 256 first-tier boxes were sold at a $1.25 each, totaling $320.00; 296 second-tier boxes at $1.00 each, totaling $296; 7,293 reserve seats at $1.00 each, totaling $7,293; 5,833 pavilion seats at $0.50 each, totaling $2,916.50; and 1,603 bleacher seats at $0.25 each, totaling $400.75. Together, 15,281 seats were sold for $11,226.25. Adding $1,633 in subscriptions and $55.35 taken in from copies of *Baseball Magazine* sold at the game, the total received from the benefit game was $12,914.60. A subsequent article noted that: "It is expected that the fund will be increased by $200 from further subscriptions within the next few days." See, "Joss Fund Will Reach $15,000," *Boston Globe*, July 29, 1911, 5.

56. "Joss Day May Yield $10,000, World's Star Players Here." Unattributed clipping from Joss' file in the Giamatti Research Center at the Baseball Hall of Fame. Another unidentified article noted that the time of the game was chosen to allow players time to return to their respective teams. It also notes the higher price for grandstand tickets but the regular price for pavilion and bleacher seats: "For this game all grand stand tickets will cost $1. The price does not include the pavilion and bleachers where the usual prices of admission will be charged."

57. "Expect Big Crowd at Joss Day Game: Greatest Stars of National Game to Appear at League Park Today," *Cleveland Leader*, July 24, 1911.

58. "Addie Joss All-Star Game," Baseball Almanac. Available at: http://www.baseball-almanac.com/tsn/addie_joss_benefit_game.shtml.

59. "Buy Baseball Magazine to Help Swell Joss Fund." Unattributed clipping from Joss' file in the Giamatti Research Center at the Baseball Hall of Fame.

60. Unidentified clipping from Joss' file in the Giamatti Research Center at the Baseball Hall of Fame.

61. "All-Stars Win at Cleveland: Joss Benefit Will Net Family $13,000," *Boston Globe*, July 25, 1911, 6.

62. "Comedian Herman Schaefer Pleases Crowd in Role of Megaphone Man." Unattributed clipping from Joss' file in the Giamatti Research Center at the Baseball Hall of Fame.

63. Ibid.

64. J.P. Garvey, "Fans Crowd Stands in Honor of Great Pitcher," *Plain Dealer* (Cleveland, OH). Clipping from Joss' file in the Giamatti Research Center at the Baseball Hall of Fame.

65. Weigand. Unattributed clipping from Joss' file in the Giamatti Research Center at the Baseball Hall of Fame.

66. Markson suggests that Cobb "showed up with a bad cold" on the day of the game and likely made a last-minute decision to play, perhaps leading to the uniform snafu. David Markson, "A Day for Addie Joss," *Atlantic Monthly*, August 1975, 37. Garvey also notes that Cobb had a "heavy cold."

67. The primary source for game play-by-play here is, "Huge Crowds Turn Out to See Diamond Stars Perform at Somers Park," *Cleveland News*, July 24, 1911. No page number given. Unless otherwise noted, all play-by-play events cited in this piece derive from the play-by-play provided in this article. Some play-by-play also derives from an unattributed clipping in Joss' Hall of Fame file, in places where the former is illegible.

68. Ibid., July 24, 1911.

69. J.P. Garvey, "Fans Crowd Stands in Honor of Great Pitcher," *Plain Dealer*.

70. "Addie Joss Benefit Game." Baseball Almanac. Available at http://www.baseball-almanac.com/tsn/addie_joss_benefit_game.shtml.

Addie Joss and the Benefit Game

71. J.P. Garvey, "Fans Crowd Stands in Honor of Great Pitcher," *Plain Dealer*.
72. "All-Stars Win at Cleveland: Joss Benefit Will Net Family $13,000," *Boston Daily Globe*, July 25, 1911, 6.
73. Garvey.
74. "Comedian Herman Schaefer Pleases Crowd in Role of Megaphone Man." Unidentified clipping from Addie Joss' file in the Giamatti Research Center at the Baseball Hall of Fame.
75. Livingston was a Cleveland-area native and also lived there in the off-season. See Longert, 77. It is occasionally suggested that Livingston's Cleveland ties were a key factor in his participation in the All-Star Game.
76. One contemporary account said that "Blanding singled and took second on Cobb's error." Blanding ultimately was credited with a double. The only two errors in the game were given to Birmingham and to Olson (though box scores which attribute Olson's error to Ball also exist). A box score of the game can be found at http://www.baseball-almanac.com/tsn/addie_joss_benefit_game.shtml.
77. The time of the game is noted in the box score from the *New York Times* on July 25, 1911, available on Baseball Almanac at http://www.baseball-almanac.com/tsn/addie_joss_benefit_game.shtml. As Green noted, the 5–3 score was "apparently a bit closer than the game really was." See Green, 82.
78. Editorials, "Addie Joss Day," *Baseball Magazine*, September 1911. No page number given. Clipping from Joss' file in the Giamatti Research Center at the Baseball Hall of Fame.
79. Editorials, "Addie Joss Day," *Baseball Magazine*, September 1911. No page number given.
80. Husman, 56.
81. J.P. Garvey, "Crowd Stands in Honor of Great Pitcher," *Plain Dealer*.
82. The All-Star Game was commonly referred to as "The Game of the Century" at the time. One example can be found at Arch Ward, "49,000 to See Game of Century: A Sellout," *Chicago Tribune*, July 4, 1933. In contemporary articles promoting that game, the Joss benefit game was seldom mentioned. Another article recounting Ward's role in the creation of the modern All-Star Game is available at http://www.chicagotribune.com/news/nationworld/politics/chi-chicagodays-allstargame-story-story.html.
83. John Drebinger, "All-Stars on Edge for Battle Today," *New York Times*, July 6, 1933, 19. Drebinger refers to the game as "Baseball's contribution to the World's Fair."
84. Drebinger, 19. Drebinger notes: "The net proceeds (for the 1933 All-Star Game) will go to baseball's charity organization." See also Ward, who said: "After expenses of the game have been deducted 100 per cent of the proceeds will be donated to the Baseball Players' Charity organization, which aids old time athletes unable to supply themselves with life's necessities." Regarding affordability of tickets, bleacher seats were sold to the public for 55 cents each. "Bleacher Seats on Sale Today for Game of Century," *Chicago Daily Tribune*, July 3, 1933.

Unraveling a Baseball Mystery[1]
JOHN THORN

The classic 1866 Currier & Ives print "The American National Game of Base Ball" (1866) is not, the writer reveals, what it purports to be, i.e., the depiction an 1865 game subtitled in the print as the "Grand Match for the Championship at the Elysian Fields, Hoboken, N.J." That game was indeed played between the Atlantic Base Ball Club of Brooklyn and the Mutual of New York: in a rain-shortened contest, the Atlantics prevailed, 13–12. Clearly the winning club is depicted at the lower right; yet in all the years since issuance of the print—today the most scarce and valuable in all baseball art—no one had thought to examine the players in the field under a looking glass. It turns out that the Atlantics opponents depicted by Currier & Ives were not the Mutuals but instead the Excelsiors, a bitter Brooklyn rival that, after abuse from Atlantics' fans, walked off the field in midgame in 1860 and never again consented to play a game with their antagonists. This is, if the writer may be permitted to say so, a dandy bit of sleuthing.

IN 2012 I LOCATED TWO new game-action images of Jim Creighton, the most famous player of baseball's early period.[2] Further snooping has revealed some truly startling information about the game's most celebrated and valuable image: the 1866 Currier & Ives lithograph "American National Game of Base Ball: Grand Match for the Championship at the Elysian Fields, Hoboken, N.J." Long believed to depict the 1865 match between the Atlantic of Brooklyn and the Mutual of New York, it has turned out be something else entirely: a fantasy game, one that the baseball world desired but that never was played.

The path of discovery began with an intriguing post to SABR's 19th century baseball committee. Bob Tholkes wrote:

Unraveling a Baseball Mystery

The American National Game of Base Ball, Currier and Ives, 1866.

"An August 1, 1860 ad by a book seller in the Buffalo Daily Courier of August 1, 1860 mentioned that pictures of the recent match between the Atlantic and Excelsior (played on July 19) appeared in the current edition of Demorest's New-York Illustrated News, which would have been the issue of July 29 [actually it was August 4]."

Grand Base-Ball Match for the Championship, between the Excelsior and Atlantic Clubs, of Brooklyn, at the Excelsior Club Grounds, South Brooklyn, on Thursday, July 19—from a sketch made by our own artist. *Demorest's New-York Illustrated News*, August 4, 1860.

I had seen and admired that picture more than twenty years ago, at the home of collectors Frank and Peggy Steele. A couple of respondents to the above posting offered digital versions of it, and I located the accompanying text. "Right glad are we to find that manly sports and exercises are becoming so popular in America," opined the unnamed scribe, who rambled on in this rather arch manner, not reporting the outcome—Excelsior 23, Atlantic 4—except through an appended box score.

Examining an enlargement of the panoramic scene, it struck me that the emblem on the pitcher's bib front looked to be single letter, not the ABBC of the Atlantic Club. He must be Excelsior and, as the box score would corroborate, he must be Creighton. Compare this cropped enlargement from the Illustrated News woodcut to the carte de visite (cdv). Note the crossed legs prior to delivery; I don't know that this stance was unique to Creighton but I have seen it depicted nowhere else. Also note the distinctive multi-paneled hat with piping in the crown. In *Baseball in the Garden of Eden* I wrote the following, based on a contemporary report:

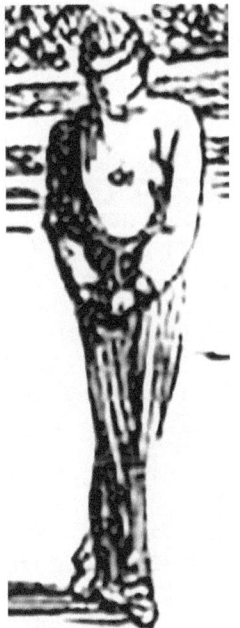

Enlargement from the previous image; Jim Creighton prepares to deliver the ball.

"Early pitchers had taken two steps in delivering the ball, and would follow it halfway to home plate until 1858, when the pitcher's line was established at forty-five feet. Until the pitcher's [rear line] came in five years later, pitchers would still throw from a running start. Creighton, however, did not move from his original position, taking only a step with his left foot and keeping his right in place."[3]

Only three other depictions of the incomparable athlete survive: a team shot of the 1860 Excelsiors; a cdv produced after his death at age twenty-one, four days after a mortal swing of the bat on October 14, 1862; and a crepe-draped portrait surmounting the notable players of 1865, offered up in *Frank Leslie's Illustrated Newspaper* of November 4 of that year. Later woodcuts were all based upon one or another of these three images.

Subsequently it occurred to me that the pitcher in the "American National Game" lithograph, who is supposed to be Richard H. Thorn of the Mutuals (formerly of the Empire and Gotham clubs) looked strangely

Unraveling a Baseball Mystery

familiar—yet I had never seen an image of him other than this. The championship game of August 3, 1865, had been hotly played, as the New York Herald headlined, and but for a sudden storm that ended the game after five innings, was a thriller:

"THE GRAND MATCH FOR THE CHAMPIONSHIP; TWENTY THOUSAND SPECTATORS PRESENT; THE FINEST CONTEST EVER WITNESSED; THE ATLANTICS STILL THE CHAMPIONS; THE PLAYERS AND SPECTATORS DISPERSED BY A HEAVY THUNDER SHOWER; EXCITING SCENES AT THE HOBOKEN FERRIES, ETC."[4]

Now the lithograph depicting this famous 1865 championship game positions the Atlantics at the bat, with identifiable likenesses of those on the sideline and in the field. Indeed, the likenesses are drawn from a cdv celebrating their championship and issued by Charles H. Williamson of Brooklyn. The Currier & Ives likenesses, drawn by an unnamed hand, are so faithful to the photograph that Peter O' Brien, who in the cdv is posed in street clothes,

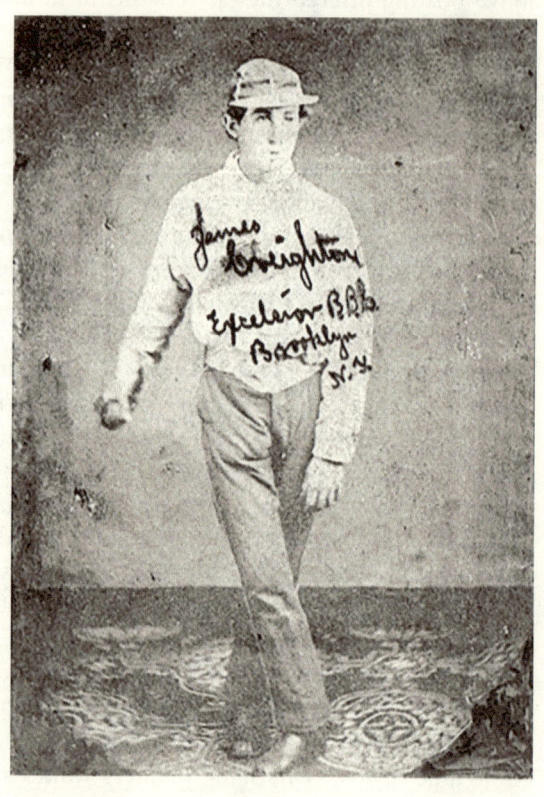

Jim Creighton carte de visite, issued posthumously.

Opposite, top: Great Base Ball Match between the Atlantic and Eckford Clubs of Brooklyn, at the Union Base Ball Grounds, E.D., Oct. 11, with Portraits of the Leading Players of the Principal Clubs of New York, Brooklyn, and Newark. The crepe-covered Creighton, three years dead, is featured. *Frank Leslie's Illustrated Newspaper,* November 4, 1865.

Opposite, bottom: The Atlantic of Brooklyn, 1865, "Champions of America," a card issued by photographer Charles H. Williamson.

Unraveling a Baseball Mystery

in the lithograph stands on the sideline, in civilian garb, even though he played center field in the championship game and struck its only home run!

It follows that the Currier and Ives pitcher must be Thorn of the Mutuals ... yet he certainly looked to me like Creighton, and he was wearing the distinctive Excelsior cap! I recalled that I had once downloaded from the Library of Congress site a high-resolution version of the uncolored lithograph, and zoomed into the pitcher's spot.

I was struck not only by the resemblance to Creighton, with his distinctively planted rear foot, but also by the two pitcher's plates. The playing rules for 1858 had called for a "flat circular iron plate, painted or enameled white" to mark the "pitcher's points." While the pitching distance had been established at 45 feet from the front foot in mid-delivery, the back distance had not yet been established. However, by 1863 the points were gone, replaced by a "pitcher's box" absent the side boundaries, three feet deep. Accordingly, these round iron plates were anomalous for a championship game of 1865, and must have been the product of artistic license.

I then looked to the batter, with the hands-apart stance that would endure into the deadball era, and saw that he too was standing at a "flat circular iron plate, painted or enameled white." It also seemed—was my imagination running away with me?—that the catcher looked like the Excelsior captain, Joe Leggett. Panning into the field, I came upon a detail invisible in the reproduced versions I had at hand of the colored lithograph. The belt of the shortstop was clearly emblazoned with the name "Excelsior."

ATLANTIC.			MUTUAL.		
Players.	O.	R.	Players.	O	R
Pearce, s. s.	2	3	Brown, 2d b.	2	2
Smith, 3d b.	1	3	Wansley, c.	3	1
Start, 1st b.	1	3	Duffy, 3d b.	2	1
Chapman, l. f.	1	2	Zeller, l. f.	2	1
Crane, 2d b.	1	2	Goldie, 1st b.	2	1
P. O'Brien, c. f.	3	1	Devyr, s. s.	1	2
Galvin, s. s.	2	0	Patterson, c. f.	1	2
Pratt, p.	2	0	McMahon, r. f.	1	1
Sid. Smith, r. f.	2	0	Thorn, p.	1	1
Total	15	13	Total	15	12

INNINGS.	1st	2d.	3d.	4th.	5th.	Total.
Atlantic	2	0	4	6	1	13
Mutual	1	2	4	1	4	12

Umpire—Mr Yates, of the Eagle Club. Scorers—Mawlein and Dongan. Home runs—P. O'Brien, 1; Put out on bases—Atlantic, 9 times, Mutual 9 times. Put out on foul balls—Atlantic, twice; Mutual, 8 times. Fly catches—Atlantic, 5; Mutual, 3. Time of game—One hour and thirty minutes.

The championship game of August 3, 1865; box score.

John Thorn

The American National Game of Base Ball, Currier and Ives, 1866, as above but uncolored.

Now I consulted the New York Public Library's singular large-scale salt print of the 1860 Excelsiors. Yes, the pitcher in the 1866 image was the long-dead and lamented Creighton; the catcher was Leggett; and the shortstop was little Tommy Reynolds. A letter from a Mr. A. Jacobi of Montgomery, Alabama, to the *New York Clipper,* published on September 4, 1875, provided the identities of each man in the 1860 salt print, from which the *Clipper* executed a woodcut:

"Through the courtesy of Mr. A. Jacobi of Montgomery, Ala., we are enabled to lay before our readers a picture of the

Enlarged detail from image above; Creighton pitches to Leggett; note iron plates.

Base Ball 10

Unraveling a Baseball Mystery

model baseball nine of the period when the game was entirely in the hands of the amateur class of the fraternity. Mr. Jacobi, in a letter to us, says he is indebted to Dr. A.T. Pearsall of Montgomery for the photograph sent us, that veteran first-baseman being still a "play list" in the South...

"The picture contains the portraits of the following players: On the extreme left is the old shortstop of the nine, Tommy Reynolds.... Next to him stands John Whitney.... The third is James Creighton—he has a ball in his hand—the pitcher of the period par excellence, and the first to introduce the wrist throw or low-underhand-throw delivery. His forte was great speed and thorough command of the ball.... This team defeated nearly every nine they encountered in 1859 and 1860, but in the latter year they had to succumb to the Atlantics..."[5]

The defending champion Atlantics and the Excelsiors split their first two contests in 1860, each winning upon its home grounds (23–4 for the latter club and then 15–14 for the former). The winner of the third game would wear the laurel. With the Excelsiors

Top: Enlarged detail from image on previous page; Excelsior shortstop Tommy Reynolds.

Wood engraving from the *New York Clipper*: THE OLD EXCELSIOR BASEBALL NINE IN 1859; published September 4, 1875.

The Excelsior Nine of 1860, salt print.

leading 8–6 in the top of the sixth inning, "a desperate party of rowdies, who were determined that the Excelsiors should not win," became so offensive that Captain Leggett withdrew his men from the field and thus forfeited the opportunity his club had to take the "championship" title from the Atlantics. Bitter enemies ever after, the two never played each other again.

The Atlantics and Excelsiors had never played each other at the Elysian Fields, so the grand Currier and Ives lithograph celebrates, perhaps, the game that ought to have settled the championship in 1860. As such it would be history's first instance of fantasy baseball.

Postscript: This image from *Leslie's*, drawn on the day of the 1865 championship game, will show what a Mutual player's uniform looked like:

Addendum: In February 2017 my friend Bob Tholkes sent me this heretofore unnoted bit from the *New York Sunday Mercury*, an important sporting newspaper not available in digital form:

"Messrs. Currier & Ives, the well-known print publishers, had a corps of artists on the ground last Thursday (2nd Excelsior-Atlantic match of 1860, in Bedford), taking elaborate sketches of the immense field, and of the players. They propose publishing a handsome colored lithograph, which will present an accurate view of the interesting scene."[6]

Because the Atlantic defeated the Excelsior in that game of August 9, a third contest to decide the championship was scheduled for August 23.[7] As Craig Waff writes: "As expected, it was another closely contested con-

Unraveling a Baseball Mystery

Actual image of the 1865 championship match; from *Frank Leslie's Illustrated Newspaper*, **August 1865.**

test—perhaps too close for a crowd that seemed to favor the Atlantics. With the Excelsiors leading 8–6 in the top of the sixth inning, 'a desperate party of rowdies, who were determined that the Excelsiors should not win,' became so annoying that Excelsior captain Joe Leggett took his team off the field and thus gave up the opportunity it had to take the 'championship' title from the Atlantics." The clubs never played each other again, perhaps quashing the market for a Currier & Ives "handsome colored lithograph" but affording them a wealth of sketches that could be repurposed.

Notes

1. This article is reprinted from "Our Game," https://ourgame.mlblogs.com/unraveling-a-baseball-mystery-b443c0541c96.
2. John Thorn, "Jim Creighton," http://sabr.org/bioproj/person/2d2e5d16.
3. John Thorn, *Baseball in the Garden of Eden: The Secret History of the Early Game* (New York: Simon & Schuster, 2011), 122.
4. *New York Herald*, August 4, 1865.
5. *New York Clipper*, September 4, 1875.
6. *New York Sunday Mercury*, August 12, 1860.
7. See: https://ourgame.mlblogs.com/atlantics-and-excelsiors-compete-for-the-championship-1860-55b9bfb89217#.kpqyc3fep.

Better Than Creighton
Eric Miklich

Who was the best pitcher during the early development of baseball? Most 19th century base ball historians are programmed to recite Jim Creighton's name which is the result of incomplete research. While he was a talented player who accumulated a larger than life reputation, Creighton was never able to lead his clubs to elite or championship status. At the same time a relatively unknown pitcher made his mark with the Eckford of Brooklyn BBC. He attained a 24-game personal winning streak, never lost a match in an Eckford uniform and helped the club capture consecutive National Association Championships and the first two Silver Ball trophies in 1862 and 1863. This pitcher then moved to the rival Atlantic of Brooklyn club, played sparingly and was part of two more championships in 1864 and 1865.

The following exposé compares these two gentlemen and reveals who was "Better Than Creighton."

NINETEENTH CENTURY BASEBALL RESEARCHERS, writers, and historians have repeatedly made it clear that Jim Creighton was the best pitcher in America from 1860 until his death on October 18, 1862. There is no disputing the evidence that he was the first to effectively pitch instead of simply "feed" the ball to the batters. He possessed speed and developed control, which was a difficult combination for batters of early baseball to adapt to. That mixture absolutely did not exist until Creighton, and he deserves a plaque in Cooperstown as a pioneer. Creighton's style irritated Henry Chadwick, baseball's most famous early journalist. Perhaps if Chadwick wrote about the importance, development, effectiveness, and strategies of Creighton-like pitching, the position of pitcher may have evolved more quickly with more players willing to adopt this approach.

Better Than Creighton

Creighton played for three clubs in two seasons during a time when club members changed venues less frequently then was done later in the mid-1860s, further fueling the belief that he was the first paid player in baseball history. Creighton gained prominence by compiling a 17-2-1 personal record in 1860 while his club, the Excelsior Club of Brooklyn, posted an 18-2-1 record, both initially impressive. Those facts have been repeated many times in numerous articles. However, there is more to these figures that is not discussed. When looking more deeply into the history of the Excelsiors, the 1860 season for both Creighton and club becomes less remarkable.

Excelsior of Brooklyn, 1858–1860 and 1862

The Excelsiors compiled a 42-11-2 record from 1858 through 1860, and 1862. The club did not appear in any matches in 1861 due to the large number of their members joining the ranks of the soldiers involved in the Civil War. The club finished 8-5 in 1858, 12-3 in 1859, 18-2-1 in 1860, and 4-1-1 in 1862, impressive on the surface. Less imposing were the opponents they chose to challenge or accepted challenges from during that period. With the exception of one club, even opponents that produced winning records each season were less-skilled clubs.

In 1858, the Excelsiors opponents overall record was 22-22-1, thanks largely to the 7-0 log of the Atlantic of Brooklyn Club. Only four of eight Excelsiors opponents posted a better than .500 record, and all five Excelsiors losses came against three of those opponents. The losses included an opening-season defeat, 31-18, to an average (4-3) Putnam Club of Brooklyn. Four matches later, the Excelsiors suffered a 17-16 loss to the 3-1 Harlem Club of New York, a weak club. The Excelsiors then ended the season with three straight losses: 19-15 to the Putnam, for the second time, and two consecutive losses to the Atlantics, 22-10 and 27-6. The losses of the Putnam and Harlem clubs came at the hands of the Atlantics and a strong Eckford of Brooklyn Club. The Excelsiors did not play any matches against the 11-1 Mutual of New York Club, the 9-1-1 Empire of New York Club, or the 6-1 Eckfords.

The record of Excelsiors opponents in 1859 was 32-36, with only two opposition clubs posting a better than .500 mark. The Excelsiors opened the season with an 18-17 loss to the (1-3) Charter Oak Club of Brooklyn, the Excelsiors' fourth defeat in a row dating back to the end of the 1858 season. After seven straight wins, including four (two each) over the anemic Baltic Club and the famous but feeble Knickerbocker Club, both of New York, the

Excelsiors lost to the 8–1 Star of Brooklyn Club and pitcher Jim Creighton by the score of 17–12. Three more Excelsiors wins over weak clubs were followed by a 19–15 loss to the Union of Morrisania Club (2–3). Two wins concluded the Excelsiors season. The club did end one streak in 1859. On September 8, they defeated the 6–3 Eagle Club of New York. This was the Excelsiors first win over a club with an above .500 record in 22 matches, dating back to September 28, 1857, when they defeated the Union Club. The 11–1 Atlantics and the 10–2 Eckfords did not appear on the Excelsiors schedule in 1859.

After suspending match play in 1861, the Excelsiors resumed in 1862 and posted a 4–1–1 record. Their opponents' overall record in 1862 was 10–12–1, but two of their six opponents were from Massachusetts where the level of competition did not approach that which existed in New York or Brooklyn. The Union Club that the Excelsiors lost to finished with a .500 record. The Excelsiors, however, did beat the 4–2–1 Star Club. No matches were played against the 14–1 Eckfords who would claim the championship in 1862, the 8–5 Mutuals or the 6–3 Gotham Club.

The Historic Season

The 1860 season was the apex for the Excelsiors and Jim Creighton. That campaign, however, began in the winter of 1859. With the memory of a summer loss to the Star Club at the hands of Creighton fresh in mind, Joe Leggett, the Excelsior team captain, catcher, and best player lured Creighton from the Stars (who had enticed him away from the Niagara of Brooklyn Club earlier in the 1859 season). With their new pitcher secured, the Excelsiors seemingly had the firepower to challenge the best clubs in New York and Brooklyn. The dearth of quality opponents appearing on the Excelsiors' schedule proved otherwise. Possibly seeking redemption for the embarrassing defeats received at the hands of the Atlantic Club in 1858, the Excelsiors added this rival to the schedule. Still, the Atlantics were only one of two clubs that the Excelsiors would face in 1860 who would boast a better-than .500 record at the conclusion of the season. Both Excelsior losses were inflicted by those over–.500 clubs.

The 1860 season opened as it had the year before with the (5–2) Charter Oak Club as the opponent. History promptly repeated itself as Creighton lost to the Charter Oaks by the score of 12–11 on May 17. The first batter Creighton faced, right fielder T. Vanderhoef, tripled to center field "and made first run for the Charter Oaks by stealing home when Leggett and

Better Than Creighton

Creighton were off their guard."[1] After surrendering a second run, Creighton struck out short fielder, (shortstop today) Sam Patchen to end the inning.[2] Creighton was not asked to start in the return match on June 21, a 36–9 Excelsior victory. Instead, the club called upon Ed Russell who had handled most of the pitching duties in 1859. With the game safely in hand for the Excelsiors, Creighton pitched the eighth and ninth innings, allowing no runs to score. Next, he whipped his former club, the winless (0-5-1) Star Club, 16–5, before the Excelsiors traveled to the Adirondack region in upstate New York to face six severely inexperienced clubs. In winning all these matches decisively, the Excelsiors outscored their opponents 189 to 56.

On July 19, the Excelsiors and Creighton each achieved their greatest victory, a 23–4 defeat of the Atlantics (who would end the season with a record of 12-2-2). Creighton was virtually unhittable and preformed as the superstar he was acquired to be, striking out the first batter of the game, left fielder Pete O'Brien.[3] The Atlantics got as close as 4–1 after 2½ innings before the Excelsiors pulled away. The contest was an important event for the sport and spawned print coverage in all the major newspapers of New York and Brooklyn. This fueled the public's interest and excitement for the return match on August 9. In the meantime, the Excelsiors traveled "south" and defeated the Excelsior Club of Baltimore, another weak opponent, and a combined club in Philadelphia, billed as the Picked Nine. The club then returned home to defeat the Putnams in preparation for the second match with the Atlantics.

The Excelsior-Atlantic return match began as the first, with the Excelsiors dominating the early going. They held leads of 8–0 after three innings, and 12–3 after five innings. Then, Creighton wilted under the heat of the day and the intensity of the match. He was lifted after seven innings, trailing 15–12. Reliever Ed Russell held the Atlantics at 15 runs, but the Excelsiors managed only two more scores and were defeated, 15–14. What is never mentioned by latter-day commentators is the fact that nine days later on August 18, the Excelsior BBC took the field against the Empire of New York Club. Creighton started but was pulled for the second straight match. In three innings, he allowed seven runs to this far weaker opponent. Russell came to the rescue for a third time, once again holding the opposition in check. But with the Excelsiors leading 13–7, the match was called after four innings due to rain.

The August 23 Excelsiors-Atlantics match, the third in their series, has been widely documented. The game was never completed and declared a draw, even though the Excelsiors led 8–6 after 5⅔ innings. Thereafter, six consecutive victories ended the Excelsiors season. These wins included a

25–0 rout of the St. George's Cricket Club, a victory which some accounts have absurdly labeled the first shutout in baseball history.

1860 Season Review

Due to the general lack of familiarity regarding the strength of baseball clubs in early 19th century baseball, Creighton's historic season can be best evaluated by applying a rating number—zero to five, with five representing the strongest—to the opposition that he and the Excelsiors faced in 1860. The ratings applied to clubs for this comparison is solely the opinion of the author. Taking into account what clubs the Excelsiors' opponents faced, their seasons' records, histories, and victories, nine of the clubs that Creighton pitched against are assigned a "0" rating. These weaklings include Creighton's old club, the Star which did not win a contest in 1860; the six clubs he faced during the upstate New York tour; the Excelsior from Baltimore, and the iconic but non-competitive Knickerbockers. Six other clubs: Charter Oak, Picked Nine of Philadelphia, Putnam, Empire, Union, and Independent clubs, have been accorded ratings between "1" and "2." The Atlantics are the only club deemed higher than a "2," and are given the highest rating of "5." By this metric, the overall strength of the opponents that Creighton pitched against amounted to a measly 1.3, with a combined club record of 27–28–3. As should be expected, there were far more average or below-average clubs competing in 1860 than there were above-average clubs. And predictably, the 15–2 Eckfords and the 8–1–4 Gothams did not appear on the schedule for the Excelsiors.

Joe Sprague

During the same period Jim Creighton was being lauded, other pitchers were refining their skills. Richard Stevens of the Knickerbockers and Equity Club (NJ) and Bernard Hannegan of the Union of Morrisania (NY) were two such pitchers. A third emerging pitcher joined a very good Eckford Club of Brooklyn for their final match of the 1861 season. The following year, he briefly served in the Union Army, returned to Brooklyn in July, and pitched the deciding match against the Atlantics of Brooklyn in September, helping secure the Eckfords first championship. He then pitched the Ecks to an undefeated season in 1863, the first time a top-flight club had achieved that distinction, and to a second-consecutive National Championship. He was one of the important ingredients in the Eckfords winning 22-straight matches over two seasons. As a pitcher, he personally complied a 24-straight game winning streak. He then joined the rival Atlantics but played only sparingly during their consecutive championship seasons of 1864 and 1865. Thereafter, he practically disappeared from baseball and was rarely mentioned until his death notice appeared in the *New York Clipper* in 1898. His accomplishments during baseball's development were truly second-to-none and he deserves to be recognized in Cooperstown. The name of this undeservedly neglected pioneer star was Joe Sprague.

The first newspaper account of Sprague as a pitcher stems from a match held on November 26, 1857, when he was only 14 years old. He appeared for the National Club of Brooklyn, a junior club, and defeated another junior club, the Montauk Club of Bedford, 61–5.[4] Scouring box scores from various newspapers for further Sprague appearances produced spotty results, mainly because of his association with junior clubs until 1861, including four clubs from 1857 through 1860, and three different clubs, National of Brooklyn, Exercise of Brooklyn, and Oriental of Greenpoint, in 1860 alone. Perhaps Sprague was one of the first paid players in baseball history, even at the junior level.

Sprague became a regular for the Exercise Club of Brooklyn in 1861, the club's first year as a senior organization, and he began his first-nine career facing two of the most powerful clubs in the coun-

This image of Joseph E. Sprague appeared in the *New York Clipper* of July 9, 1898, not long after his death. "Thirty-five years ago ... he was the noted pitcher of the old Eckford Club, of Williamsburg, L.I. He was a large man, of fine athletic appearance, and his great strength just suited him for the arduous duties of pitching. He was cool and fearless in facing swiftly batted balls, and possessed 'brains' that enabled him to meet any emergency." In 1865 "he became interested in cricket, joining the Manhattan Cricket Club, and giving up baseball entirely. Being a speedy underhand bowler, Mr. Sprague soon took a front rank as a cricketer."

try: the Eckford and the Atlantic. Sprague was defeated in all three matches, twice by the Eckfords and once by the Atlantics. Ironically, he debuted against the Eckfords, losing 27–20 (tied at 17 after six innings, Sprague surrendered five home runs in the match).[5] He rebounded to win his next two matches against significantly weaker clubs, the Hamilton of Brooklyn and the Woodlawn of the Bronx. Another match against the Hamiltons is mentioned in multiple sources, but no line or box score has been located. While it can be deduced that Sprague was the winning pitcher, it cannot be confirmed. When his epitaph was printed in the *New York Clipper*, it stated that Sprague remained with the Exercise Club through the 1861 season and joined the Enterprise Club for the start of the 1862 season.[6] Neither of those statements proved to be true.

On the Move, Again

Sprague's victory over the Hamilton Club on October 22, 1861, was his final for the Exercise Club. As reported in *Wilkes' Spirit of the Times*, he then turned up as the winning pitcher for the Eckford Club against the Hudson River Club (Newburgh, NY) in Brooklyn on November 4, 1861.[7]

"The Eckfords were not out in full force, although they rallied, as they generally do, a strong nine. Beach, as catcher, was in his usual first-class play; Sprague, formerly of the Exercise Base Ball Club, made his *debut* in the Eckford Club, as pitcher, and fully sustained the good name which he has long enjoyed..."[8] For the second time in two seasons, Sprague made appearances for more than one club, this time at the senior level. Had he been paid for perhaps the fourth time to dress for another club? Pitching for five clubs in two seasons would almost guarantee that money was a factor in his travels.

"The Streak" Begins

The outstanding achievements of Joe Sprague were neglected during his playing days and remain overlooked by modern historians. Without the benefit of newspaper public relations, he proved on the field that he was perhaps the best pitcher in the 1860s. One of his pitching accomplishments commenced with a victory over the Woodlawn Club on October 9, 1861,[9] and would not be matched until Tim Keefe of 1888 New York Giants won

Better Than Creighton

A 21st century image of the form Joe Sprague used to win 24 straight matches. This image shows Eric Miklich pitching in an 1864 match at Old Bethpage Village Restoration.

19 straight matches. In fact, two other Sprague streaks began with that same win over Woodlawn. His October 1, 1861, loss to the Eckford Club while pitching for the Exercise Club[10] would be the last time Sprague would be on the losing end of a baseball match, either pitching or playing the field, until he retired. That winning streak would reach 34-consecutive matches, and end only with his "retirement" in 1865. As the 1861 season neared conclusion, Sprague began a three-match personal winning streak.

1862

Sprague started the 1862 season winning two Eckford intra-squad matches before crossing paths with a living legend. On May 22, Sprague and Creighton played on the same side for the only time in their careers, but neither pitched. Rather, they were stationed at shortstop and second base, respectively, for the winning side.[11]

After pitching and winning a third Eckford intra-squad match,[12] Sprague left the club and joined the Union Army for a three-month tour

> CHARTER OAK CLUB.—Another fine practice game was had on the grounds of this club, in Brooklyn, on Thursday, May 22d, in which members of the Excelsior, Eckford, Star, Hamilton, &c., took part, the fielding being the best seen on the grounds this season. Nine innings were played, in the unusually short time of *one hour and fifty minutes*, the scores being 11 to 6. Piper's side, which was by no means a weak one, were put out six times in succession, with a single run being scored, and there were five innings on Skaats' side, in which no runs were obtained. Every fine afternoon, almost, just such excellent pratice games as the above are had on the Star ground, and, in consequence, the place has been quite a favorite resort of base ball players.

PIPER'S SIDE.	H.L.	RUNS.	SKAATS' SIDE.	H.L.	RUNS.
Piper, s s.........3	2		Skaats, p............4	1	
Randolph, 2d b......2	0		Oswald, c f..........5	0	
Vanderhoof, l f.....3	1		Waddell, 3d b........3	0	
Mitchell, r f.......3	1		McKenzie, 1st b......5	1	
Galpin, c f.........3	1		Creighton, 2d b......1	3	
Flanly, 1st b.......3	0		C. Bergen, l f.......1	3	
Kelly, p............4	0		Sprague, s s.........3	0	
H. Brainard, c......3	1		Nicolson, r f........2	2	
Gilbert, 3d b.......3	0		Henry, c.............3	1	
Total...............		6	Total...............		11

RUNS MADE IN EACH INNINGS.	1st	2d	3d	4th	5th	6th	7th	8th	9th	
Piper's side......	3	2	0	0	0	0	0	0	1	6
Skaats' side......	0	5	0	1	0	4	0	1	0	11

Umpire, Mr. Duval.

New York Clipper, May 31, 1862.

of duty.[13] At the time, it was not uncommon for baseball players to enlist, and those from the New York area generally joined Northern ranks.

During his stint with the Thirteenth Regiment, New York State Militia, Sprague found time to pitch and win a match played among two New York Regiment nines.

> BALL-PLAYERS OFF TO THE WAR.—But few of the fraternity, in comparison with the number who left in May, 1861, have gone off to the war this time in the militia regiments. Of the first nines of the Brooklyn clubs, the Eckford lose Sprague, the Enterprise, Cornwell; the Star, Kelly; the Hamilton, Bergen; Holt, too, the catcher of the Henry Eckford's, has left. All the clubs have their representatives in the several regiments, especially in the Thirteenth Regiment; but the hegira of warlike ball-players is nothing near as great as in 1861, the necessity not being as pressing as it was a year ago, or otherwise the clubs would have suffered considerably in the loss of members through the departure of the State Militia.

New York Sunday Mercury, June 1, 1862.

> **MATCHES AMONG THE SOLDIERS.** — It will be seen by the following letter that the members of the Thirteenth Regiment, N. Y. S. M., and the Fourth, N. Y. S. V., have been enjoying themselves:
>
> CAMP CROOKE, VA., July 20.
>
> We had a good afternoon's sport here yesterday. The selected nine of the Fourth N. Y. S. V., came into our camp to play us a game of ball, feeling quite confident of success. We were unable to turn out in our full strength, but we paraded a very good nine notwithstanding. The Fourth boys played a very strong game, their pitcher and catcher being first rate players; but they were out-batted, our men doing some very tall things in the way of batting. Lieut. Fuller treated the visiting party handsomely, in his tent, and they departed in right good spirits, though feeling a little sore at their defeat, having hitherto beaten every nine they have played against.
>
> Captain T. S. Dakin operated as umpire, and did his duty thoroughly.
>
> I send you the score, which is as follows:
>
> | 13TH REGIMENT. | O. | R. | 4TH REGIMENT. | O. | R. |
> |---|---|---|---|---|---|
> | Sprague, P. | 4 | 2 | Ward, C. | 3 | 1 |
> | Murphy, C. | 3 | 1 | Murray, P. | 4 | 1 |
> | G. Holt, 2d b. | 3 | 2 | Nape, 1st b. | 2 | 2 |
> | Hendrickson, r. f. | 3 | 2 | Boyd, 2d b. | 5 | 0 |
> | S. Patchen, 1st b. | 2 | 3 | Farrell, 3d b. | 3 | 2 |
> | Bergen, c. f. | 3 | 2 | Hanson, s. s. | 3 | 1 |
> | Fountain, 3d b. | 3 | 2 | McCullum, c. f. | 3 | 1 |
> | Selleck, l. f. | 3 | 1 | Hunt, l. f. | 2 | 1 |
> | Kelly, s. s. | 3 | 1 | Smullen, r. f. | 4 | 2 |
>
> | INNINGS | 1 | 2 | 3 | 4 | 5 | 6 | 7 | 8 | 9 | |
> |---|---|---|---|---|---|---|---|---|---|---|
> | Thirteenth | 0 | 1 | 3 | 2 | 5 | 2 | 1 | 1 | 1 | —16 |
> | Fourth | 1 | 1 | 0 | 0 | 1 | 6 | 0 | 1 | 1 | —11 |

New York Sunday Mercury, July 27, 1862.

September 18, 1862

While Sprague was mustering, a very good Eckford club amassed a 7–1 record that included a split with the powerful Atlantics. The loss was an embarrassing one, 39–5, and came 10 days after a 14–10 victory in the first match of the series. The Eckfords postponed the third and deciding match with the Atlantics until Sprague returned to Brooklyn and had time to regain his pitching form.[14] Although his reappearance on the field on September 18, 1862, has been romantically but incorrectly recorded as his debut with the club, the 19-year-old did pitch the Eckfords to victory in front of a reported 10,000 spectators.[15] In perhaps the greatest game of the early 1860s. Sprague held the Atlantics to the lowest run total in their eight-year history (3), and blanked them in six of the final seven innings. This bettered the four-run effort that Creighton had held the Atlantics to in 1860. Their

8–3 victory brought the Eckfords to the precipice of their first championship. The rules of the time regarding the anointing of a champion stated that in order to be declared the champion, a challenging club had to beat the accepted champion two-of-three matches, all played while that club was recognized as the title holder. Sprague defeated the Union of Morrisania, 13–10, and next beat the Mutuals, the second win over the Mutes ensuring the 1862 championship. The Eckfords then headed to Philadelphia for a four-game tour.

The Champions

The Eckfords played four matches in four days, October 21 through 24. Sprague sat out the first match but won the final three with little difficulty. The Eckfords ended the season with a 12-game winning streak. Sprague himself had won nine-straight senior matches, 13-straight including exhibitions, and had been on the winning side 14-straight times. Sprague's pitching effectively halted opponents' offensive output. Prior to his arrival, Eckford opponents had scored 15 or more runs five times in eight matches. In the six matches that Sprague appeared in, opponents scored 15 or more runs only once. Since the Eckfords had very little trouble scoring runs, the addition of Sprague and his pitching abilities quickly vaulted the Eckfords to the top of the baseball fraternity.

1863

Sprague pitched the entire 1863 season for the Eckfords, and the club defeated all ten of its challengers. In these matches, opponents scored more than 10 runs only twice. Sprague easily defeated the Atlantics twice in a span of seven days; 31–10 and 21–11, for his second and third wins in a row over the historic club. It was the first time in the Atlantics history that they lost to the same pitcher in three consecutive matches. Sprague also defeated the Mutuals and the Union of Morrisania, each for the third straight time. His domination was again on display on September 16, when the Eckfords were forced to start a game against the Resolute of Brooklyn with only eight players, due to Sprague being off bowling in a cricket match in Hoboken.[16] He arrived after four innings of play with his club clinging to an 11–8 lead. Once Sprague took over, the Resolutes were unable to get a runner to first for the remainder of match.[17] In securing their second consecutive championship, the Eckfords outscored their opponents 217 to 80, allowing only eight runs per game, an unheard-of number for bare-handed early baseball. With Sprague, the Eckfords easily dominated all challengers, winning 22-straight matches over a season and a half.

Post-Eckford

Sprague played sparingly for the Atlantics during the 1864 and 1865 seasons, never experiencing a loss. In 1864, he appeared in seven matches, with the final match of a three-game upstate trip was called after four innings due to rain. In all, Sprague made the least amount of outs during those matches (6), and was third in total runs scored with 16. He also appeared on the winning side of a 19-11 Old Atlantic Nine (1860) win over the New Atlantic Nine (1864) on October 13.[18]

Although it has been often reported that Sprague never pitched for the Atlantics during his spotty tenure with the club, he in fact pitched against the Lowell Club in a game at the Capitoline grounds on July 20, 1865.[19] Tom Pratt, the Atlantics regular pitcher, was unable to attend the match, forcing left fielder John Chapman to pitch the first three innings. A late-arriving Sprague was inserted between the lines in the fourth inning, with the Atlantics leading 26-4 and coasted to a 45-17 victory.[20] The Atlantics won all three games Sprague appeared in during 1865.

Sprague's Numbers

Applying the same formula used to determine Creighton's opponents' overall rating, the six that Sprague faced in 1862 compiled a 17-17 record and had a strength rating of 2. The 10 opponents Sprague faced in 1863 amassed a 32-25 record and a strength rating of 2.5. At the conclusion of the 1863 season, Sprague had accomplished the following: two-consecutive championships, 23-straight pitching wins (19 at the senior level), while the clubs that he dressed and played for won 25-straight matches. Adding in his time with the Atlantics, Sprague's career figures expand to four-straight championships, 24-straight pitching wins (20 at the senior level), while the clubs that he dressed and played for won 34-straight matches.

Creighton and Sprague

The bases of comparison between Creighton and Sprague involve a relatively short playing period because of Creighton's untimely demise. The 1860 season has been used for Creighton, while the end of the 1862 season coupled with the entire 1863 season was utilized for Sprague.

In 1860, Jim Creighton produced the following stats: pitched 166 innings; allowed .88 runs per inning; had 17 strikeouts; and produced a 17-2-1 record against opponents who were a combined 27-28-3, with a rating strength of 1.4. Creighton was 1-1-1 against the Atlantics, but never faced the Mutuals or the Eckfords.

Creighton Pitching for the 1860 Excelsior Club of Brooklyn

5/17—L—12-11: Charter Oak (Brooklyn), recorded two strikeouts.
6/21—W—36-9: Charter Oak (Brooklyn), pitched the eighth and ninth innings.
6/28—W—16-5: Star Club (Brooklyn), recorded six strikeouts.
7/2—W—24-6; Champion (Albany, NY).
7/3—W—13-7: Victory (Troy, NY).
7/5—W—13-7: Niagara (Buffalo, NY).
7/7—W—50-19: Flour City (Rochester, NY)
7/9—W—21-1; Live Oak (Rochester, NY), recorded two strikeouts.
7/11—W—59-14: Hudson, River (Newburgh, NY).
7/19—W—24-3: Atlantic (Brooklyn), recorded two strikeouts.
7/22—W—51-6: Excelsior (Baltimore, MD).
7/24—W—15-4: Picked Nine (Philadelphia, PA).
8/4—W—23-7: Putnam (Brooklyn), recorded two strikeouts.
8/9—L—15-14: Atlantic (Brooklyn), pulled after seven innings, losing 15-12.
8/18—Called due to rain, ahead 13-7 (4 innings): Empire (New York), pulled after three innings.
8/23—T—8-6: Atlantic (Brooklyn), ended in the top of the sixth (with two runs in); pitched five innings.
8/25—W—32-9 (8 innings): Knickerbocker (New York).
9/1—W—23-7: Empire (New York).
9/7—W—7-4: Union (Morrisania).
9/15—W—46-14: Independent (Brooklyn).
9/29—W—23-7: Empire (New York).
11/5—W—25-0: St. George Cricket Club (New York).

Better Than Creighton

From 1862 (final six games) through 1863, Sprague produced the following stats: pitched 132 innings; allowed 1.05 runs per inning; had 31 strikeouts; and produced a 16-0 record against opponents who were a combined 49-47, with a rating strength of 2.25.

Sprague Pitching for the 1862 Eckford Club of Brooklyn Club

- 8/18—W—8-3: Atlantic (Brooklyn) Atlantic's lowest run total; recorded two strikeouts.
- 9/24—W—28-10: Mutual (New York).
- 10/7—W—13-10: Union (Morrisania).
- 10-22—W—39-13: Olympic (Philadelphia PA).
- 10-23—W—32-25 (6 innings): Athletic (Philadelphia, PA), recorded two strikeouts.
- 10-24—W—26-2: Keystone (Philadelphia, PA), recorded two strikeouts.

Sprague Pitching for the 1863 Eckford Club of Brooklyn Club

- 6/17—W—13-10 (6 innings): Athletic (Philadelphia), recorded three strikeouts.
- 7/22—W—10-9: Mutual (New York).
- 7/30—W—8-4: Union (Morrisania), recorded nine strikeouts.
- 8/4—W—50-13: Hudson River (Newburgh, NY).
- 8/14—W—16-5: Resolute (Brooklyn).
- 9/2—W—31-10: Atlantic (Brooklyn), recorded four strikeouts.
- 9/8—W—21-11 (8 innings): Atlantic (Brooklyn).
- 9/16—W—24-8: Resolute (Brooklyn), pitched final 5 innings, no batter reached first base.
- 9/24—W—29-5: Union (Morrisania).
- 10/6—W—18-10: Mutual (New York), recorded five strikeouts.

Unfortunately, detailed box scores are unavailable for four Sprague outings during this period. His strikeout total would easily be over 40 with those games included. He struck out nine batters against the Union of Morrisania on July 30, 1863.[21] Sprague consistently faced stronger competition than Creighton, defeating the Atlantics, Mutuals, and Union of Morrisania, three times each.

These two pitchers were the best early 19th century baseball produced. The reputation of one benefited from a tragic early death. The other was overshadowed by a print media legend. Creighton essentially maintained his new club's performance level, while Sprague made a good team invincible.

The following source was used in the assistance of the compilation of the pitching opponents for Jim Creighton and Joe Sprague:

Wright, Marshall D. *The National Association of Base Ball Players, 1857–1870*. Jefferson, NC: McFarland, 2000.

Notes

1. *Mears Base Ball Scrap Books*. Vol. 1, 1860–1861, 26.
2. *Ibid.*
3. *New York Times*, July 20, 1860, 8.
4. *New York Clipper*, December 5, 1857, 263.
5. *New York Clipper*, September 21, 1861, 179.
6. *New York Clipper*, July 9, 1898, 311.
7. *Wilkes' Spirit of the Times*, November 11, 1861.
8. *Ibid.*
9. *Wilkes' Spirit of the Times*, October 19, 1861, 100.
10. *New York Clipper*, October 12, 1861, 202.
11. *New York Clipper*, May 31, 1862, 50.
12. *Mears Base Ball Scrap Books*. Vol. 1, 1862–1863.
13. *New York Sunday Mercury*, June 1, 1862.
14. *New York Clipper*, September 27, 1862, 186.
15. *Ibid.*
16. *New York Sunday Mercury*, September 20, 1863.
17. *Ibid.*
18. *Mears Base Ball Scrapbooks*, Vol 1, 1864–1865.
19. *Wilkes' Spirit of the Times*, July 29, 1865.
20. *Ibid.*
21. *Wilkes' Spirit of the Times*, August 8, 1863, 356.

Ballplayer for Hire
The Life and Times of Charles "Famous" Krause

Justin McKinney

> This article examines the life of Charles "Famous" Krause, a charismatic and erratic ballplayer on the fringes of professional baseball from 1894 to 1910, whose major league career consisted of one game with the 1901 Cincinnati Reds. Krause played for at least 16 different professional clubs, relying on his gift for self-promotion, networking and persistent letter writing campaigns to prospective ball clubs in order to find his next gig. Krause's knack for self-aggrandizement was matched by his ability to get into controversy, including his frequent contract jumping and his expulsion from the Canadian League in 1905 due to game fixing allegations. Krause's story reveals the importance of "soft" skills in finding employment as a baseball player at the turn of the last century.

CHARLES "FAMOUS" KRAUSE WAS a bizarre yet today virtually unknown figure in the annals of professional baseball. Krause was a baseball nomad, who played one game for the 1901 Cincinnati Reds in the midst of a 15-year career that saw him play for at least 16 professional teams and numerous semi-pro teams from 1894 to 1910. Krause's career was marked by his uncanny ability to find work despite relatively limited ability, as well as his erratic behavior and a penchant for controversy. The story of Krause demonstrates the power of "soft" skills including self-promotion, networking, and persistence for finding employment as a baseball player at the turn of the last century.

Charles Frederick Krause was born on October 2, 1873, in Detroit, Michigan, the son of German immigrants, August Krause and Augusta (Grubba). Detroit in the 1860s and 1870s was home to a wave of German immigration, and the Krauses arrived in 1873. They arrived in Detroit just in time to see the birth of Charles, their eldest child. The Krause family was working class and father August was employed as a laborer once he arrived in America and would hold similar roles for the rest of his life. The Krauses would eventually have five more children.

Little is known about Charles Krause's early life. The earliest public mention of Krause occurs in 1894 in the *Detroit Free Press* sporting pages. That year he began his baseball career with the Detroit Athletics, one of the leading semipro teams in the city. The Athletics were one of the longest tenured clubs in all of Michigan, having been formed in 1886. (Detroit was home to a thriving semi-professional and amateur community in the 1890s, with numerous teams competing regularly throughout the state.) In his debut for the Athletics, Krause, listed as "Krouse" in the box score,[1] played third base and had three hits in five at bats against the Michigan Athletic Association. Krause played various infield and outfield positions for the Athletics in 1894 to 1896, while also playing for other top teams including Monroe, Yale and Muskegon.

During this period of Krause's career, from 1894 to 1910, professional baseball saw high levels of growth, as numerous teams and leagues were formed across North America. In 1894, there were 27 leagues in organized baseball and by 1910 that number had more than doubled to 56 leagues. This is in addition to the multitude of semipro and amateur leagues that dotted the country. Within this growth, there was also great instability, as one can see by looking at Krause's first foray into organized baseball, with the 1897 Kalamazoo entry in the newly re-formed Michigan League.

The Michigan League was initially founded in 1889 but folded in 1890. It was re-formed in 1895 but folded before the 1896 season. The league was reconstituted in 1897 as a six-team circuit with teams in Bay City, Saginaw, Port Huron, Kalamazoo, Lansing and Jackson. The Kalamazoo team would be managed by German-born Fred Popkay, who was a titan in the Detroit and Michigan baseball community. During a long playing, umpiring and managing career in the minors and various Michigan semipro leagues, Popkay helped numerous Michigan-based ballplayers land jobs. An article in the April 7, 1897, *Kalamazoo Gazette* was optimistic about the team formed by Popkay, singling out Krause: "Charles Krause will gather in the flies to the admiration of the base ball public, in centre field. He is a youngster full of ambition and promise. His hitting will assist in winning many a close game. He hails from the popular Athletic club of Detroit."[2]

The Kalamazoo club made its regular season debut on April 29, with Krause leading off and manning center field in an 11 to 4 loss to Jackson. Krause was hitless in four at-bats. The Kalamazoo club got off to a poor start, winning only one of their first 15 games. Krause did not remain with the club for long and appears to have been released in mid–May, making his last appearance on May 11. The reason for his release was not given in the local papers, though he does not appear to have played particularly well in his two weeks with the club.

In spite of his release from Kalamazoo, Krause remained much in demand in his native Detroit, where he rejoined the Detroit Athletics in mid–May and would also play for several semipro clubs including Buick and Sherwood, East Side Brewing Company, and the West Side Locals throughout the 1897 season. Krause earned positive reviews for his hitting, while also playing center field and third base. Krause demonstrated his ample foot speed when he won a 100-yard dash at the West Side Locals picnic in mid–August.[3] Seemingly content with staying in his hometown, Krause did not play professionally in 1898. In April of that year, he rejoined his former manager Popkay, who was slated to manage the Detroit Athletics. Krause batted .352 for the Athletics that year.[4] Krause was firmly established as a mainstay for the Athletics and would return as their third baseman in 1899 as well.

Krause was a lifelong bachelor, who like his father, worked a series of blue collar jobs throughout his life. The 1900 census has him living at home with his parents and several siblings. (In fact, Krause lived at home with his parents until their deaths in the early 1920s.) It is possible that the stability of his home life and lack of dependents enabled his renewed pursuit of a professional career in the coming decade. As the 1900 season started, the 26-year-old Krause had played six years of semipro ball and apart from his two-week stint with Kalamazoo in 1897, had no professional experience. In 1900 Krause once again starred with the Detroit Athletics and played the hot corner for the majority of the season.

In September, Krause made his return to the minor leagues, when he joined the American League's Minneapolis Millers. It is not clear how Krause ended up with the Millers, since there is no apparent Michigan connection on the club and no announcement of his signing. He made his debut on September 2 against Buffalo, where he went hitless in a 9 to 8 loss but was praised for his errorless play at second base. Krause stayed with the club for the remainder of the season as a utility man, batting .172 and playing shortstop, second, left field and center field in his nine games with the club.

The year 1901 would prove to be the real beginning of Krause's nomadic pursuits and the first evidence of his erratic tendencies. Krause placed an ad requesting work in the March 2, 1901, issue of *Sporting Life*.[5] This was a common tactic for hungry ballplayers of the era. Despite Krause's underwhelming performance with Minneapolis, Krause received a glowing recommendation from team owner C.H. Saulspaugh, and on the strength of this recommendation was signed for the 1901 season by Hugh Nicol, former American Association star and current manager of the Rockford Red Sox of the Three-I League.[6] Upon signing, Krause was listed at a height of 5 feet 8 (he was 5 feet 6), age 24 (he was in fact 28) and was credited with having played 17 games with Minneapolis and a .284 average.[7] These false "facts" could be the result of journalistic exaggeration, but may also hint at Krause's own inflated sense of self, a trait which soon became evident.

This signing was not without controversy, as Krause also signed a contract with the rival Terre Haute club when his Rockford contract failed to arrive promptly.[8] The dispute over his services lasted for several weeks before a resolution was reached with Nicol retaining the shortstop's services. Nicol was praised for bringing the young shortstop into the fold and notes of congratulations were reportedly sent to Nicol from various sources.[9]

Krause was given the nickname "Germany" due to his ancestry during his time with Rockford. He became known for his "ginger" in the field and speed on the base paths, at one point boasting that he would steal one base each game.[10] The shortstop's time with Rockford would be short-lived however, as on May 18, he asked for his release.

A 1901 illustration of Charles Krause documenting his time with the Rockford Illinois club (*Rockford* [Illinois] *Republic*, April 27, 1901).

The Life and Times of Charles "Famous" Krause

When asked why he wanted his release, the impulsive Krause indicated that he was in a rut and stated, "I quit simply because that's the way I feel."[11] The local papers speculated that Krause was disheartened by crowd criticism whenever he made an error in the field. Krause indicated that he expected to join Evansville in the Three-I League or Toledo of the Western Association.[12] He headed instead to Chicago to pursue his next opportunity and joined the semipro Aurora club.[13] Krause spent June and July with Aurora before heading back to Chicago in the hopes of finding his big break. The wayward infielder got his chance on July 27, 1901, when he made a memorable appearance for the Cincinnati Reds in Chicago.

The means by which Krause landed a spot with the Reds reveal Krause's penchant for exaggeration and ability to self-promote. According to the *Cincinnati Post*, Chicago Orphans manager Tom Loftus had received a letter a week from Krause since the season started and apparently Chicago president Jim Hart expressed interest in the persistent shortstop.[14] Cincinnati manager Bid McPhee recounted that Krause met with him early on July 27, and claimed to be such a prominent player in Aurora, that "they were going to give him the waterworks."[15] McPhee in dire need of a second baseman, with regular Bill Fox having injured his finger the day before, enlisted Krause for a trial.

Krause's performance was so poor in the Reds' 9 to 3 loss on July 27 to the Chicago Orphans that it was still being discussed days later in the local papers. At the plate, Krause had one hit in four at-bats against Jack Taylor. But in the field he really made his mark. Filing in at second base for the injured Fox, Krause made two errors, one on a ground ball that caused him to "lobsterize" and stumble backwards and another drop on a lazy pop fly which was described colorfully by the *Cincinnati Enquirer*: "Childs hoisted a little fly, and Mr. Krause ran for it. Just as he reached the ball he stopped stock still. He stood there like the Silver King when the Chee-ild says 'They say my father killed a man,' and the ball fell while two runs came in. The crowd had fits and the Reds told Mr. Krause that Aurora was full of thieves and men who were only sorry that there were but 10 commandments to be fractured."[16]

The *Enquirer* speculated he "may never be seen in a professional uniform again, but while he lasted he was the Weber and Fields, put together, of the diamond."[17] The *Cincinnati Post* mockingly dubbed him the "Aurora Borealis" and noted that any claim to Krause's services by the Orphans was immediately rescinded after that day's debacle.[18] The vitriol directed at Krause seems to suggest a sort of comeuppance for a braggadocious young ballplayer who talked his way into an opportunity far above his actual worth.

Krause does not appear to have returned to the Aurora club and there are no records of him playing again that year. In November, Krause wrote to his former manager Nicol, expressing regret for leaving the club and asked for a recommendation to help him to catch on with another club.[19] In early 1902, perhaps on the strength of Nicol's reference, Krause signed with the Concord Marines of the New England League.[20] He never played for Concord, however, and when the season opened Krause was the starting shortstop for the rival Lawrence Colts.

Krause's time with Lawrence would be tumultuous and short-lived, as he batted a meagre .222 in 27 games with the club. Krause demonstrated a fiery temper during his time with Lawrence, getting kicked out of a game on May 15 for "using vile language."[21] He earned national notoriety for an incident in a game at Lowell on May 22. Krause got into an argument with umpire Hassett and in response, Hassett walked towards Krause and tweaked the shortstop's nose.[22] The following day, Krause was kicked out of a game in Manchester, New Hampshire, for arguing.[23]

Krause left the club sometime in June, for unknown reasons and resurfaced the following month as an infielder and outfielder for Decatur of the Three-I League. His former manager and teammate Popkay was the club's first baseman and likely served as a connection for the impetuous baseballist. In what was becoming a familiar pattern, however, Krause's tenure would be brief for reasons of his own making. Krause played 22 games for Decatur and batted a modest .256 but asked for his release in early August. His stated reason was "not finding some of his teammates personally agreeable."[24] The *Decatur* [Illinois] *Herald* noted that Krause "imagined that the other members of the team were knocking on him and wanted his release. The knocking story is said to be imagination pure and simple, but he nursed that theory and didn't play ball."[25] Krause quickly joined rival Evansville on August 5 but was released just two days later.[26] He appears to have returned to Detroit and appeared for the Detroit Professionals 10 to 8 victory on October 19 over a very young Eddie Cicotte and the Detroit Independents.

Thus far in his career, Krause had demonstrated a remarkable talent for locating opportunities to play professional baseball, and an equally remarkable ability to squander those chances through impetuousness, short sightedness and self-absorption. The season began with the now familiar news that Krause had signed with a new club, in this case the Marion, Indiana, club of the Central League.[27] Meanwhile, Krause also agreed to play for two local Detroit teams, the Popkay-managed Detroit Athletics and the Detroit Wheelmen. Krause ended up not reporting to Marion and stayed in

The Life and Times of Charles "Famous" Krause

Detroit. In early May, it was reported that Krause had signed with the Anderson, Indiana, club of the Central League.[28] The club was managed by Chip Handford, who was a former teammate of Krause on the 1901 Rockford club.

Anderson ended up relocating to Krause's home state of Michigan, where the club was reconstituted as the Grand Rapids Orphans on May 30. It is not clear if Krause played for the club that year, as there is no record of him playing for the Anderson/Grand Rapids Orphans in 1903 and he does not appear on the Grand Rapids reserve list published in October. Nonetheless, the ramifications of his signing would have severe consequences on his career.

The 1904 season would find Krause in a bizarre predicament. In January, Krause signed with the Dayton Veterans of the Central League under the name of Charlie McGau. The moniker of McGau first appeared in October 1903, when the *Detroit Free Press* received a letter addressed to someone of that name, so it is apparent that Krause was using the alias to obtain work.[29] In March 1904, Krause created a new baseball club, the Athletics No. 2, announcing his intention to play the original Athletics for rights to the name.[30] Around the same time, McGau/Krause was receiving interest from two American League teams and had requested his release from Dayton.[31] The club refused to sell McGau and denied him his release.[32] It was in Dayton, where he would enjoy arguably the most success of his professional career, but in typical Krause fashion, it would not last long.

"McGau" began the season as Dayton's starting shortstop and quickly made a positive impression. The April 23 issue of the *Dayton [Ohio] News* stated confidently and somewhat ironically, that "McGau of course at short is a fixture, and will remain throughout the season."[33] In the same issue, a drawing of McGau appeared, depicting him with bandit mask, flashlight and pistol, and holding second base, alluding to his speed and ability as a base stealer.[34] In his first month with Dayton, McGau's hitting stood out, as he batted .320. But he also made numerous errors in the field.[35]

The reason for Krause's ruse would become clear on May 9, when the *Grand Rapids Press* commented on McGau's true identity:

> Notice has been served on Dayton that that club must at once turn over to Grand Rapids Shortstop McGau, last year with the local team, but who jumped and went with the Pacific coast outlaws. This year he started in with Dayton, but some of the old Grand Rapids players recognized him there.... McGau, or Crouse, as he called himself here, must now play with Grand Rapids or with no league team in the United States, as the national agreement covers them all.[36]

Krause jumped the Dayton club to go to Grand Rapids, where he played one game on May 21, before he was suspended by Central League President

George W. Bement while the situation waited to be resolved.³⁷ According to Krause's own account, he felt he was free to jump to Grand Rapids from Dayton, since he had signed with Grand Rapids the previous year, but had not come to terms with the club over the winter.³⁸ As a result, he had signed with Dayton, while waiting for the terms to be resolved with Grand Rapids.³⁹ The logic of Krause's account and the fact that he played under an alias demonstrate a strange sense of ethics and dubious understanding of contract law. Krause was released by Grand Rapids and reportedly sought reinstatement with Dayton.⁴⁰ By the time his suspension was lifted in late June, Krause had returned to Detroit.⁴¹ Back home, he rejoined the Athletics, his feud with his former nine having apparently subsided. Krause was claimed by Rochester of the Eastern League in September, but did not report, choosing to remain in Detroit.⁴²

A caricature of the mysterious Charles McGau—Krause's alias during his short-lived stint with Dayton in 1904 (*Dayton News*, April 23, 1904).

The controversy of 1904, should seemingly have spelled the end of Krause's professional career, given his spotty performance and questionable behavior. Yet 1905 would prove to be even more tumultuous for the oddball Krause. The infielder signed with Terre Haute of the Central League in January and would quickly demonstrate his ability to embroil himself in controversy.⁴³ Krause began the season as Terre Haute's starting shortstop, but by May 5, he had lost his starting job to a local amateur, John Brown.⁴⁴ Krause was released the following week, then quickly re-signed when another player failed to report.⁴⁵ When Terre Haute traveled to Grand Rapids on May 16, Krause jumped the team. The *Dayton Daily News* commented on Krause's disappearance, calling him "a disturbing element [who] … caused trouble in the team here and later with Terre Haute" and claimed that his real name was "Fonmagau."⁴⁶ This strange revelation regarding his identity does not appear to have any grounding in truth, but simply adds another layer to the tangled web that Krause wove everywhere he went. Krause hit a meager .060 in ten games with the club, but that did not stop him from landing his next opportunity.

The Life and Times of Charles "Famous" Krause

From there, Krause went north to Canada, where he joined the Woodstock Maroons in the newly formed Western Ontario League, which began play in late May. Krause joined fellow Detroiter Joseph Cocash on the club, which quickly established itself as the top team in the league. Krause manned second base and both somehow found time to form a local junior club to manage, the Famous Krause Juniors.[47] This is noteworthy because it is the earliest appearance of his nickname "Famous," though there is no indication how he received the moniker. The Maroons continued their strong play into July, when Krause became the center of scandal once again.

On July 15, the first place Maroons traveled to Brantford, where they lost 7 to 0 to the third-place club. Both Cocash and Krause played poorly

Charles Krause pictured in the front row with the London Tecumsehs in September 1905 a few months after his banishment for game-fixing in the Canadian League (*Detroit Free Press*, September 3, 1905).

in the loss and were released after the game. It was quickly revealed that both men had not given their all during the game and this was the reason for the release. The Woodstock *Daily Sentinel Review* explained the situation, while alluding to Krause's unsavory reputation:

> The principal cause and root of the trouble on Saturday is traceable to one Charles Krause. He simply did not try to play ball and his sole object seemed to be to see how "rotten" he could make the game. He has always been a hard fellow to handle although at times a good ball player. He wrote here in the spring for a situation. After two or three letters from him the management sent him a ticket. He been used well by them, and the thanks they received for their kindness is to have him virtually throw them down. He received his pay Saturday [July 15], and immediately handed in his uniform. Secretary Muir persuaded him to go to Brantford. This was a mistake, as a "dummy" would have been more useful than the erratic player proved to be.[48]

Rumors around Brantford were that the players had been "bought up to throw the game, and that efforts were made to bet on Brantford."[49] Krause and Cocash were released that day and suspended by the league.[50] Both men denied the charge shortly after in the *Detroit Free Press*.[51] The *Grand Rapids Press* also accused Krause of throwing a game for Terre Haute earlier in the season.[52] Seemingly these accusations should have cemented Krause as a character of ill-repute and had some consequence on his career. Yet Krause was back with the Athletics for their July 23 game and later in the month was reportedly being courted by the same Terre Haute club he had deserted.[53] In August, he was back in Ontario, this time starring for the semipro Tecumseh club. In October, Krause joined Bill Armour's Detroit All Professional squad where he joined such stars as Sam Crawford, Wild Bill Donovan and Nig Clarke.[54]

As 1906 started, Krause remained a highly sought-after player. It is worth examining why this was the case, given what we know of his career thus far. Evidence shows that Krause was persistent in his pursuit of work, as he frequently wrote letters to prospective teams, as well as former teammates and managers. His name regularly appeared in the *Detroit Free Press* as the recipient of letters of interest. Given his propensity to attract new opportunities, it seems he must have been quite a persuasive writer. One can imagine that a man who called himself "Famous" and managed to talk his way into a major league game, must have had a certain confidence. How else could he have gotten chance after chance despite his consistently poor performance, unreliability, and questionable ethics?

Krause kept moving as 1906 started, signing with the Youngstown club

The Life and Times of Charles "Famous" Krause

of the Ohio and Pennsylvania League in early March. In a notice heralding his signing, Krause is listed as 25 years old, seven years younger than his actual age of 32.[55] Krause did not last long as he was among the first cuts in mid–April. Krause blamed his release on "a slight attack of malaria [that] detained him from training."[56] Despite this setback, Krause was hired in late April to serve as manager of the Alma (Michigan) College team.[57] Whether Krause actually coached the team is unknown as no further mention is made of him leading the Alma squad.

Krause remained busy playing for local semipro teams and joining the strong Petoskey independent club in Northern Michigan during the summer. The club relocated to Charlotte, Michigan, in August due to a lack of money.[58] In spite of Charlotte's success on the field, Krause remained an enigmatic presence and in mid–September, he and pitcher John Kiel quit the team.[59] The *Grand Rapids Press* put it succinctly noting that "Krouse ... has a reputation as a disorganizer."[60] Despite all this, Krause remained a sought-after commodity and was signed along with Kiel for the 1907 season by the Battle Creek Crickets of the Southern Michigan Association.

Krause started the 1907 season as the Crickets starting second baseman and was with the club through May. He last appeared for the Crickets on May 30 against Kalamazoo, though no reason was given for his disappearance. In 11 games with the Crickets, he hit a modest .252. Krause soon rejoined the local Athletics for what would be his thirteenth season with the club. He also played several games for other top semi-pro clubs in Detroit and started to umpire local games. On September 7, he replaced guest umpire and world heavyweight boxing champion Tommy Burns in a game between the Everetts and the Delray Athletics.[61] In the coming years, Krause would become a much sought-after umpire throughout Michigan.

The year 1908 brought more offers for the aging Krause. Now in his mid-thirties, he was "known to every ball player in Michigan."[62] His fame apparently crossed state borders, as he was offered the dual role of manager and third baseman with the Rockford Reds in the Wisconsin-Illinois League. He did not accept the position, instead playing out the year with the Athletics and umpiring around Detroit. In March 1909, upon the recommendation of former Detroit Wolverines star Sam Thompson, Krause was signed by the Winchester Hustlers of the Bluegrass League.[63] Krause does not appear to have reported and did not play with the club. Krause's professional playing career was over, but he continued to play and umpire locally for the next several years.

Krause did enjoy one last and very brief hurrah in professional baseball, when he became an umpire in the Central Association in 1914. Krause relocated to Keokuk, Iowa, as the season started in May, but Krause's tenure as a professional umpire was just as brief as most of his professional stints, as he quit after four games due to health troubles and returned to Detroit.[64]

Very little is known about the rest of Krause's life. He worked in 1910 as a laborer in an iron foundry and he listed a title of watchman on his 1917 World War I draft registration card. He is listed as a machinist in a motor shop on the 1920 census, still living in the same residence as his parents and several brothers. Krause's mother died in 1920 and his father died in 1924. At some point after this, Krause was institutionalized for mental illness at the Eloise Hospital in Nankin Township and would remain there for the rest of his life. Krause died of a stroke on March 30, 1948.

Krause was a colorful figure in baseball, seemingly bulletproof in his ability to overcome scandal and find work. What he lacked in on-field skill, he made up for with self-promotion and a demonstrated ability to network and leverage his baseball contacts to find new opportunities. His tactics included advertising, branding, letter-writing campaigns, getting recommendations, networking, contract jumping, and playing semi-professionally. Krause was exceptionally adept at these skills and managed to furnish a 15-year career and a place in the major league record books, based more on these "soft" skills than anything he accomplished on the field.

Notes

1. Krause's name would appear frequently as some variation of Krouse, Crouse, or Kruse throughout his baseball career.
2. "Popkay's Players," *Kalamazoo Gazette*, April 7, 1897.
3. "West End Locals Won at Tashmoe," *Detroit Free Press*, August 17, 1897.
4. "City League Figures," *Detroit Free Press*, November 12, 1898.
5. "For Managers and Players," *Sporting Life*, March 2, 1901, 7.
6. "Speedy Players Required," *Rockford* [Illinois] *Register Gazette*, March 5, 1901.
7. "Comes from Detroit," *Rockford Register Gazette*, April 5, 1901.
8. "Nicol on Hunt in Sand Hill," *Rockford* [Illinois] *Morning Star*, March 15, 1901.
9. "Nicol's Team of Young Hustlers," *Rockford Morning Star*, March 24, 1901.
10. "Gossip of the Game," *Rockford Morning Star*, May 5, 1901.
11. "Krouse Is Released," *Rockford Morning Star*, May 19, 1901.
12. "Notes of the Day," *Rockford Register Gazette*, May 21, 1901.
13. "Note Book Briefs," *Rockford Republic*, June 10, 1901.
14. "First and Last of Krouse," *Cincinnati Post*, July 29, 1901.
15. "Hahn, Given Bad Support," *Cincinnati Enquirer*, July 28, 1901.
16. *Ibid.*
17. *Ibid.*
18. "First and Last of Krouse," *Cincinnati Post*, July 29, 1901.
19. "Nicol Hears from Shortstop Krouse," *Rockford Register Gazette*, November 13, 1901.
20. "Krause, of Detroit, Signed by New England Manager" *Detroit Free Press*, January 15, 1901.
21. "New Engl'd League," *Sporting Life*, May 31, 1902, 22.
22. "New Engl'd League," *Sporting Life*, June 7, 1902, 22.
23. "New England," *Boston Post*, May 24, 1902.

24. "Notes," *Decatur Herald*, August 1, 1902.
25. "Dickey Out of It," *Decatur Herald*, August 5, 1902.
26. "Little Things in Baseball," *Indianapolis News*, August 8, 1902.
27. "Marion Players Signed," *Indianapolis Journal*, March 1, 1903.
28. "Splinters of Sport," *Decatur Herald*, May 7, 1903.
29. "All Sorts of Sports," *Detroit Free Press*, October 17, 1903.
30. "Newly Organized Nine," *Detroit Free Press*, March 10, 1904.
31. "After M'Gau," *Dayton News*, March 16, 1904.
32. *Ibid.*
33. "Sporting Review," *Dayton Daily News (Ohio)*, April 23, 1904.
34. "A Lively Week Throughout Sporting World," *Dayton News*, April 23, 1904.
35. "McGau Heads the Dayton Bunch," *Dayton News*, October 24, 1904.
36. "Play at the Lake," *Grand Rapids Press*, May 9, 1904.
37. "Central League Gossip," *Sporting Life*, June 4, 1904, 21.
38. Dyer, Wallace C., "News and Gossip of the Evansville Team." *Evansville* [Indiana] *Courier*, May 21, 1904.
39. *Ibid.*
40. "Just a Little Dope." *Evansville Courier and Press*, June 4, 1904.
41. "Central League News," *Fort Wayne* [Indiana] *News*, June 30, 1904.
42. "Eastern League," *Detroit Free Press*, September 14, 1904.
43. "Central League Notes," *Fort Wayne* [Indiana] *Journal Gazette*, January 15, 1905.
44. "Central League Has Made a Good Start," *Indianapolis News*, May 6, 1905.
45. "Changes at Terre Haute," *Indianapolis News*, May 11, 1905.
46. "Protest," *Dayton Daily News (Ohio)*, May 17, 1905.
47. "Two Let Out," *The* [Woodstock, Ontario] *Sentinel Review*, June 23, 1905.
48. "Burlesque at Brantford," *The* [Woodstock, Ontario] *Sentinel Review*, July 17, 1905.
49. "Three Gone," *The* [Woodstock, Ontario] *Sentinel Review*, July 17, 1905.
50. *Ibid.*
51. "Detroit Duo Suspended," *Detroit Free Press*, July 19, 1905.
52. "Krause at His Old Tricks," *Grand Rapids Press*, July 19, 1905.
53. "Amateur Ball Briefly," *Detroit Free Press*, July 29, 1905.
54. "Armour Names His Men," *Detroit Free Press*, October 13, 1905.
55. "Crouse with Hogan's Team," *East Liverpool* [Ohio] *Evening Review*, March 2, 1906.
56. "Alma Nine Secures Coach," *Grand Rapids Herald*, April 29, 1906.
57. *Ibid.*
58. "Change Their Home," *Grand Rapids Press*, August 2, 1906.
59. "After Two Layers," *Grand Rapids Press*, September 11, 1906.
60. *Ibid.*
61. "Everetts Best Delray," *Detroit Free Press*, September 8, 1907.
62. "'Famous' Krouse as a Manager," *Detroit Free Press*, April 2, 1908.
63. "Signs Good Infielder," *Winchester* [Kentucky] *News*, March 26, 1909.
64. "'Famous' Krouse Will Return to Detroit," [Keokuk, Iowa] *Daily Gate City*, May 10, 1914.

Mother Watson
A Look Back at One of 19th Century Baseball's Most Obscure Players

BILL LAMB

> *This article was adapted from a presentation given by the author at the Fred-Ivor Campbell 19th Century Committee conference in April 2017 and profiles Mother Watson, a two-game pitcher for the 1887 Cincinnati Reds. Watson is one of 19th century baseball's most obscure figures, with even his pitching arm being unknown to modern day researchers. The Watson images reproduced in the text are the only ones of him known to exist and have not been widely seen in 130 years.*

HIS PROFESSIONAL PLAYING CAREER was brief, distinguished only by one of the most peculiar nicknames in major leagues baseball history. Otherwise, Mother Watson, a two-game pitcher for the 1887 Cincinnati Reds of the American Association, was a nonentity, a performer who left an impression on the game so indistinct that modern reference works cannot even tell us which way he threw or batted. Watson's life away from the game was similarly shrouded in obscurity, penetrated only by the brief spasm of press attention that surrounded his death from gunshot wounds in November 1898. Still, the historical record is fragmentary, not silent, and traces of Watson's life can still be extracted from century-old reportage, census data, and surviving shards of circumstantial evidence. Through use of these sources, this essay will endeavor to present a coherent, if less-than-complete, profile of one of 19th century baseball's least-known figures.

The Watson life story begins with his birth on January 27, 1865, in

Mother Watson

Middleport, Ohio, a small but bustling Ohio River outpost located on the southeast border of the state. Christened Walter L. Watson, our subject was the youngest of the 11 children born to riverboat engineer Elisha Watson (1818–1899) and his wife Martha Jane (née Cotsman, 1820–1907), both native-born Ohioans.[1] Despite the size of his brood, father Elisha's income was apparently sufficient to permit several of his sons to continue their education beyond the eighth-grade level common for boys of the time. This included youngest son Walter, whom the 1880 U.S. Census records as still in school at age 15. Apart from that, nothing is known of his early life except that when it came time for Walter to enter the work force, he did not follow his father and older brothers onto the river. Rather, his first known employer was a nail manufacturing plant.[2]

Like countless teenagers, the youthful Watson spent much of his leisure time playing baseball. He soon developed a local reputation as a pitcher, a positional choice perhaps dictated by the fact that he was "not strong in baserunning and batting."[3] Of average height, but lightly-framed (5-feet-9, 145 pounds), Watson did not throw hard, relying instead on a baffling assortment of breaking pitches and cool-headedness in tight spots.[4] He first attracted wider attention during the 1886 season pitching for an independent club in Zanesville, Ohio.[5] In reporting on a 17-strikeout no-hitter thrown at the Columbus Browns, the *Zanesville Signal* captioned its story: "Sissy Watson At Home."[6] For the most part, however, the local paper referred to the club's star hurler as *Mother Watson*.[7] Later often described as "the Zanesville phenomenon,"[8] Watson reportedly racked up 52 victories in 58 starts against top amateur and semipro clubs in Ohio and the adjoining regions.[9] Particularly eye-catching were a pair of exhibition game outings wherein he held the American Association champion St. Louis Browns to four hits each time. Elevated to prospect level by these two impressive showings, Watson thereafter signed contracts with both the AA Cincinnati Reds and the Syracuse Stars of the minor International League, with the ensuing inter-club dispute being resolved in Cincinnati's favor.[10]

The Reds had finished a non-contending (65–73) fifth in 1886 American Association standings, and improvement was needed in all playing departments. This included the pitching staff, where the club ace, the talented but temperamental Tony Mullane, needed support. Young Watson was one of a host of newly-minted professionals who would be auditioned by the Reds. He joined the club as something of an unknown commodity, as word of his Zanesville prowess had not carried to many ears in Cincinnati. His prospects of sticking with the Reds, moreover, received decidedly mixed reviews in the better-informed baseball press. A non-bylined piece in *Sporting Life* related: "Watson, one of Cincinnati's young twirlers, played with Zanesville last season and won a wide reputation. He is beyond doubt, a good pitcher but it remains to be seen how" he will fare against major league batsmen.[11] Far less hopeful about Watson was the weekly's Wheeling, West Virginia, correspondent, who wrote: "I see [Cincinnati manager] Gus Schmelz is expecting great things from Watson ... but I am afraid that he will not last long. In the first place [Watson] has but little speed, and the success he had last season was the result of headwork mainly. ... The reason why he won so many games for Zanesville was not because he was an extraordinary pitcher, but because he had a superior team behind him, one that seldom got rattled."[12]

But as the regular season approached, a more optimistic tone was adopted by the *Cincinnati Commercial Gazette*. It cited Watson's impressive pitching performances against the St. Louis Browns the previous year: "Watson is speedy in his delivery and uses great headwork for so young a player. ... Should he prove a failure it would be quite a damper to the sanguine hopes of the management."[13] Accompanying the *Commercial Gazette's* thumbnail bio of Watson was the inked portrait of him reproduced herein. Until recently, this was believed to be the only image of Watson known to exist.[14]

Commenting on Watson's chances with the Reds, the *Cincinnati Enquirer* observed: "The people here [in Zanesville] are wondering what Cincinnatians think of 'Mother' Watson's personal appearance. He is not a dude, but he can twirl a ball to perfection."[15] Then on April 11, the *Sandusky* (Ohio) *Register* advised readers that: "Zanesville will probably have a chance to secure their old pitcher 'Mother' Watson before the season is far advanced. He has not shown very well in Cincinnati and will likely be released."[16] Four days later, the paper revised that forecast following a strong Watson pre-season outing against Columbus, relating that "'Mother' Watson seems to have been a Jonah for the Capital City boys in yesterday's game."[17]

This *Mother* moniker, obviously, was a peculiar one, but at the time the conference of a feminine nickname upon a ballplayer was not

Mother Watson (*Cincinnati Commercial-Gazette*, April 24, 1887).

Mother Watson

unprecedented.[18] Indeed, only a few seasons before Watson's arrival in Cincinnati, Reds catcher Phil Powers had been called *Grandmother*. But the reason why Walter Watson was nicknamed *Mother* is far from clear. The nickname did not originate in Middleport. To hometown friends and acquaintances, he was "Wal [or Wall] Watson, the ball player," the appellation later employed in local newspaper coverage of Watson's shooting in an area saloon and subsequent death.[19] In *Major League Players: 1871–1900, Volume 2*, eminent baseball scholars David Ball and David Nemec maintain that Watson was "nicknamed 'Mother' because fellow players felt he needed his mother with him at all times. ... [He] was a complete greenhorn when signed by Cincinnati for $1,500 in the winter of 1886–87 and had been victimized by 'half a dozen bunko men before he had been in [Cincinnati] a week.'"[20] Well, maybe. But the description of Watson as a "complete greenhorn" is questionable, as Watson was not some bumpkin come to town from the farm, whatever his appearance. He had grown up in a small but busy river port, and had the life example of six older brothers to guide him as well. By the time that he joined the Reds, moreover, Watson already had a season away from home and parents under his belt. Last but perhaps most important, Watson acquired the *Mother* nickname BEFORE he connected with the Cincinnati Reds, as the *Zanesville Signal*, *Cincinnati Enquirer*, and *Sandusky Register* articles noted above clearly indicate that he was called *Mother Watson* while playing for Zanesville.

An alternative theory asserts that "'Mother' was a nickname for those who did not indulge in the typical vices of smoking, drinking, swearing or brawling. By all accounts, Watson conducted himself as a 'gentleman.'"[21] The placement of Watson in the virtuous player class also finds support in his *Commercial Gazette* profile: "Watson is a strictly temperate young man."[22] There is, of course, something incongruous about this paragon of temperance later dying as a result of a saloon shooting. More to the point, if *Mother* was a generic nickname applied to players who avoided debauchery and ungentlemanly conduct, how is it that Walter Watson is the only one of the multitude of such players in baseball history to have ever been called *Mother*? In short, the claim that *Mother* was a common soubriquet for the virtuous ballplayer, while neat, is unpersuasive.

Because those critical of the nickname interpretations of other contentions bear the responsibility of offering a plausible alternative to them, the writer will offer his own pet theory—one unencumbered by hard evidence but with a certain logic grounded in the experience of sports: *Mother* was a pejorative sandlot nickname—1880s trash talk—that probably began as soon as Watson advanced beyond the neighborhood pickup game stage of his career. Crucial to the argument here is the fact that the name *Mother Watson* was already in the public domain by the time that young Walter Watson took up playing baseball. One of the popular Horatio Alger novels, for example, contained a villainess named *Mother Watson*.[23] And *Mother (Mrs. H.A.) Watson* was also the much-publicized head mistress of a Los Angeles home for wayward girls.[24] Given the foregoing and the mean-spiritedness then rampant in American sporting culture, saddling a young opponent named Watson with the discomforting, effeminate nickname *Mother* would have been a natural put-down, the kind of cutting but period-appropriate mockery indigenous to 19th century baseball. (Such mockery was standard practice at the time—witness *Nig* Cuppy, *One-Arm* Daily, *Piano Legs* Hickman, etc.) Thereafter, the baseball press would have had no compunction about adopting the *Mother* nickname and putting it into newsprint once there was cause to bring Watson's existence to reader attention. Sadly, no evidence validating this novel but engaging theory has been found. In the end, the obscurity of our protagonist and the passage of more than a century since his demise make discovery of a definitive explanation of how Mother Watson got his nickname probably beyond reach. We will just likely never know.

However he got his moniker, Mother Watson was projected as one of the staff members who would support Reds ace Mullane in 1887. But club plans for the new season were promptly jeopardized when Watson and fellow hurling prospects Billy Serad, Elmer Smith, and Mike Shea came down with arm miseries once spring camp opened.[25] And when he was fit to enter the box, Watson pitched inconsistently. He was hit hard in an early intra-squad game but then shut down league rival Columbus in a more-seriously played pre-season contest. All in all, Watson showed just enough in camp for management to place the name Walter L. Watson on the Reds' roster for the 1887 season.[26]

Watson made the team but saw no action in Cincinnati's first 24 games. He finally got his chance on May 19, courtesy of a Tony Mullane hissy fit. The mercurial Mullane refused to accept the ball for a home game against Brooklyn, complaining that it was not his turn to pitch. Mullane was suspended on the spot by manager Schmelz, who then seized upon the untested Watson as an emergency replacement. In his major league debut, Watson lasted five innings, leaving the game with Cincinnati ahead, 9–6. The following day, wire service reports stated that "Watson, the Zanesville phenomenon, did extremely well for a few innings. His arm gave out and [Pop] Corkhill came in to pitch."[27] The hometown press concurred, the *Cincinnati Post* stating: "Watson, the new Cincinnati pitcher, did well."[28] The glowing reviews, however, are difficult to reconcile with the game's box score. Same reveals that Watson surrendered six runs on six base-hits, walked four, struck out none, and threw three wild pitches. He also muffed two of his three fielding chances. Still, Watson could have been credited with a victory, had not Corkhill surrendered the lead before the Reds rallied to win, 14–10. Also on the plus side, Watson, ordinarily a near-helpless batsman, had managed a single and a walk in six plate appearances against Brooklyn right-hander Hardie Henderson, and had done no harm as Corkhill's replacement for two innings in left field (as no balls were hit Watson's way).

Mother Watson made his second and final big leagues appearance eight days later. Given a start against the Philadelphia Athletics, "the Zanesville phenom Watson pitched a fair game but was miserably supported by [catcher Kid] Baldwin" who had five passed balls.[29] Watson went the route and lost, 9–5, but only two of the runs charged against him were earned. But he also surrendered 16 base-hits, and the contest had not been a particularly close one. The following day, Cincinnati announced the signing of Bill Widmer, a hard-throwing right-hander from the amateur ranks in nearby Cumminsville.[30] The acquisition signaled the end of Mother Watson's stay with the Reds, and he was given his release shortly thereafter.

The Cincinnati Reds of 1887 were in their sixth year of play in the American Association; the city had been a charter member of the AA in 1882 after a year's absence from National League play.

Unbeknownst to the 22-year-old Watson, his career as a major league pitcher was over. In his two appearances, he had posted a 0–1 record, with an unsightly 5.79 ERA in 14 innings pitched. His log also showed 22 base-hits and six walks surrendered, while he had struck out only one opposition hitter. In his May 27 outing, no balls had been hit back to him, leaving the Watson fielding average at a dismal

.333. He finished 1-for-8 as a hitter (with a .125/.200/.125 slash line), and one run scored. Still, the experience was sufficient to permit Mother Watson to rightly claim the status of former major leaguer in the years thereafter.

Although the historical record is muted, it appears that Watson returned home to Middleport following his release and resumed working at the nail manufacturing plant.[31] And he apparently did no further pitching in 1887.[32] But the following January, Watson was back in uniform, a member of the Zanesville Kickapoos of the newly-formed minor Tri-State League.[33] Before the 1888 season started, however, it was widely reported that Watson had been released by Zanesville.[34]

When the Kickapoos got off to a poor start it was Watson to the rescue. Following a 6–4 Zanesville triumph over Kalamazoo, *Sporting Life* reported: "The poor showing of the home team the first week of the season was rather disappointing, but Thursday 'Mother' Watson slipped into the pitcher's box and his appearance seemed to inspire the team with confidence as they put up an elegant game. It was Watson's first for almost a year, and taking it all in all, was decidedly creditable to him. Twelve hits were made off him but he kept them scattered and his old time coolness did a great deal for him at crucial points."[35]

Mother Watson, *Cincinnati Commercial-Gazette*, April 24, 1887.

Mother Watson during his 1888 year with the Zanesville Kickapoos.

Mother Watson

Three weeks later, the *Canton Repository* proclaimed: "'Mother' Watson, a phenomenon who failed with the Cincinnatis of 1887, has come again and is pitching Zanesville's best ball."[36]

In time, Watson settled in as Zanesville's second pitcher, a steady helpmate of staff ace Ad Gumbert. A personal highlight for Watson was a June 18 exhibition game victory (8–2) over the National League Pittsburgh Alleghenies and future Hall of Famer Pud Galvin.[37] The Kickapoos were a pennant contender until late-August when Gumbert was sold to the St. Louis Browns.[38] A week or so before the season ended, the Zanesville club disbanded, its successful 63–39 record notwithstanding.[39] Final Tri-State League pitching stats have not been uncovered,[40] but examination of published Zanesville Kickapoos box/line scores puts the Watson record in the neighborhood of 12–13.

After his 1888 tour with Zanesville, Watson never played another game in Organized Baseball. And with that, the light on the life of Walter "Mother" Watson goes dark. He withdrew to the anonymity of private life. His name would not appear in newsprint for the next 10 years, leaving his whereabouts and activities during that time period almost entirely unknown.[41] But from snippets of information published at the time of his shooting and subsequent death in November 1898, it can fairly be said that he lived the remainder of his life with his parents and various siblings at the family residence in Middleport; that he never married; that he became a member of the town's volunteer fire department; and that he continued to do some pitching for independent and semipro teams in the southern Ohio–West Virginia region. Watson's last known engagement was with the Mason Citys, a crack Charleston, West Virginia, nine.

Watson reemerged from the shadows on November 7, 1898. It was Election Day, and after the polls closed he repaired to Gardner's Saloon, a popular watering hole in nearby Pomeroy. While there, he encountered Louis Schreiner, 32, once a clerk at the Middleport post office. The two men were long acquainted, but, according to one source, there had been "a slight altercation" between them several days earlier.[42] Another report had the two men quarrelling "about politics" that evening.[43] Whatever the underlying circumstance, things turned violent at about 1:00 am. Schreiner uncovered a pistol and fired three shots at Watson. Watson returned fire with his own weapon, shooting twice.[44] Only one round found its target, with Watson being struck in the chest or stomach, news accounts varied. He managed to stagger to the saloon door but then collapsed onto the floor. Sometime thereafter, Watson was borne on stretcher to the family residence, but given little chance of recovery.⁴⁵ Schreiner, meanwhile, quickly fled the saloon and disappeared, reportedly to the mountains of West Virginia,⁴⁶ if not out of the country entirely.⁴⁷

A week later, Watson was still alive, with recovery now predicted.⁴⁸ Fate was not so kind. On the morning of November 23, 1898, Walter Watson died in his bed from the effects of his gunshot wound. He was 33. The obituary subsequently published in the *Middleport Republican Herald* described the deceased as "of a kind disposition and [he] numbered his friends by the score."⁴⁹ Funeral services were conducted by two local clergymen, the Reverend Brainard, pastor of the Middleport Christian Church, assisted by Reverend Williams of the Methodist-Episcopal Church. Among the throng in attendance were Watson teammates from the Mason City ball club and the Middleport Fire Department dressed in full uniform, their presence attesting to the "high esteem in which Walter Watson was held in his home town."⁵⁰ Interment was at Hill Cemetery, Middleport. Survivors included his elderly parents and five siblings.

Several days after Watson had been laid to rest, Meigs County Coroner Scott released the findings of his inquest. Post-mortem examination revealed that the fatal ball had passed through the liver, damaged the kidney, and then exited the body.⁵¹ Sometime thereafter, the fugitive Schreiner was apprehended. The disposition of any criminal charges against him, indeed whether or not formal charges were even instituted, is unknown.⁵² Whatever the case, Lewis Schreiner was a free man, living openly and unmolested by the law in Columbus, Kansas, at the time the 1900 U.S. Census was collected. By then, the memory of the two-game Cincinnati Reds pitcher named Watson had already dimmed, and today he is long-forgotten. Still, 130 years-after-the-fact, our subject retains one modest distinction: he is still the only player in major league history ever nicknamed *Mother*.

Sources

The sources of the biographical info provided herein include the Mother Watson profile published in *Major League Profiles: 1871–1900, Volume 2*, David Nemec, ed. (Lincoln: University of Nebraska Press, 2011); U.S. Census data, Watson family posts accessed via Ancestry.com, and various newspaper articles cited below. Unless otherwise noted, stats have been taken from Baseball-Reference.

Mother Watson

Notes

1. Walter's older siblings were: William (born 1842): Charles (1845); John (1849); Mary (1850); Elisha (1854); Jonas (1857); Madora (Dora, 1858); and Robert (1861). Two other Watson children, names unknown, did not survive infancy.

2. Watson's off-season engagement at the nail manufacturing plant was mentioned in *Sporting Life*, March 21, 1888, and in the Watson profile contained in *Major League Profiles: 1871–1900, Volume 2*, David Nemec, ed. (Lincoln: University of Nebraska Press, 2011), 411.

3. As per *Sporting Life*, February 9, 1887.

4. The writer subscribes to early baseball scholar David Nemec's dictum that because left-handedness was a relatively uncommon 19th century playing trait likely to be noted by the baseball press, the absence of press mention that a particular player threw lefty supports the presumption that the player was right-handed, the same as roughly 90 percent of the American population. Thus, the fact that Watson was never described as left-handed by the baseball press seems telling. And while Watson's pitching repertoire featured the deceptive curveball nowadays associated with the crafty lefty, a puzzling assortment of breaking pitches was frequently attributed to any pitcher rising to fast company in the 19th century.

5. See, e.g., the *Cleveland Plain Dealer*, May 28, 1886, taking note of a three-hit shutout pitched by Watson against the semipro Cincinnati Clippers. Other mentions of outstanding Watson hurling efforts for Zanesville were published in the *Cleveland Leader*, August 12 and 25, 1886, and *Cleveland Plain Dealer*, September 11, 1886.

6. *Zanesville Daily Signal*, August 20, 1886. The writer is indebted to baseball historian/author Rick Huhn for finding and synthesizing the Zanesville reportage on Watson.

7. See, e.g., the *Zanesville Signal*, August 25 and September 7 and 13, 1886.

8. See, e.g., the *Cleveland Plain Dealer*, May 16, 1887, and *Canton [Ohio] Repository* and *Sporting Life*, May 16, 1888.

9. Nemec, 410.

10. *Ibid.*

11. *Sporting Life*, February 9, 1887.

12. "Pickwick," *Sporting Life*, March 16, 1887.

13. *Cincinnati Commercial Gazette*, April 24, 1887.

14. A headshot of Watson in the team photo of the 1888 Zanesville Kickapoos was discovered by Carson Lorey and published in *Reflecting the Past* (the newsletter of SABR's Pictorial History Research Committee), June 20:1, 16.

15. "Ohio League Notes: Zanesville," *Cincinnati Enquirer*, March 20, 1887. Again, many thanks to Rick Huhn for tracking down Cincinnati reportage inaccessible to the writer.

16. *Sandusky [Ohio] Register*, April 11, 1887. The writer is indebted to baseball author and historian Dennis Snelling for unearthing and supplying the Sandusky reportage about Watson.

17. *Sandusky Register*, April 15, 1887.

18. For more on feminine nicknames in early baseball, see James K. Skipper, Jr., "Feminine Nicknames: Oh You Kid: From Tilly to Minnie to Sis," *Baseball Research Journal*, Vol. 11 (1982). Perhaps the most bizarre of these monikers was the one attached to National Association outfielder Charlie Pabor: *The Old Woman in the Red Cap*.

19. See, e.g., the *Pomeroy [Ohio] Tribune Telegraph*, November 8 and 23, 1898, *Pomeroy Democrat*, November 9, 1898, and *Pomeroy Leader*, November 10, 1898.

20. Nemec, 410. As the writer understands it, the Watson profile was researched by David Ball, a Cincinnati native and a scrupulous baseball historian. Regrettably, the underlying sources of the profile passages placed in quotes are not provided, and Ball's untimely death in 2011 has prevented their identification.

21. Mike Shannon, *Moments from the Cincinnati Reds History* (Chicago: Triumph Books, 2008), 3. The Bullpen section of the Baseball-Reference entry on Mother Watson also mentions the virtuous person hypothesis.

22. See again, the *Cincinnati Commercial Gazette*, April 24, 1887.

23. Mother Watson was the hero's cruel landlady in *Mark, The Match Boy, or Richard Hunter's Ward*, published in 1869.

24. See, e.g., the *Los Angeles Times*, May 17, October 23, and December 9, 1887.

25. As reported in *Sporting Life*, April 6, 1887, and the *Baltimore Sun*, April 7, 1887. The Cincin-

nati *Enquirer,* June 12, 1887, later maintained that Watson's arm had gone lame prior to spring camp, and others attribute the problem to an injury suffered at the nail manufacturing plant the previous winter. See Nemec, 410.

26. As per *Sporting Life,* April 13, 1887.
27. See, e.g., the *Cleveland Plain Dealer, New York Herald,* and *New York Tribune,* May 20, 1887.
28. *Cincinnati Post,* May 19, 1887. The *Cincinnati Enquirer,* May 19, 1887, was less impressed, deeming the performance of "Watson, the Zanesville wonder" neither a "glittering success" nor "a dismal failure."
29. *Philadelphia Inquirer,* May 28, 1887. The box score in the *Cincinnati Enquirer,* May 28, 1887, charged Baldwin with six passed balls.
30. As reported in the *Cleveland Plain Dealer,* May 29, 1887.
31. See *Sporting Life,* March 21, 1888.
32. The Watson who anchored the pitching staff of the 1887 Kalamazoo (Michigan) Kazoos of the Ohio State League was Art Watson, not our subject.
33. As reported in the *Wheeling* (West Virginia) *Register,* January 2, 1888, and *Canton Repository* and *Cleveland Plain Dealer,* January 8, 1888. Zanesville had entered Organized Baseball the season before as a member of the Ohio State League.
34. See, e.g., the *Sandusky Register,* March 20, 1888, *Wheeling Register,* March 22, 1888, and *Canton Repository,* March 27, 1888.
35. "Zanesville Zephyrs," *Sporting Life,* May 9, 1888.
36. *Canton Repository,* May 16, 1888.
37. As reported in the *Canton Repository,* June 19, 1888.
38. As reported in the *Wheeling Register,* August 20, 1888. Gumbert would go on to have a solid nine-season major league career.
39. The Kalamazoo and Sandusky clubs also abandoned play before the season's close. The champion of the 1888 Tri-State League was the 74–35 Lima (Ohio) Lushers.
40. Baseball-Reference provides no stats regarding Watson's 1888 season in Zanesville.
41. The search for the post-baseball Watson is handicapped by the unavailability of the 1890 U.S. and Ohio state censuses, both lost long ago to fire.
42. According to the *Pomeroy Leader,* November 10, 1898. The writer is indebted to Wanda Ashley of the Meigs County (Ohio) public library system and Mary Cowdery of the Meigs County Historical Society and Museum for their generous help in securing local reportage of the incident and the Watson funeral.
43. See the *Cincinnati Post,* November 9, 1898, and *Sporting Life,* November 19, 1898..
44. As per the *Pomeroy Tribune-Telegraph,* November 9, 1898. The *Pomeroy Leader,* November 10, 1898, stated that Schreiner had fired only twice, but with "little provocation."
45. The assessment of the *Pomeroy Democrat* and *Pomeroy Tribune-Telegraph,* November 9, 1898, and *Pomeroy Leader,* November 10, 1898.
46. According to the *Denver Post,* November 23, 1898.
47. *Cincinnati Post,* November 9, 1898.
48. By the *Pomeroy Democrat,* November 16, 1898.
49. *Middleport Republican Herald,* November 25, 1898.
50. *Middleport Republican Herald,* December 2, 1898.
51. As reported in the *Pomeroy Tribune-Telegraph,* November 30, 1898. Despite a "diligent search" of the saloon, the fatal pistol ball was not recovered.
52. A dissertation on the application of penal statutes is beyond the scope of this profile. Suffice it to say that not every homicide constitutes a criminal offense. Certain types of killing—combat in war, or acts of self-defense, defense of a third person, accident, and/or misadventure—may be legally justified or excused. Regrettably, the documentary record needed to say more about the Watson-Schreiner affair could not be obtained by the writer.

Doctoring the Ball
The Underrated Role of Physicians in the Rise of Early Baseball
THOMAS W. GILBERT

A surprising number of Amateur Era (pre–1871) baseball players, especially in leadership positions in the first clubs and associations, were physicians. Many of these, including Joseph B. Jones of the Excelsiors of Brooklyn and Daniel L. Adams of the Knickerbockers of New York City, viewed sport as a tool for public health reform. Like other East Coast cities, mid–19th century New York City suffered from declining life expectancy and regular deadly cholera and yellow fever epidemics. Lacking a modern scientific understanding of infectious disease, reformist physicians of the time believed that cleanliness, fresh air and physical fitness were the keys to improving public health. They saw the potential of organized adult participant sports, which barely existed in the United States before the 1850s—the exception being cricket, whose disqualifying flaw was its foreignness—to popularize exercise nationally. After failing with boxing and gymnastics, they succeeded with baseball, which expanded with stunning rapidity beyond the New York City area, establishing itself before the Civil War as America's first national team sport.

THE GAME WE KNOW AS baseball evolved from a folk game into a modern sport in the New York City area before the Civil War. The earliest players called themselves amateurs. This does not mean that none of them were paid or compensated in some way, but it does mean that nearly all were part-time athletes with full lives and occupations outside of baseball. A surprising number of them, especially in leadership positions in the first clubs and associations, were physicians. To explain why, we need to look outside of sports. Early and mid-19th century America was a time of sweeping reform movements, including abolitionism, temperance and public health reform. Like other East Coast cities, New York City suffered from declining life expectancy and deadly cholera, yellow fever and other epidemics. Lacking a scientific understanding of infection, reformist physicians believed that cleanliness, fresh air and physical fitness were key to fighting disease and improving public health. Along with elements of the clergy and other non-medical allies, they saw the potential of adult participant sports, which barely existed in the United States before the 1850s, to popularize exercise nationally. Eventually, they succeeded with baseball, which became America's first national team sport.

When baseball historians talk about the Amateur Era, they mean the historical period that ended on St. Patrick's Day of 1871. On that day, the first national professional baseball league, the National Association of Professional Base Ball Players, was formed in New York City. It is less clear when the Amateur Era began. Conventional baseball histories usually start with the founding of the Knickerbocker Club in New York City in 1845. There were earlier clubs. We do not know a lot about them, but we do know that some of their key members were physicians. In 1887, Knickerbocker co-founder William Wheaton, a New York lawyer who had moved to California in the Gold Rush in 1849, told the *San Francisco Examiner* of playing in the 1830s in a pickup baseball game on the lower East Side of Manhattan involving "merchants, lawyers and physicians."[1] When this game was formalized as the "New York Base Ball Club" in 1837, one of its founders was John Miller, an 1829 graduate of the College of Physicians and Surgeons (or CPS), today the medical school of Columbia University. Descended from Quakers who had settled in Flushing, Queens in the 1650s, Miller was a popular neighborhood doctor who lived and practiced at 186 East Broadway until his death in 1863. William Wheaton lived around the corner from Dr. Miller at the intersection of East Broadway and Rutgers Street. Like so many early baseball clubs, the New York Club grew out of a casual neighborhood game that went back who knows how long. (Incidentally, this is the same New York Club that in Hoboken, New Jersey, on June 19, 1846, defeated the Knickerbockers in what is often misidentified as the first interclub baseball game.) The New York Club went through several permutations, also using the names Gothams and Washingtons.

An 1896 interview with Daniel "Doc" Adams, who moved to New York

Physicians in the Rise of Early Baseball

from New Hampshire shortly after his 1838 graduation from Harvard Medical School, corroborates Wheaton's story that the New York/Gotham/Washington Club antedated the Knickerbocker Club and that physicians played important roles in both clubs. Adams recalled playing with the New York Club as early as 1839, before he and "several of us medical fellows"[2] switched to the newly formed Knickerbockers in the autumn of 1845. He did not name names, but the Knickerbockers' membership records contain several prominent physicians, including William B. Eager, Chief of Staff of the City Hospital on Blackwell's (now Roosevelt) Island and Professor of Gynecology at Bellevue, and Francis Upton Johnston, Sr., a trustee of the CPS. As we will see, both men had professional connections to Adams and to the cause of public health reform. By 1848 Doc Adams had become the Knickerbockers' president and most influential member. This mattered because unlike many Knickerbockers, who were interested only in intramural play—remember, the early clubs were essentially organized pickup games in which members played against other members—Adams supported both the spread of the game to other clubs in the New York City area and the natural result, interclub competition. He presided over the first annual convention of baseball clubs in 1857, whose main purpose was to regulate matches between clubs that had differing cultures and playing rules. From this convention evolved the National Association of Base Ball Players, or NABBP, the sport's first governing body.

For Doc Adams and his fellow physicians, baseball was, in the words of sportswriter Henry Chadwick, "a powerful lever ... by which our people could be lifted into a position of more devotion to physical exercise and healthful outdoor recreation."[3] Such a lever was necessary because before baseball went national in the late 1850s, American adults were decidedly uninterested in exercise or play as such. Horse

New York Knickerbockers president and public health activist Daniel "Doc" Adams.

racing and boxing were popular, but Americans participated in these by gambling on them, not by competing in them.

Along with Protestant ministers who preached "Muscular Christianity"—the religion-based physical fitness ideology that created the YMCA in the 1840s—progressive physicians set out to change this. Early 19th century American physicians were neither as technically accomplished nor as well paid as today's doctors. Without modern antibiotics, anesthetics and surgical technology, they had few weapons with which to combat sickness and disease. They did, however, have a broad sense of mission. Inspired by the ideas of Englishman Sir Edwin Chadwick—the father of public health science and Henry Chadwick's half-brother—who believed that physical and social ills could be cured by reforming education, sanitation and other human systems, they campaigned to clean up American cities.

There was a lot to clean up. Early 19th century New York City had no water or sewer systems. Human waste was buried or collected in wooden crates and carted away by hand; the New York custom of building stoops and elevating the first floor of row houses was a response to the fact that compacted horse dung and other refuse continuously raised street levels. Wild pigs roamed the streets, feeding on garbage and providing the poor with the only meat they could afford. English and American public health activists believed in reforming the human body as well as the environment. "Whoever takes [exercise] regularly," wrote future Brooklyn public health officer and Excelsior baseball club president Dr. Joseph B. Jones in 1852, "may bid defiance to consumption [tuberculosis] and all its handmaids."[4]

An important goal was to put physicians, not political appointees, in charge of public health. "Are officers of our government, employed in the conservation of public health, competent persons?" asked surgeon Dr. Valentine Mott, co-founder of the NYU School of Medicine, "Not men of science, not of learning, but some political artist, some worker in the dark caverns of political villainy, is always the chosen one for this task ... [is] it not necessary that medical men should be employed to divine and arrest the causes of disease?"[5] By the 1830s, crusading New York City doctors, working without pay and independently of the government, had established a system of health districts, each with a dispensary that provided free treatment and medicine to the poor, including vaccinations, and collected public health data. In 1847, the New York dispensary system served 28,277 patients, more than five percent of the city's population. Free from the exigencies of Tammany Hall's political patronage system, it did so at the shockingly low cost of $3,476—about ten times the annual salary of an unskilled laborer.[6]

Physicians in the Rise of Early Baseball

The New York Dispensary,
Northwest corner of Centre and White streets.

The New York Dispensary, located at Centre and White Streets in Manhattan, the workplace of several physician members of the New York Knickerbockers. Doc Adams lived around the corner.

Supported by private charity, these dispensaries are the forebears of the present public hospital system and municipal health departments.

Behind the story of the forgotten dispensary system, there are connections to baseball. Wealthy Quaker watchmaker Samuel Demilt, a major dispensary benefactor, was a relative of William W. Demilt, a member of the Gotham baseball club. In 1840 two Knickerbocker Club M.D.s, Doc Adams and Francis Upton Johnson, held supervisory positions at the central New York Dispensary at the corner of White and Centre Streets; in the 1850s Doc Adams became co-medical director of the dispensary; on his staff was another Knickerbocker, Dr. William B. Eager.

Physical fitness advocates labored long and hard to convince American adults to exercise. Boxing and gymnastics were their first choice of weapons. Interestingly, when we look closely at these two sports, we find names that later appear on the membership rolls of early baseball clubs such as the

Knickerbockers and Gothams. As early as the 1820s, public boxing facilities opened in Boston, Philadelphia and New York. Proponents of boxing tried to market the sport to respectable gentlemen as the "manly art of self-defense," but boxing never achieved broad popularity as a participant sport. Physicians and entrepreneurs made another attempt to sell exercise by importing gymnastics and weight training from Great Britain and the Continent. In 1833 Englishman William Fuller opened one of the first New York City gymnasiums to feature gymnastics at 29 Ann Street, near City Hall. He took out this advertisement in the *New York Evening Post*:

> We esteem exercise, as an essential means to the preservation of health, and as one of the most certain prophylactics against those innumerable diseases, which result from a want of it. We, therefore, cordially recommend all sedentary persons, whose professional avocations debar them from the pursuit of health by the more common forms of exercise, to resort to this Gymnasium, where every species of muscular invigoration can be readily obtained, from the gentlest to the most athletic exercise.[7]

Not only was Fuller using the language of public health reformers, but he also added a testimonial—"We fully concur in the value of Gymnastic [sic]

The Crosby Street Gymnasium opened in New York City in 1845. Several Knickerbocker baseball players were members.

Physicians in the Rise of Early Baseball

An 1859 double team portrait of the New York Knickerbockers and Brooklyn Excelsiors. Dr. Joseph B. Jones, in top hat and dark coat, is the umpire, at center; Doc Adams is 4th from left; Samuel Kissam is 8th from left; 8th from right is physician Andrew Pearsall; weight training advocate Joe Leggett is fourth from right.

exercises"—signed by Dr. Valentine Mott and nine other pillars of the New York City medical establishment. In the 1840s, Charles Ottignon, another Englishman, taught gymnastics at gyms on Canal Street and, later, on Crosby Street. In 1852, Ottignon held a gymnastic competition in which prizes were won by Knickerbocker baseball club members James Montgomery and Edward Cone; another prize winner, Henry Bogart, may have been the man of the same name who belonged to the Knickerbockers. In 1856 Ottignon went into partnership with Montgomery, who was also an early proponent of weightlifting.

James Montgomery was not the only baseball player with an interest in gymnastics and weight lifting. In 1849, Joseph B. Jones opened Brooklyn's first state-of-the-art gymnasium at the corner of Pineapple and Fulton Streets in what is now Brooklyn Heights, a five-minute walk uphill from the New York ferry landing. Tall and thin, Jones was a good amateur boxer and an excellent gymnast who judged and performed in exhibitions at Ottignon's gymnasium. He promoted his gym with advertising and public lectures to a sometimes-skeptical public. When Jones hired trousers-wearing English feminist Madame Beaujeu Hawley to teach females, he provoked a public outcry. Jones responded by promising to keep the sexes strictly separate at his facility, and published a statement in the *Brooklyn Daily Eagle* from abolitionist preacher Henry Ward Beecher and other prominent Brooklyn clergy endorsing the moral probity of gymnastics for women and girls.

Like boxing, however, gymnastics ultimately failed to capture the imagination of the public as a participant sport. Jones sold his gym and entered the CPS, where he switched his focus to baseball. Graduating in 1855, he practiced medicine in Brooklyn and joined a club called the Esculapians, who played near the present site of Brooklyn's Carroll Park. As its name suggests, this club was made up of young physicians and medical students. Their members included doctors who staffed and ran the Brooklyn Dispensary, Long Island College Hospital, Brooklyn Medical Association and other institutions; as well as public health officers and Kings County coroners. The very existence of the Esculapian club, possibly the earliest baseball club made up of members of a single profession, testifies to the special relationship between early baseball and medicine.

Dr. Jones was a good enough ballplayer that he soon joined the Excelsiors, Brooklyn's first baseball club and one of its most competitive. Founded in 1854, the Excelsiors began as a kind of satellite of the New York Knickerbockers. Many of the early Excelsiors had family, professional or social connections to the older New York club. One of them was Dr. Daniel Albert

Dodge, visiting surgeon at Long Island College Hospital. Another was CPS graduate Van Brunt Wyckoff, who made a fortune in Brooklyn real estate and never practiced medicine. Dodge's cousin Samuel Kissam lived in Brooklyn, very near Carroll Park. Although a prominent member of the Knickerbockers, he appears, without explanation, in two box scores playing for the Excelsiors. Kissam was a stockbroker, but he came from a famous medical dynasty; more than two dozen of his family members were physicians and CPS grads.

The socially exclusive Knickerbockers were choosy about which other clubs they played, but in both 1858 and 1859 they played home-and-away series with the Excelsiors. Coverage of a postgame banquet in the 1858 *New York Times* gives an idea of the friendship between the two clubs, as well as the public health reform ideology that they had in common:

> "Mr. [James Whyte] Davis, having presented the ball with appropriate remarks to Dr. Jones, President of the Excelsior Club, proposed "Health and success to the Excelsior Club," with three times three [i.e., "hip, hip, hip, hooray" three times]. Dr. Jones made a pertinent and witty reply, and proposed three times three for the "Parent of base-ball clubs, the Knickerbockers." Dr. Adams … recommended the practice of the game by Americans, old and young…. Mr. Burtis, of the Excelsior

Brooklyn Daily Eagle box score for an 1858 game between the Esculapians and the Excelsiors' second nine. The Esculapian lineup includes physicians Andrew Pearsall, the future Excelsiors star and Confederate surgeon; William F. Swalm, attending physician at the Brooklyn Dispensary; and Deputy Brooklyn Health Commissioner William Otterson.

Club ... alluded to an article from the *London Times* in which it was stated that for the want of out-door athletic exercises and sports, the youth of America had physically deteriorated and ... he hailed the game of baseball as the panacea for their loss of physical powers."[8]

For an ambitious young doctor looking for a way to sell Americans on exercise, Joseph B. Jones was in the right place at the right time. New York City, baseball's birthplace, was the biggest and richest city in the United States. Then an independent city, Brooklyn was catching up fast, doubling its population each decade and beginning to see itself as New York's competitor in all things. That included baseball, even if before 1854 the world of competitive New York baseball consisted of three clubs, with a total of 90-odd members. When baseball crossed the East River in that year, it kicked off a new era of interclub and intercity rivalry. This is the watershed event to which we can trace baseball's success as a national team sport, as well as its eventual transformation into an entertainment industry.

Events moved quickly. Before the mid–1850s, baseball games rarely attracted spectators beyond a handful of club members and gamblers. In July of 1858, journalists reported with surprise that 3,000 people had come to Carroll Park in Brooklyn to watch Brooklyn's Excelsiors defeat New York City's Knickerbockers, 31 to 13. Later that same summer, an all-star series pitting Brooklyn against New York City drew crowds of well over ten thousand. In a powerful cycle, interclub and intercity rivalry—that is, rivalry between New York City and Brooklyn—generated spectator and media interest, which raised the competitive stakes, which inspired the formation of new clubs eager to prove themselves against other clubs.

A colleague of Dr. Joseph Jones and a fellow New York physician, Dr. William H. Bell, was a particularly energetic club organizer. Bell was raised in Manhattan's 11th Ward, home to many of New York City's shipyards. He may have been related to one of several Bell families in shipbuilding and related trades. In the 1850s, at the same time as the baseball explosion, the booming shipbuilding industry was moving, yard by yard, across the East River to Greenpoint and Williamsburg, now neighborhoods on north Brooklyn, in search of room to expand. In 1855, Dr. Bell founded the Eckford baseball club, together with six self-described "shipwrights and mechanics" from the old neighborhood.

Along with the rival Atlantics and Excelsiors, the Greenpoint Eckfords became one of the top clubs in Brooklyn and in the country, winning championships in 1862 and 1863 and lasting long enough to compete in the first national professional league in 1872. Dr. Bell left the Eckfords and founded

Physicians in the Rise of Early Baseball

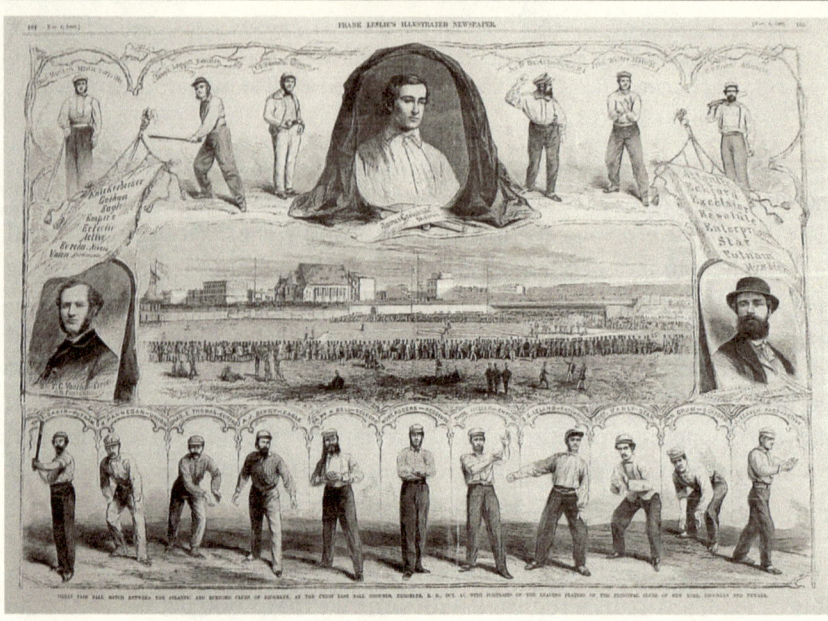

Dr. William H. Bell, "slow pitcher," prolific baseball club organizer and co-author of the "sixth rule" (called balls), a key step toward the modern strike zone.

the New York City–like Henry Eckford club, as well as the Social and Eclectic clubs. An exemplar of what was known as "slow pitching" (we are not sure what it was, but it got good hitters out), the stout Bell pitched effectively for these and other clubs well into his 40s. In the mid–1860s Drs. Bell and Jones convinced the NABBP Rules Committee to pass the so-called "sixth rule," which introduced called balls, an important step toward the modern strike zone.

Dr. Jones had a plan to build the Excelsiors into a dominant club and use it as a vehicle to convert the entire country to the New York version of baseball. In November 1857, Dr. Jones took control of the Excelsior club in a special officers election. He represented the club as president at the 1858 NABBP convention. Despite calling itself the *National* Association of Base Ball Players, the NABBP was still a regional baseball organization. Scattered clubs in Boston, Philadelphia and other towns and cities were playing their own versions of the game. The second step was to upgrade the Excelsiors' playing talent. Jones recruited promising athletes through his personal and professional connections, including from his alma mater, New York City's

College of Physicians and Surgeons. The finest of these was first baseman Andrew Pearsall, whose superb fielding—in a time before the invention of baseball gloves—was attributed to his surgeon's hands. Pearsall's preceptor, or personal tutor, at CPS was none other than Dr. Joseph B. Jones. The Excelsiors acquired team captain and catcher Joseph Leggett via a club merger. Leggett pioneered the use of weight training for baseball and put the Excelsiors on a rigorous training regimen. We do not know if Leggett, a Brooklyn fireman, had any connection to Jones's gymnasium, which was two blocks from his firehouse, but we do know that policemen and firemen of the time were particularly active in boxing, gymnastics and weight lifting. After Leggett persuaded young prospect James Creighton to use weights, Creighton developed a dominating fastball and became the greatest pitcher of his time. In another innovation, Jones made farm system–like arrangements with Brooklyn junior clubs that provided the Excelsiors with a supply of young talent. The ostensibly amateur Excelsiors also compensated their best players.[9] But they did so discreetly. Thanks to the political connections of men like Van Brunt Wyckoff, for example, James Creighton and his father held no-show patronage jobs in the New York Customs House.

Going into the 1860 season, Brooklyn was home to the best of the New York baseball clubs and the Excelsiors were as good as any of them. Now president of both the NABBP and the Excelsiors, Jones exported New York

The 1858 Brooklyn Eckfords, with star pitcher Frank Pidgeon at center, holding the ball.

baseball to the rest of America through a series of tours—an entirely new idea—in which the games were played by NABBP rules. The 1860 Excelsiors challenged local nines from Albany to Boston to Philadelphia and Baltimore and went undefeated, routing them by scores such as 24–6 and 50–19. James Creighton became baseball's first national star. Forged in the crucible of the hyper-competitive New York–area baseball scene, the Excelsiors' thrilling and athletic play convinced clubs across the country to convert to the Excelsiors' brand of baseball. Before the end of the Civil War, the New York game had driven most other regional bat and ball games into extinction. It was now known, simply, as baseball. A game that fifteen years earlier had been known to fewer than a hundred residents of Manhattan was played and watched by hundreds of thousands from coast to coast.

By 1870, with baseball firmly established and the founding of the first professional leagues around the corner, America no longer needed to be sold on sports or the benefits of exercise. The physicians who had helped create baseball in the Amateur Era continued to practice medicine, but most disappeared from the baseball scene, at least at the top competitive levels. The Esculapians kept playing in Brooklyn into the 1870s. As Brooklyn's chief public health official, Dr. Joseph B. Jones directed that city's response to the cholera epidemic of 1866, lobbying for improved sanitation laws, conducting aggressive health inspections and cleaning up dirty city streets, tenements and vacant lots. We know now that none of this in fact prevents cholera, which is spread through water contaminated by bacteria, but Jones's sanitation and public health reforms improved lives just the same. Clearly practicing what he had always preached about staying in shape, Jones appeared in baseball old timers' games into his 50s. In 1898, when he was 75, he won a citywide bowling tournament. Walking home late one night in the 1860s, the former amateur boxer was assaulted by a pair of muggers. One got away; the other he beat so badly that Jones declined to press robbery charges.

In 1862 Doc Adams retired, due to marriage or physical injury, from the Knickerbockers and baseball. He moved to Connecticut, where he died in 1899. Dr. William H. Bell continued to play baseball and continued to gain weight through the 1860s. In an 1864 "heavyweight" inter-city match made up of fat men, Bell pitched the New York side to a 37–32 victory over Brooklyn. Physician and Excelsiors star first baseman Andrew Pearsall fought in the Civil War. This was not unusual; over 90 of his clubmates, including Dr. Jones, also served in the armed forces. However, while

Pearsall's Excelsior teammates wore blue, he wore grey. The reason, it seems, was Pearsall's support for the institution of slavery.[10] After the war broke out in early 1861, he continued practicing medicine and playing baseball in Brooklyn. Then, late in 1862—at about the time that President Abraham Lincoln revealed his intention to abolish slavery—Pearsall suddenly disappeared, resurfacing in the Confederate capital of Richmond, Virginia. We know this because he ran into an old friend there.

> The Excelsior Base Ball Club of Brooklyn recently expelled one of its members, A.T. Pearsall, for deserting the flag of the Union, and going over to the rebels.... During the past winter he left, and no one knew where he had gone. Some time since he was heard from in Richmond, Va., as a Brigade Surgeon, on the rebel General Morgan's staff. He had charge of some Union prisoners... when he recognized a gentleman of Brooklyn, formerly a member of the Excelsior Club, and entered into conversation. He asked particularly about Leggett, Flanley, Creighton, and Brainard, whom ... he wished particularly to be remembered to.[11]

After the war, Pearsall settled in the South, where is remembered as a founder of the first baseball clubs in Richmond, Virginia, and in Alabama, his wife's home state.

The Knickerbockers, Excelsiors and Eckfords followed similar trajectories in the post–Civil War years. All fell behind the competitive curve in baseball and transitioned over time into social clubs. The Knickerbockers folded in the 1880s. The Excelsiors failed to survive the Great Depression of the 1930s. The Eckfords lasted long enough to donate their Amateur Era game balls and trophies to the National Baseball Hall of Fame in Cooperstown. They closed their doors in 1961. As for the dispensaries, as governments gradually took responsibility for public health and the care of the poor in New York City, Brooklyn and other cities, they were gradually replaced by public hospitals and state and local agencies. The last American dispensaries closed in the 1920s.

NOTES

1. *The San Francisco Examiner*, November 27, 1887.
2. *The Sporting News*, February 29, 1896.
3. Henry Chadwick, *The Game of Baseball* (New York, 1868) 10.
4. *Brooklyn Daily Eagle*, October 13, 1852.
5. *New York Times*, November 13, 1858.
6. E.P. Belden, *New-York: Past, Present, and Future* (New York: Putnam, 1849), 116.
7. *New York Evening Post*, April 17, 1833.
8. *New York Times*, August 23, 1858.
9. T.W. Gilbert, *Playing First: Early Baseball Lives at Brooklyn's Green-Wood Cemetery* (Brooklyn, 2015), 85*ff*.
10. Ibid., 114 *ff*.
11. *New York Clipper*, July 4, 1863.

Baseball's Financial Revolution of 1866 and the Rise of Professionalism

RICHARD HERSHBERGER

> *Baseball underwent a financial revolution in 1866, when clubs discovered that the public was willing to pay 25 cents to see a game. The previous standard price of ten cents, established in the Fashion Course matches of 1858, was sufficient to pay for the playing ground but left no surplus for the participating clubs. The higher rate spurred the growth of professionalism and a scramble by the top clubs to establish enclosed grounds under their control.*

BASEBALL UNDERWENT A financial revolution in 1866, when clubs started charging 25 cents to attend games, rather than the previous 10 cents. Admission fees were not new. They had been business practice, at least for some games, for years, but the higher admission rate was not entirely new. It had been charged for occasional special events. The novelty was the normalization of the higher rate. This resulted in changes to the physical environments where top clubs played and in the rise of fully professional teams.

Professionalism Up to 1866

The beginnings of professional baseball are hidden. This was deliberate. The National Association of Base Ball Players (NABBP) in 1859 enacted a rule barring any player "who shall at any time receive compensation for his services." With the principle of amateurism made baseball law, it followed that any player compensation would be secret. Baseball historians have worked to pierce the veil around early professionalism.

The identity of the earliest professional players is an evergreen topic. While of undoubted interest, this can obscure the fact that early professionalism, prior to the financial revolution, was a marginal aspect of the game. This was not due to the need for secrecy, but due to lack of funds. Once clubs had a revenue stream, the paying of players quickly moved from scandalous secret to open secret. From there it was a short step, soon taken, to the NABBP throwing in the towel and legalizing the practice.

The only sources of revenue for the earliest clubs were membership dues and initiation fees which generally paid for rental of playing grounds and the purchase of equipment. The mid-1850s saw the rise of the "match game" between two clubs. Early match games were social affairs as much as they were competitive, with one club taking the role of host and the other of guest, then switching roles for the return match. The game itself was followed by a dinner provided by the host. The ritual inevitably led to competitive hospitality, with clubs striving to outdo one another in lavish entertainments. Such events seem to have been paid for by donations from wealthier members or patrons of the club. They soon outstripped the willingness of the funders to pay, and in 1865 the New York, Brooklyn, and Newark clubs called a cease fire, abolishing such entertainments among themselves and keeping them only for clubs visiting from other locales.[1] The agreement freed up resources that could now potentially go to paying players.

The avenue for early professionalism was members or supporters providing jobs for players. Better yet were politicians able to provide patronage positions. Political patronage would be an important source of funding for top clubs through the 1860s, most notably the Mutual Club of New York, which had ties to the city coroner's office, and the National Club of Washington, with ties to the Federal Treasury Department. This era came to an end with the fall of Tammany Hall and the end of the Andrew Johnson administration, respectively.

These early resources were limited. Even generous employers were only willing to take on so much dead weight (and if the player actually performed his job duties, then this was not so much an example of professionalism as of networking through club connections). But were patronage jobs unlimited. Political patronage positions were the lifeblood of machine politics. A politician might find advantage in being seen as a benefactor of a

Baseball's Financial Revolution of 1866

popular club, and he might even be an enthusiast personally, but there still were only so many patronage positions to be distributed.

The result was that even the wealthiest clubs could only pay a handful of players. The best information available is with respect to the Athletic Club of Philadelphia, whose dirty laundry was aired following the falling out between the club and Thomas Fitzgerald, its former president. Fitzgerald was also the owner of the Philadelphia *City Item* newspaper, and took full advantage of the power of the press to make his displeasure known.

Fitzgerald claimed in an open letter to the club that "There are four playing in the nine who are paid for their services—two are regularly paid, and two are paid constructively," the latter two presumably being given jobs.[2] Astute readers might have noted that these hirings would have occurred when Fitzgerald was president. He later claimed that he had fought against the idea, but had been overruled by the board of directors, and this is why he resigned.[3] Fitzgerald followed by filing a formal charge to the NABBP judiciary committee that three players were paid, naming names: Lipman Pike, Patsy Dockney, and Dick McBride, claiming that they received $20 a week.[4]

Fitzgerald's story is probably substantially true, with Pike and Dockney being the paid players. Fitzgerald had previously claimed that Dockney had been offered a conductorship on a street car but insisted on a direct salary.[5] His paper later claimed that Pike resigned from the club due to unpaid back wages.[6]

McBride is unlikely to have been paid directly, but it is plausible that he was one of the players paid "constructively," holding a position in the Philadelphia City Comptroller's office. On the other hand, McBride seems to have actually performed the work. The day following an Athletic victory by a score of 31–12 over their arch-rivals, the Atlantics of Brooklyn, McBride arrived at work to find "his desk beautifully festooned with flags, and with the magical numbers, 31 × 12, with other devices, in commemoration of the engagement of the day previous. The surprise to Dick was an agreeable one, and was arranged by his fellow clerks, with whom Dick is justly popular."[7] This shows that he had a desk, and was rightly expected to come to work that day. On the other hand the game was played in Brooklyn, so clearly he had the day of the game off. Thus McBride's constructive pay seems to have been a real job, but with flexible scheduling.

The second "constructively" paid player probably was Al Reach. The Athletics had recruited Reach away from the Eckford Club of Brooklyn in 1864, and in early 1866 he had received a loan—either from Fitzgerald directly, or arranged by him—to go into business.⁸ It was obvious that he had received compensation of some sort under Fitzgerald's presidency. Fitzgerald likely omitted his name from his charge so as to avoid this embarrassing detail.

This sets an upper range to early professionalism. The Athletics were a wealthy club. We will see below that they had a unique source of revenue. It is no coincidence that they also were one of the only clubs outside the New York metropolis that could compete on the highest level. Even at this level there were but two players paid directly, and two given financial assistance of other sorts. This is professionalism, but constrained by the limited resources available to clubs seeking to hire players.

Enclosed Grounds and Gate Receipts

The expansion to full professionalism would come when clubs started receiving gate receipts. The first games to with an admission charge were the famous Fashion Course games of 1858. This was a series of three games between "picked nines" of New York City and Brooklyn. The late 1850s saw the first flush of enthusiasm for baseball as a spectator sport, making these games a huge attraction. They were held on a neutral ground, the Fashion Race Course in Queens. The games' expenses (probably mostly rental of the race course and advertising) were to be defrayed by charging admission of ten cents per person, with extra charges to bring vehicles onto the grounds. The profits were donated to the widows' and orphans' funds of the New York and Brooklyn fire departments.⁹

The series was a success, with about 7,800 paying admission for the three games, resulting in a surplus of $35.55 paid to each of the two fire department funds.¹⁰ The precedent thus was set that spectators were willing to pay to see a baseball game, at least if it was the right game.

Important as this precedent was, the idea was to lie fallow for several years. There were barriers yet to be overcome. Charging admission required a ground enclosed by a fence. Gate receipts, after all, require a gate; and a gate requires a fence to function. Charging admission to horse races was an established practice, so the Fashion Course had the necessary fixtures. It was not, however, really suited for baseball. It was not easily accessible. This was acceptable for special events, but not for week in and week out play. In any case, the layouts for racing and for baseball are not really compatible. Most of all, the series turned a profit, but not a large one. Bad

Baseball's Financial Revolution of 1866

weather or a decline in interest could have resulted in financial disaster. While proclaiming a great success, the organizers did not repeat the experiment.

The next development came in 1862. William Cammeyer was the proprietor of the Union Skating Pond in the Williamsburgh district of Brooklyn. Ice skating was sufficiently popular to support this commercial skating pond, enclosed by a fence. Cammeyer's idea was to adapt it for baseball in the warmer months. His business model was to offer the grounds free to three clubs, each having use of it two days a week, and he charged spectators ten cents a head.[11]

This arrangement was mutually beneficial. Clubs were having increasing difficulty in locating and holding suitable grounds: "The great disadvantage attached to the Ball Clubs—which every year is increasing—is that of procuring grounds. The vacant lots and unfenced fields in the suburban districts and the vicinity of the city are every year becoming in more demand, and the Ball Clubs have to make way for the giant of Time—improvement—and as he makes rapid strikes, are deprived of their grounds."[12]

Under Cammeyer's arrangement the club was provided with grounds that were well laid out and maintained, and with crowd control:

> The preparations made on the ground for the convenience of the spectators and players were admirable. The former were supplied with three rows of seats on each side, out of the way of the catcher in taking foul balls, and no one was allowed to encroach upon the field anywhere, an uninterrupted and fair field being given the players. The chalk line, for foul balls, was extended beyond the bases into the field, on each side, so that there could be no mistake as regards foul balls—the umpire and spectators alike having a fair view of the ball when it struck near the line. The outside crowd, occupying the hill-side surrounding the inclosed grounds, was an immense one; but nevertheless there was a goodly number occupying seats inside, there being seats furnished for over 1,500 people. The scorers and reporters had a place to themselves, and the entire arrangement was excellent and highly satisfactory.[13]
>
> The arrangements to keep the crowd from interfering with the players were excellent, and were in striking contrast to the neglect shown by the New York clubs on Hoboken in this respect, the Gotham Ground Committee entirely neglecting their duties on Tuesday last. But for the good order of the crowd that day, great inconvenience would have resulted from the want of proper arrangements. We hope our clubs will manifest an improvement in this respect in their next matches, as Brooklyn—which has hitherto not been celebrated for the order of its assemblages, especially in the Eastern District, where the veriest lot of blackguard boys ever seen, collect on these occasions—has got ahead of New York in these games. This, by-the-by, is one of the advantages derived from the inclosed grounds at

Williamsburgh; the noisy, rag-tail boys are thereby kept from annoying the players as they did on the Eckford grounds at Greenpoint.[14]

The experiment proved successful. The clubs benefited from access to the ground. The admission fee made it worth Cammeyer's while, while being low enough that there was little resistance from potential spectators (and those unwilling or unable to pay it could watch from the hill overlooking the grounds). This business model was so successful that two years later, Hamilton Weed and Reuben Decker copied it, opening the Capitoline Grounds a bit over a mile away hosting the Atlantic and Enterprise clubs.

There was one other enclosed baseball ground at this time: that of the Olympic Club of Philadelphia, opened in 1864, and which it also sublet to the Athletic and the Mercantile clubs.[15] The Olympics were a socially (if not competitively) elite club. They enclosed their ground for privacy rather than revenue. The Athletics were not so demure. A visit by the Atlantics of Brooklyn in 1864 was the highlight of the season. The Athletics attempted to take advantage by charging ten cents admission, Fitzgerald placing two of his sons as gate keepers. The experiment was not a success: "The receipts of the afternoon were $14. This was not a heavy return, considering especially that the crowd was greater than had ever up to that time attended a match in that city. But the entrance charge was considered more or less as a joke by nearly everybody."[16]

The Athletics moved onto their own ground the following year. They, and perhaps some other clubs, seem to have charged the ten cent admission, as shown by the suggestion that in return, they should start their games more promptly: "Gentlemen, you ask a reasonable charge in admitting spectators to your matches, let us ask you to confer a favor on the public who attend your games so freely, 'Open the ball' a little earlier; commence punctually at 3 o'clock, and not keep the 'plebe' waiting for an hour after time. The days are getting shorter, and the dusk comes on rapidly."[17]

Introducing the Twenty-Five Cent Admission

The ten cent admission paid for the ground, but it did not leave a surplus. Even a club such as the Athletics, which controlled its own ground directly, still had to pay rent and maintenance. Clubs soon began experimenting with higher admission fees.

The early experiments also used charity to provide cover from charges of crass commercialism. This took two forms. The profits could be donated

Baseball's Financial Revolution of 1866

to a worthy organization, as with the Fashion Course games, or the game could be a benefit for a player. The benefit match was a practice borrowed from cricket. It could have developed as a way both to provide funds to pay the player while working around the prohibition on professionalism. In practice, open professionalism quickly eliminated both issue. Benefit matches were therefore rare. In later years they typically were played for causes such as the widow of a deceased player.

The first benefit match was played September 24, 1863, for Harry Wright by the Atlantic Club of Brooklyn and the Mutual Club of New York on the enclosed grounds of the St. George Cricket Club in Hoboken. Wright was a member of the Gotham Club of New York and played cricket professionally for the St. George Club (the cricket community not sharing baseball's qualms about the subject). The game served as a dual benefit, with his cricket employers providing the site and the baseball community the game itself. The admission was ten cents, all of which was profit since there were no expenses to cover.

The first match to charge twenty-five cents admission was the inaugural game played on the Olympics' new grounds in Philadelphia on May 25, 1864. The sides were picked nines of Pennsylvania and New Jersey (mostly Philadelphia and Camden) players. The proceeds went to the Sanitary Commission (the Civil War equivalent of the modern Red Cross), preempting any potential criticism of the admission charge by cloaking the affair within the flag:

> It is a well known fact that no class in the community have excelled the base ball players of the chief cities of the North in the fervor of their patriotism, or in the cheerful willingness to tender their services, and if need be, offer up their lives in defense of the national honor and the glorious banner of the Union. Hundreds of ball players fill the honored graves of those who have thus nobly fallen, and thousands are now in the ranks of the Union army. This week we are to have their patriotism shown in another form, viz.: that of contributing to aid the funds of the Fair for the United States Sanitary Commission, the proffered assistance being in the form of a series of grand matches at base ball.[18]

The reported attendance was about 2,000, an excellent turnout at that time. The price thus was not a barrier, at least for a good cause. The original plan was for a series of three games, but the subsequent games were rained out and not rescheduled. No one knew how well attendance would hold up.

The next twenty-five cent game was more controversial. This was a season-closing game between the Atlantic Club and a picked nine on

November 27, 1865. The game lacked a charitable cause, being a benefit for the Atlantic players. The admission hike was inadequately advertised ahead of time. Hard feelings resulted. "The club unwisely increased the charge of admission to twenty-five cents, greatly to the dissatisfaction of the hundreds to went up there supposing the usual fee of ten cents would only be demanded. The increased charge, of course, led to greater profits, but second experiment of the kind won't succeed."[19] "It is to be hoped that this is the last time such an entrance-fee will be asked to a base-ball match, save for a charitable purpose."[20]

Going into the season of 1866, there were, as we have seen, about a half-dozen clubs playing on enclosed grounds and charging ten cents admission, plus a handful of additional clubs playing on enclosed grounds but not routinely charging admission. Where admission was being charged, it usually went to the proprietor of the ground, not the club. The sole exception was the Athletics, who collected admission directly. This, as much as wealthy patrons, explains the Athletics' wealth, with the treasurer reporting a total of $2,200 from gate receipts for the 1865 season. They let no moss grow under their feet, using some of their wealth to recruit players. Other clubs noted the Athletics' business model. The Keystone Club of Philadelphia enclosed their grounds and started charging ten cents. So too did the Union Club of Lansingburgh, outside of Troy, New York.[21] This option was closed, however, to the New York and Brooklyn clubs, as there were no suitable grounds available.

The only way to replicate the Athletics' revenue, especially for clubs that did not control their grounds, was to raise prices. The idea was in the air. Cammeyer proposed organizing a tournament (which never came off) charging the higher fee.[22] It was the Athletics who finally made the leap, despite being the club least in need. The Athletics and Atlantics had formed a great rivalry, and their games were huge attractions. The Atlantics traveled to Philadelphia for a game October 1, 1866. The Athletics charged the higher admission, justifying it on the grounds that is would "keep the boys out, for our juveniles are so badly brought up that they are the foremost in creating disturbances at exciting ball matches."[23] The match was a failure, but not because the high admission price kept people away. Quite the opposite: there was a frenzy of excitement about the game. The Athletics got greedy, and let too many people inside the enclosure. The crowd spilled onto the playing field and broke down the fence, making the game impossible to play.[24]

The return game in Brooklyn came off successfully, also charging

Baseball's Financial Revolution of 1866

twenty-five cents, with careful preparations for crowd control. Once again the higher admission was no obstacle. Crowd estimates ran as high as 20,000.[25] This was undoubtedly exaggerated, but nonetheless reflects the high level of public interest in the game. The two clubs then replayed the game in Philadelphia with the grounds repaired and a new fence installed. The Athletics this time charged a full dollar admission. A reported 2,500 spectators paid this admission, but the consensus was that it was exorbitant.[26]

But the genie was out of the bottle. No one tried charging a dollar admission again for over twenty years, when this premium price was introduced for the 1887 World Series.[27] The twenty-five cent admission, however, was rapidly normalized. The Atlantics charged it for additional games later that season, against the Irvington and the Eureka clubs. These were not charity games, nor were they special events like the Athletics-Atlantics games. It was simply that twenty-five cents was now the standard entrance fee. In 1867 Cammeyer routinely charged twenty-five cents "on the occasion of all first-class matches."[28] By the end of the season, this was the normal price charged by top clubs, or clubs that aspired to being at the top.[29]

The Scramble for Enclosed Grounds

One immediate effect of the new admission rate was that clubs scrambled for enclosed grounds. The Philadelphia clubs had been in the position to lead the way because a new passenger rail system was extended into northern Philadelphia, past the fully developed neighborhoods. This made land available at affordable rents, yet accessible to spectators. The Union Club of Lansingburgh, outside Troy, New York, and the Irvington Club, outside Newark, were able to replicate this and enclosed their grounds in 1867.[30]

The Union Club of Morrisania provide a cautionary tale of how this could go wrong. The Unions were a top club, winning the unofficial championship for 1867. Morrisania is in what is now the Bronx but was then part of Westchester County, not far from modern Yankee Stadium. Their old ground was not suitable for commercial use, being undersized and sandwiched between railroad tracks. The club responded to the new incentive by constructing a new ground on a grand scale:

> The Union Club of Morrisania has made arrangements for an inclosed ground at Tremont, Westchester County, which are now being graded, and will be in first-

MATCH GAME BETWEEN THE YALE COLLEGE BASE BALL CLUB AND THE UNION CLUB OF MORRISIANA, N. Y., JULY 17, 1868.

The Union of Morrisania Club's Tremont Grounds in what is now the Bronx. This ground was opened at great expense in 1868 during the scramble by the top clubs to control enclosed grounds. It proved a white elephant, being difficult to reach from downtown Manhattan and having poor drainage.

> class order by the opening of next season. The grounds leased by the club cover a space of ten acres. On a portion of the grounds will be erected a spacious saloon, dressing-rooms, etc., and etc., and the ball-field will accommodate nearly twice as many spectators as could be either into the Capitoline or Union grounds of Brooklyn. The location of the grounds is such as to be very conveniently reached. The horse cars from Harlem Bridge go direct the grounds, and the Tremont station of the Harlem steam cars is within two minutes walk of the ball-field. The enterprise of the Union club in securing these grounds will be amply repaid.[31]

This optimism proved ill-founded. Accessibility from lower Manhattan proved more difficult than advertised, and people preferred the boat ride to the enclosed grounds in Brooklyn. The ground itself was not wisely chosen, with poor drainage making it unplayable after even a modest rain:

> The grounds of the Union Club, at Tremont, are almost useless, a day's rain making them so wet and muddy that play is impossible for a week afterward. We have not seen them really dry and in first-class condition once this season, and unless more perfect drainage can be effected, the boys had better return to the old "trian-

gle" at Melrose, or find some more suitable sport for play. A good coat of turf would do much to improve the ground, and we hope that next season we shall find green grass instead of mud.[32]

The Union Club thus had a white elephant on its hands, one that dragged down the entire organization. The club had been in line with the trend for covert professionalism. Going into the 1869 season when, as we shall see, professionalism was made legal, the Unions were forced to reverse course and instead fielded an amateur nine.[33] They again tried professional competition in 1870 with modest success, but closed the season in early September. They attempted in 1871 to continue as an amateur club, but soon faded away. Their end years are not well documented, but it is not unreasonable to believe their failure to solve the ballpark problem explains much of their failure.

The most curious episode of the scramble for enclosed grounds was the political escapades around the Mutual Club. The Mutuals were a New York City club, but played on the Elysian Grounds in Hoboken. This was a traditional and popular site for New York clubs. The Mutuals were the only top-tier club using the ground, and its owner had no interest in enclosing it. The club needed to find a new place to play and looked to Brooklyn.

Surprisingly, the Mutuals found a site that was both suitable and available: the Satellite Grounds.[34] This was the third enclosed ground in Brooklyn, adjacent to the Union Grounds. It usually escapes notice because it was controlled by the Satellite Cricket Club. Two baseball clubs were based there in 1867, but they were relatively minor clubs, the Resolute and Constellation.[35] It is not clear whether they charged admission, but if they did it is unlikely that the could command the higher rate.

Going into the 1868 season the Mutuals were able to secure a lease to the ground, placing it under the club's direct control. The lease would prove poorly drafted, from the club's perspective. Direct control had an important advantage over using the Union or Capitoline grounds. With clubs now collecting gate receipts, financial terms had to be negotiated while arranging games. Terms varied, but the most common arrangement came to be a three-way split between the two clubs and the proprietor of the ground. If the club controlled its own ground it would take the proprietor's share. This would, for a popular club, more than make up for the expense of leasing and maintaining the ground themselves.

This explains the Mutuals' interest in controlling the Satellite Grounds. It also explains Cammeyer's interest in preventing them from controlling the grounds. He didn't want a major attraction such as the Mutuals next to his grounds. He wanted them inside his grounds. The Mutuals went about that spring preparing their grounds, improving the playing field and constructing a club house. Then in early April an unidentified buyer purchased lots in the middle of the field and hired a surveyor to stake them out for development. The Mutuals offered to buy back those lots at a premium, but this was refused. The circumstances of the purchase were murky, but there was a widespread (and likely correct) suspicion that Cammeyer was behind it. The Mutuals protested, but in the end were forced to accede and play at the Union Grounds. This remained their home ground the rest of their existence, through 1876. Along the way, at some time in the 1870s, Cammeyer ended up with control of the club.[36]

The Rise of Full Professionalism

The other effect of the new admission rate was the rise of full professionalism. In 1866 even the wealthiest clubs could only afford to pay a fraction of their first nine, and professionalism was presumed to be shameful. This changed rapidly once the money started flowing. Late in 1867 two picked nines of New York and New Jersey players competed in a game sponsored by the New Jersey State Fair for $250 a side, with no pretense that the players weren't being paid to play.[37] The New Jersey State Fair game evoked disapproving clucking of the tongue, but it was soon followed by defenses of professionalism and a proposal to legalize it:

> We shall first present to our readers the argument in favor of changing the rules so as to allow a club to compensate any of their players for special services rendered, or, in other words, the reasons given for an amendment abolishing the restrictions prohibiting the services of professional players in match games. In the first place, the existing rules in reference to paid players in match games are mere dead letter laws, having no effect beyond that of leading to dishonest practices in disguising the method of compensating professionals of a nine. Secondly, we do not see anything more discreditable in paying a man for his services in a base ball match than there is in doing the same thing in cricket, and cricket professionals are, as a class, as honest as any that can be found—the Wright family, for instance. The most potent reason for the change, however, is that there is no rule that can be adopted that will prevent players from being paid, and the only question, therefore, is whether it is not better to make a law to regulate that which cannot be prevented, if legally prohibited, or to have rules on our statute books which are regularly violated season after season, thereby bringing all our rules into contempt.[38]

The NABBP voted down the proposal, but defenses of professionalism escalated through 1868, and the pretense of amateurism grew ever thinner. No clubs proclaimed themselves professionals, but openly professional picked nine games sprang up:

> This match was arranged for the pecuniary benefit of the two nines who took part in it. It was in this respect an experiment, and as such it was an undoubted success. It was publicly announced that a grand match would take place between the noted players of the principal clubs of Brooklyn and New York, and though among the last-named were several amateurs, it was well known that the majority had adopted base ball as a means of earning a livelihood, and had therefore become professional ball players. As this was plainly apparent, and in view of the fact that twenty-five cents admission was charged, it was equally plain that the object of the match was to earn money, the proposed contest became a test game whereby it was to be ascertained how far the public would go in patronizing an affair of this kind, and by patronizing it, of course, endorsing the system of professional ball playing; and, inasmuch as nearly a thousand spectators were congregated on the ground at the cost of a quarter of a dollar admission fee, that alone was proof of the approval of the system, and hence we may set it down as a fact that two classes of ball players have been practically created, viz., professionals and amateurs, the former being those who play for money or place, and the latter those only who play the game of the healthful exercise and the exciting recreation it affords.[39]

The general public proved less offended than the moralists. The practice spread beyond the top clubs. A meeting of the Excelsior Club of Chicago was held to discuss how to "retrieve the good name of the Club." Where formerly keeping a good name would mean denying paying players, the point of this meeting was to raise funds. "They already had five first-class players in the organization." The issue was what it would cost to recruit four more.[40] While there was no explicit admission that they were paying their players, there isn't any other way to take this. The press began casually characterizing some clubs as "professional" without provoking the indignant denials this would have a few years earlier. The new reality was thus summarized:

> A year or two since, we gave it as our opinion, that Base Ball would become a regular profession. Events since then, assure us we were right. Base Ball is already a profession and a very important and lucrative one. Often $1000, $2000, $3000, $4000, and even $5000 are received at the gate for entrance fees to matches. This proves that the amusement is more attractive than any other field sport. The result will be the formation of firms with capital, who will employ nines, and play them against opponents, the firms paying the nines and giving them at the rate of from $1000 to $3000 per annum, according to their value. Two such nines as the Athletics or Atlantics, ought to bring in every year about $50,000, if ably managed. Give half of this sum to the players and a good round $25,000 will remain to the capitalists or managers. ... Certainly the National Game is a profession, and nothing else![41]

That winter the NABBP faced the inevitable and voted that clubs could legally declare themselves to be professional. The vote involved its share of backroom dealing, and some delegates were outraged, but there was no avoiding the inevitable, and no going back.

Conclusion

The rapid and decisive rise of professional baseball was made possible by the discovery that not only would spectators pay to watch baseball, but that they would pay enough to provide popular clubs with an important revenue stream that would be the basis of organized baseball.

Notes

1. *New York Clipper*, March 4, 1865.
2. *Philadelphia City Item*, September 1, 1866.
3. *Philadelphia City Item*, September 15, 1866.
4. *New York Clipper*, December 22, 1866.
5. *Philadelphia City Item*, September 15, 1866
6. *Philadelphia City Item*, November 3, 1866
7. *Philadelphia Sunday Mercury*, October 28, 1866.
8. *Philadelphia City Item*, April 21, 1866, announces his new store. *Philadelphia City Item*, September 8, 1866, discusses the loan.
9. *New York Sunday Mercury*, July 11, 1858.
10. Thorn, John. *Baseball in the Garden of Eden* (New York: Simon & Schuster Paperbacks), 2011, 117.
11. *Brooklyn Eagle*, April 10, 1862. The price of admission is not stated, but later discussions make clear that ten cents was the usual fee.
12. *Brooklyn Eagle*, April 7, 1862.
13. *New York Sunday Mercury*, July 27, 1862.
14. *New York Sunday Mercury*, June 8, 1862.
15. *New York Clipper*, June 4, 1864.
16. *New York Clipper*, November 1, 1879. The story should be taken with some skepticism. The account is from fifteen years later, and clearly exaggerated to some degree for effect. Contemporary accounts of the game make no mention of any admission fee. On the other hand, the failure to advertise the fee might also explain the failure of the attempt to collect it.
17. *Philadelphia Sunday Mercury*, July 23, 1865.
18. *The (Philadelphia) Daily Age*, May 25, 1864.
19. *New York Sunday Mercury*, December 3, 1865.
20. *New York World*, November 28, 1865.
21. *Philadelphia City Item*, June 16, 1866; *New York Clipper*, September 8, 1866.
22. *Brooklyn Eagle*, August 14, 1866.
23. *New York Tribune*, October 1, 1866.
24. The failed match was widely reported. Representative reports include *Philadelphia News*, October 2, 1866; *Philadelphia City Item*, October 6, 1866; *Philadelphia Sunday Mercury*, October 7, 1866; *New York Clipper*, October 13, 1866.
25. *Philadelphia Sunday Mercury*, October 14, 1866; *New York Herald*, October 17, 1866.
26. *Philadelphia City Item*, October 27, 1866.
27. *The Sporting Life*, October 12, 1887.
28. *New York Clipper*, July 20, 1867.
29. *New York Clipper*, July 20, 1867, for games on the Union Grounds; *New York Sunday Mercury*,

Baseball's Financial Revolution of 1866

August 11, 1867, for games of the Irvington Club, outside Newark; *Philadelphia Sunday Mercury,* August 25, 1867, for games of the Athletic Club; *New York Clipper,* November 2, 1867, for games of the Union Club of Lansingburgh, outside Troy.

30. See note 29.
31. *New York Sunday Mercury,* November 24, 1867.
32. *New York Dispatch,* October 25, 1868.
33. *Philadelphia Sunday Mercury,* February 14, 1869.
34. *New York Sunday Mercury,* March 15, 1868.
35. *Brooklyn Eagle,* April 24, 1867.
36. The controversy was extensively reported. See *New York Sunday Mercury,* April 12, 1868; American *Chronicle of Sports and Pastime,* April 16, 1868; *New York Sunday Mercury,* April 19, 1868; *New York Dispatch,* April 19, 1868; *New York Sunday Mercury,* April 26, 1868; *New York Dispatch,* May 3, 1868.
37. *New York Sunday Mercury,* November 10, 1867; *New York Clipper,* November 16, 1867.
38. *Ball Players' Chronicle,* December 5, 1867.
39. *American Chronicle of Sports and Pastime,* April 30, 1868.
40. *Philadelphia Sunday Mercury,* August 2, 1868, quoting the *Chicago Tribune.*
41. Philadelphia City Item October 3, 1868.

Early Baseball and Journalism in the Midwest
Illinois College and Illinois Baseball

STEVE HOCHSTADT and
JAMES BRANDON TERRY

Baseball and journalism developed together at Illinois College in Jacksonville, and at other colleges in Illinois, in the late 1870s and 1880s, about a decade after town baseball spread through Midwestern communities. The student newspaper at Illinois College gradually developed baseball journalism, expanding reports and statistical summaries of games. Many of the student journalists were also players, who often complained about insufficient enthusiasm and organization. Baseball contests typically were paired with other intercollegiate competitions, especially oratory. Attempts at creating regular schedules for intercollegiate competition were unsuccessful, so most of IC's games were against local high school and town teams, as rivalries developed with the local high school and with the Illinois School for the Deaf. Baseball was a popular activity among college students in the late 19th century, although few continued playing after graduation.

AT ILLINOIS COLLEGE (IC) IN Jacksonville, Illinois, the second college founded in the state but the first to grant a degree in 1835, baseball and journalism developed as siblings in the late 1870s. The baseball team and college newspaper there were not firsts, but they showed up early in the history of both forms of public community activity in the Midwest. There were no rules, or even conventions, about how best to report, comment on, and encourage the playing of baseball. The first decade of baseball at Illinois College and among Illinois colleges, as reported by the newly established *Rambler*—created, written and edited by students —exemplifies the national birth of baseball journalism. Illinois College, moreover, appears to have played a central role in baseball's development in Jacksonville and among Illinois colleges more generally.

The details are worth noting. Looking closely at these early baseball players and games allows us to see college teams and careers being invented and re-invented. Student journalists, who were friends of the players or the players themselves, learned how to report a baseball game and talk about a player's performance. The *Rambler*, whose birth in 1878 was encouraged by baseball players, was an enthusiastic source of detailed information on the earliest years of baseball at Illinois College, in Jacksonville, and among Midwestern colleges and universities. Playing what was becoming the national game fit in perfectly with a classical education, literary societies, oratorical contests, and vigorous masculinity.

The Game Spreads in the Midwest

In the antebellum Midwest baseball was already a public sport. The first baseball clubs in Illinois were the Union team in Chicago in 1856, followed in 1858 by Excelsior in Chicago, Plowboys in Downers Grove, and the Alton Baseball Club. There were "organized fraternal games" in the Chicago area after 1856, and a game was reported in Davenport, Iowa, in 1858.[1] At that time there were already a few collegiate baseball teams in the East.[2] During the Civil War, baseball spread further. The Hardin Club was organized in Jacksonville, Illinois, in 1863, according to the Jacksonville *Daily Courier*.[3]

After war's end, men and boys flocked to baseball diamonds across the Midwest and began to organize amateur teams. Serious players from Illinois, Indiana, Michigan, and Iowa met in Chicago in 1865 to create the Northwestern Association of Base Ball Players. The *Illinois State Register* reported that the Hardin Club was defeated by another Jacksonville club, Hercules, by a score of 78–42, on May 29, 1866. Later that year, there were newspaper reports about other clubs in Jacksonville, the Union and the Morgan. Hardin met many teams from Illinois, Milwaukee and Louisville at a tournament in Bloomington, Illinois, in September 1866.[4] In 1867 alone, over 50 town clubs were formed across Illinois.[5] By 1867, players created the Iowa State Base Ball Association, and there were nine clubs in Des Moines.[6]

Steve Hochstadt and James Brandon Terry

Because the only form of public media, newspapers, tells us little about early baseball in Illinois, scattered bits of memory grew into oral legends. In his history of Illinois College written in the 1920s, President Charles Henry Rammelkamp retold what he had heard: "The person who, according to tradition, introduced the sport into Jacksonville was 'Line' Chandler from Chandlersville." Chandler had attended Phillips Academy in Andover, MA, and returned home to the preparatory department at Illinois College in 1865–1866. Rammelkamp credits Chandler with creating the first two teams in Jacksonville, Hardin and Hercules.[7] Since Chandler was not in Illinois and only a teenager when Hardin was first organized, he was not "the person" but probably one of many participants. He personifies one possible early link between school baseball in the East and town baseball in Jacksonville.[8]

Adopted by the Colleges

As town baseball was growing throughout the Midwest, the sport was also developing in the nation's colleges. Before the Civil War, intercollegiate contests of any type were rare. The first recorded intercollegiate athletic event was a rowing match between Harvard and Yale in 1852. Amherst College and Williams College played the first intercollegiate baseball game in 1859. Union College played against a Schenectady baseball team in 1860.[9]

During and after the war the pace of college baseball's expansion quickened. First, baseball teams were organized in the oldest northeastern institutions: Princeton, Yale and Harvard in 1864, then University of Pennsylvania in 1866 and Columbia in 1868.[10] Smaller colleges quickly followed: Wesleyan University in 1865; Bates College in 1872.[11] Many Midwestern colleges also created baseball teams in the late 1860s: Coldwater College (MI), Kenyon College (OH) and Beloit College (WI) in 1866; Shurtleff College (IL), Asbury College (IN, now Depauw University), and McKendree College (IL) in 1867; Geneva College (OH) and Grinnell College (IA) in 1868; and Monmouth College (IL) and St. Louis University in 1869.[12] A number of Illinois colleges played against each other in the late 1860s—Monmouth played Lombard in 1868. These two colleges, plus Knox, played each other occasionally in the early 1870s. Abingdon, which became Eureka College, joined the group in 1878. But in Illinois there was still little formal organizational development of the game at the college level.[13]

College baseball began as one among many forms of athletic and intellectual recreation and competition. The Amherst-Williams game in 1859 was part of a two-day social event that also included a chess match.[14] In Illinois, organized intercollegiate competition began informally as oratorical contests among literary societies. In 1872, societies at Knox and Monmouth planned an oratorical competition, but nothing happened until the next year, when Knox hosted a contest among several schools. In 1874, those colleges formed the Illinois Inter-Collegiate Oratorical Association (IICOA), and held their first annual contest in Bloomington on November 20.[15]

Baseball and Journalism at Illinois College

At Illinois College, significant new extracurricular activities for students were developed under the presidency of Rufus Crampton 1876–1882, part of a nationwide trend. The student newspaper, the *Rambler*, was founded, a YMCA club was formed, and baseball began.[16] New student activities were encouraged when students from different colleges met. At the fall 1877 Inter-Collegiate Oratorical Contest held at Monmouth, the delegates accompanying Illinois College's orator included the junior Harold W. Johnston. They brought back to campus copies of the Monmouth *College Courier* which described the contest. There had been short-lived student-produced newspapers at IC, but this time the College Association took matters more seriously. A committee was appointed to "consider the advisability and practicability of publishing such a paper," whose first issue appeared in January 1878, with Johnston as one of five editors of the new *Rambler*.[17]

In the second issue of the *Rambler* in February, Johnston wrote in his regular column, "Ramblings on the Campus," that "The captain of the ball club summons his nine to the gymnasium."[18] That captain was Thomas Powell Antle of the class of 1879. Antle was from Petersburg, IL, and became the pitcher on the earliest Illinois College teams.[19] Edward Hart Crampton '81 was an additional pitcher, who was also President Rufus Crampton's son.[20] In the spring Johnston urged the creation of "a strong base ball organization." He happily reported in March that Antle was leading practices, but by May he was disappointed. "Not a ball has been hit, not a muff been made, not a run been scored this year on the college base ball grounds."[21]

Although Johnston was not listed among the first players in spring 1878, he was in fact a baseball enthusiast. His journalistic criticism came from inside the circle of baseball players, influenced by his experience with intercollegiate oratorical competition. He was a delegate from Illinois to the Inter-State Oratorical Contest in St. Louis on May 8, where the winner of the Illinois Inter-Collegiate Contest met other Midwestern orators.[22] Not all student journalists were as excited about baseball. In the *Rambler*'s first issue, another editor, C.L. Morse, criticized Monmouth's *College Courier* for its emphasis on athletics: "the extent to which the exercise of the muscles, in place of the exercise of the mind, has been carried in some colleges, is, to say the least, very detrimental to both the students and the college."[23]

Faculty were allowed to belong to college teams. Also on that first team in spring 1878 was George R. Walker, who played 2nd base and was called "Tut" by his teammates. He was an instructor in English and Latin at Illinois College, and continued to play in 1879.[24] After he left in 1880, faculty leadership was taken over by Johnston, who become principal of Whipple Academy in 1880, the preparatory school attached to Illinois College.

A lot of baseball was played in the next season, fall 1878. The first game reported in the *Rambler*, perhaps Illinois College's first official intercollegiate varsity sporting event, took place in Alton against Shurtleff College on October 26, 1878. The result was a 1–1 tie, which the *Rambler* wrote "has set the ball in motion."[25] Other games were played at Illinois Wesleyan and Monmouth, but nothing was reported about them. Meanwhile, Knox College, McKendree College and the University of Chicago also expressed an interest in baseball. While there is no evidence about specific games, according to Johnston an intense rivalry developed immediately with the team from Jacksonville's Washington High School. The younger team was better at first.[26] That was several years before the alleged "first game between Illinois high schools," according to the Illinois High School Association.[27]

Many other students played baseball on the IC campus, as at many other colleges, on a less official basis. In fall 1878, the junior class divided up into those concentrating in the scientific program and those in the classical program, with the "scientifics" winning 10–5. The freshmen played against Brown's Business College, which had been founded by Professor Rufus Crampton in 1866 and taken over by George W. Brown when Crampton became IC's President in 1876. Many games were played between IC and the Business College over the next few years, and the rivalry was closely contested, as indicated by this game's score, 24–22 for the Business College. The IC seniors defeated the junior class. After half an inning the seniors led 9–0, and the juniors had to quit because their catcher was hurt.[28]

Intercollegiate Baseball in Illinois

By the spring of 1879, there were enough teams in Illinois for the IC team to plan a tour, including games against Champaign, Wesleyan, Knox, Monmouth, Northwestern University, and University of Chicago. But no intercollegiate games actually materialized for IC that season.[29] IC won its first few games that spring. They met their first defeat when they played a team from Havana, IL, in May. The game stayed tied all the way through 9 innings, but IC fell short in the 10th. In 1886, Johnston remembered the spring 1879 team as the best ever, the champions of the city. He singled out Antle and Walker as the most dedicated baseball men.[30] A *Rambler* article from 1885 called the 1879 team "the best that the students of Illinois College ever had."[31]

In fall 1879, the Knox team made its first intercollegiate road trip to Jacksonville, where they defeated IC 20–13 on October 24.[32] At the annual meeting of the Illinois Inter-Collegiate Oratorical Association in Champaign, where baseball joined with oratory as competitive sports, the IC team lost again to the Havana Reds 13–7 in 6 innings. IC began a game against the Illinois Industrial University (IIU), which later became the University of Illinois, but rain cut it short.[33]

Baseball continued to be paired with oratory as equally important extra-curricular activities in Illinois. In spring 1880, Illinois College and IIU called for a bigger and more organized tournament to be held at the annual IICOA meeting. Knox and Monmouth agreed, but no tournament was held. Through the 1880s, there were repeated attempts at more organization, but only a few teams showed up at these meetings.[34] Nevertheless, the annual meetings organized around oratorical contests included many of the intercollegiate baseball games played in Illinois in the 1880s, matching teams from IC, Knox, Monmouth, Blackburn, Illinois Wesleyan and IIU.

In these early days, there remained uncertainties about who was eligible to play on college baseball teams. At Knox, locals could play with students on the squad.[35] In fall 1880, at that year's Oratorical Association meeting in Galesburg, the captains of the Illinois College and Knox College teams agreed that both students and faculty could play. But local semi-professional ringers were excluded from college teams.

Little was written in the *Rambler* about baseball in 1880 and 1881, perhaps because the team was poorly organized. Football was just beginning to be mentioned as a recreational activity, and some football "games" were played with loose and variable rules in 1881, notably between the freshmen and the High School team.³⁶ But, according to the *Rambler*, football was a brutal sport. Injuries began to appear among the students: bruised shins, broken toes, sprained ankles and overexertion in general were the attendant evils. Over the next few years, the *Rambler* often noted that "the football," apparently the only one available, could no longer be used.

In spring 1882, a new local baseball rival appeared, the team from the Illinois Institution for the Education of the Deaf and Dumb, established a few hundred yards from Illinois College in 1839. *Rambler* writers called the institution "Deaf and Dumb" or the "Dummies." Illinois College lost a game on March 4 and played them again in April. Over the next few years, frequent games between these west side rivals were played. IC scheduled a game against the downtown Brown's Business College, but it was rained out.³⁷

In April 1882, the *Rambler* mentioned baseball being used in the College as a new method of settling disagreements or creating bragging rights. Class teams had appeared at other colleges: Harvard's first baseball team were the freshmen in 1862, who called themselves the "66 Baseball Club." At IC, the sophomore and freshmen classes scheduled a game against each other, but that was rained out. The College nine did not play in these intramural games.³⁸

Blackburn College played its first intercollegiate contest in Jacksonville on April 29, 1882. "A large crowd viewed the game," including a delegation from the Young Ladies' Athenaeum, an innovative women's college established in Jacksonville in 1864. Professor Johnston served as umpire, and Illinois College won 10–3.³⁹ The *Rambler* now reported more information than previously about the full lineups and the progress of the game. The story gave an inning-by-inning summary and printed the number of runs each player scored.

Whipple Academy moved from downtown Jacksonville to the campus in 1876 and into the new Whipple Hall in 1882. H.W. Johnston had become principal in 1880, and his influence was surely a major factor in the creation of a baseball team. In May 1882, Whipple lost to a "downtown nine" 18–9.⁴⁰ A varsity rematch against Blackburn College in Carlinville on May 20 was rained out, and that appeared to be the end of the spring season.⁴¹

Another notable spring event which was to affect the development of baseball at IC was new President Edward Tanner's decision to rip up the Osage orange hedgerow which divided the campus. Classes were canceled on May 5, 1882, and students went out to help uproot the hedge.

The first IC game of fall 1882 mentioned in the *Rambler* was against

Brown's Business College on September 30. Some scouting must have been done on the Business College team, because the *Rambler* noted that their pitcher could throw a curve, still an unusual ability. Unfortunately, IC's regular pitcher Charlie Reynolds could not play.[42] A chemical accident in one of his classes had burned his hand and made him take some time away from the diamond. That fall, Bedford Brown, the catcher, was captain, and third baseman Frank Lincoln Birch was business manager.[43]

Later that month, the Illinois College team traveled to Chicago for the planned tournament, but only played against Knox and Monmouth, losing both games on the same day. The *Rambler* reported inning-by-inning line scores for the first time, and listed runs scored and outs made by each player. Bedford Brown scored 5 of the team's 11 runs. Reynolds pitched both games, and J.W. Dalbey, a future star, is mentioned for the first time, although he scored no runs and made 8 outs.[44]

On October 21, wearing new uniforms, the IC team lost to Bluff City from across the Mississippi in Hannibal, Missouri. The game began with a coin toss to decide who took the field and who was first to bat. Bedford Brown again scored 3 runs, but IC lost 15–11. Whipple Academy defeated a team named the Alerts from the School for the Deaf 8–2.[45] That was the first time that a team name appeared; later the ISD teams were called the Athletics and the Browns. In the final game that fall, the men defeated the Business College.[46] The *Rambler* expressed hopes for the team playing better in the spring.

By fall 1882, amateur baseball was being played across the country, from St. Paul Island in Alaska to Yuma, Arizona, to Lewiston, Maine. Over 130 teams had been founded in New Jersey, with Illinois and New York in second place with about 100.[47] Higher education was still getting into the act, as colleges and universities continued to expand official student activities beyond the classroom. Eight colleges in Illinois planned to replace the haphazard scheduling of games by creating a league and a weekend tournament. Juniors Allen Gilbert Dunaway and Henry William Hand were chosen as delegates to the October 6 meeting in Chicago of what became the Illinois Inter-Collegiate Base Ball Association, but this organization was short-lived.[48]

Inventing Organization in College Baseball

It was always a struggle in these early years to field a consistent team of experienced players, possibly because players could not get permission from the faculty to miss many class days during a semester. Only five players from the IC team which played Knox and Monmouth in early October 1882 were in the lineup later that month against Bluff City. In February 1883, when the IC baseball players were out on the field as soon as the ice melted, the nine lost two players before the season began. The pitcher Reynolds left for the spring semester and 2nd baseman Goodspeed went West until the fall, "chasing the buffalo," as the *Rambler* put it. Three players joined the team from Whipple Academy, minor leaguers getting their chance at the majors.[49]

IC's first games that spring were against local teams, victories over ISD and the Business College. The *Rambler* wrote that the team was not quite invincible yet, and urged captain Bedford Brown to schedule more practices. The star of IC's first teams, T.P. Antle, who had pitched for the University of Michigan in 1882, now a doctor, returned to campus and "astonished some of the amateur base ballists with a few examples of curve pitching." He was offered $1200 plus expenses to play for a club in Peoria.[50] Taking the *Rambler*'s advice, the team set up a heavier than usual practice schedule. They played two more games against ISD. To celebrate the anniversary of the uprooting of the Osage orange hedges, the College organized a day of activities on May 5, which developed into an annual event, Osage Orange Day. Among the many track and field events was "throwing the baseball," which was won by Captain Bedford Brown.[51] The varsity defeated their younger brothers from Whipple Academy.[52]

The core of the team in spring 1883 was catcher and captain Brown, Alfred Tomlin Capps in the outfield, and the sophomore Dalbey at first base, who had quickly become the team's offensive leader. Some skilled players appeared in the lineup who chose not to formally join the team, including Slater at shortstop, who scored four runs against Whipple and made no outs. Alfred Tomlin Capps was an officer of Phi Alpha, associate editor of the *Rambler*, and president of the senior class. He graduated in 1885 as salutatorian. Capps later served as president of Illinois Legislative Voters League and the Anti-Saloon League of Illinois.

Whipple's right fielder, Edward Capps, brother of A.T. Capps, was about to graduate from the Academy and start a long and successful academic and athletic career at Illinois College.[53] Edward also became president of Phi Alpha, was editor of the *Rambler*, and graduated in 1887. He earned a PhD from Yale University in 1891 and taught there as professor of Greek language and literature until 1907, when he became professor of classics at Princeton University. He was president of the Classical Association of the

Atlantic States 1909–1910 and became the first president of the American Association of University Professors in 1920. After World War I, he became chair of the board of the American School of Classical Studies at Athens 1919–1939, where he organized the excavation of the Agora of ancient Athens. He was also American Red Cross Commissioner in Greece for two years and was then appointed by President Woodrow Wilson as U.S. Minister to Greece and Macedonia in 1920–1921. Edward Capps served on the Illinois College Board of Trustees 1935–1948. He was the author of many books on Greek drama.

Even at the earliest stages of the development of baseball as a popular sport, journalists offered both encouragement and criticism. The *Rambler*, acting as both reporter and cheerleader, sometimes expressed aggravation that the team did not practice more and play better. An editorial said the team needed a leader, not just a captain, but someone who would coach and focus on the team.

In September 1883, Illinois College students tried to infuse more organization into baseball. When the College Association met to elect delegates to the IICOA meeting in Rockford in October, the students also elected officers for the baseball team. The Association elected Dalbey, first baseman for the past two years, as captain, and Dunaway, a former contributor to the outfield, as the financial manager. Students also voted for a new method of selecting the team: Captain Dalbey chose one player; those two picked the third player together; and so on. The varsity was 3–1 against local teams, but no other games were reported that fall.[54]

By March 1884, warm weather returned and the team was back at practice. In April, they leveled the field with a heavy roller, a perennial chore, making it ready for the upcoming season. There were lots of ballplayers on the campus: the freshmen beat the sophomores 14–8, and later in the month played against a pick-up team. But the varsity faced a critical recruiting challenge. The *Rambler* reported, "Reynolds has left college and consequently the nine is in want of a pitcher." Students were encouraged to try out, just give it a shot.[55] Three new players showed up on the spring roster. Pitching duties were handed to the veteran Sterling Price Bond, a junior outfielder, but his arm gave out in the 6th inning of a game against Jacksonville High School.[56]

On May 8 the varsity again played the High School and took an early lead as the High School men failed to score in the first 4 innings. Bond wore out again, and the shortstop Graham came in for the last two innings. Illinois College squeaked out the win 12–11. IC outhit the High School and reached base more often on errors, especially by the third baseman. Dalbey was the offensive star, going 4 for 5. The *Rambler* bragged about the "championship of the city."[57] The large number of errors was not unusual for early baseball: in an 1876 professional game between the Boston Red Caps and the Philadelphia Athletics, 28 errors were made, with a final score of 19–11 for Boston.[58]

But more interesting than the boosterism in the reporting was the development of a much more detailed box score, which finally allowed readers to see each player's performance and understand the nature of the contest, even without a play-by-play. The *Rambler* now copied the way regular newspapers reported professional games.

The last baseball game of the spring season 1884 was part of a wider group of athletic events connected with the second Osage Orange Day on May 9. The usual slate of track and field events included the baseball throw, when Bedford Brown, about to graduate, was barely beaten by L.A. Gray '88, who never played for the varsity. The classical majors played against the scientifics, and most of the varsity team participated.[59]

May 8, 1884
ILLINOIS COLLEGE

player	position	at bats	runs	basehits	putouts	assists	errors
Brown, B.	C	5	2	1	1	5	2
Graham, H.M.	SS	5	3	2	3	7	1
Dalbey, J.W.	1B	5	1	4	17	0	3
Bond, S.	P	4	1	0	2	3	3
Galbreth, R.	2B	4	1	0	3	4	2
Capps, A.T.	RF	5	1	1	0	0	0
Wilcox	3B	5	2	2	1	0	0
Smith, T.W.	LF	5	1	0	0	1	2
Dugan	CF	5	1	2	0	0	0
	total	43	12	12	27	20	12

HIGH SCHOOL

player	position	at bats	runs	basehits	putouts	assists	errors
Alcott	C	5	1	0	5	1	3
Sanderson	RF	4	1	1	0	0	0
Jones	1B	5	1	2	5	0	1
Kent	SS	4	2	1	5	1	2
Davenport	LF	5	2	0	2	0	3
Waddell	P	4	0	0	2	2	1
Hunter	3B	4	0	0	2	0	5
Kinnett	CF	4	2	2	1	0	0
Turley	2B	3	2	1	2	3	1
	total	37	11	7	24	7	17

The students who wrote for the *Rambler* were delighted when the baseball team did well, but showed little respect during lackluster seasons. In September 1884, a number of the previous season's players did not return. The *Rambler* complained, "All love of baseball seems to have been eliminated from the characters of members of the old nine who are in college." The team consisted of underclassmen and Whipple Academy students, without veteran leadership. Reporting that the club was demoralized, the paper pleaded, "Let them organize and begin at once to practice together and before the year of their graduation has come 'Old Illinois' will have a ball nine of which she may well be proud." Only one game was reported that fall season, a 19–17 loss against Knox at the annual intercollegiate meeting in Lincoln.[60] Perhaps in a show of frustration, the *Rambler* wrote that Illinois College ought to have a football team.[61]

In March 1885, reorganization of baseball was tried again, as students met in the chapel and formed a Base Ball Association. IC senior A.T. Capps was selected as president, and a sophomore and two freshmen were elected to the other offices. Capps was captain, with H.M. Graham as assistant.[62] In April, the varsity played two games against the ISD Athletics, trouncing them first 34–7, but only tying them 13–13 later that month. On April 30, the local Jacksonville Blues scored 7 runs in the first inning and won 16–5.[63]

The connection between oratory and sports was emphasized in the increasing importance placed on Osage Orange Day as a major Illinois College celebration, including oratorical competition between the literary societies and a serious track meet. A baseball game on May 8 against former players who returned for the celebration had been planned since March. The varsity beat the alumni 22–6. The downtown clothier Lafayette Seeberger paid for a new backstop.[64] Local financial support for early baseball teams was crucial.

Playing baseball and complaining about the team in print were intimately connected. In its final issue of the school year, the *Rambler* groused that the team was not serious, did not practice enough and needed a better captain. "The base-ball nine of this season was so elated with its victory on May 8th that it has not been on the diamond since."[65] But this was not a student rejection of too much emphasis on muscles. Again, the displeasure came from within. The new editor-in-chief of the *Rambler* was Thomas W. Smith, the shortstop; other editors were Edward Capps, Henry W. Denison, and Robert H.K. Whiteley, all connected to the team. The next year, Capps became editor-in-chief.

A new baseball association was created in September, with a strong constitution and by-laws: its goal was to "organize and perpetuate a base ball league among the colleges of Central Illinois."[66] The new slate of officers was young. *Rambler* editor Smith, a sophomore who had played for a year, was elected President.[67] Junior Rush Denny Galbreth became team captain.[68] The freshman Norman Triplett was already so impressive that he was elected treasurer.[69] Denison and Whiteley, both from the class of 1887, became vice president and secretary.

For the first time, the manager was given full control of the men at all times, not just when a game was in progress. He selected the nine who would play, and excuses for absences from practices or games had to go through him. He could punish players by keeping them out of a game or making them exercise. A committee was appointed to correspond with other central Illinois colleges and to send delegates to the Inter Collegiate Convention at Carlinville on October 2. The delegates would arrange a series of games for the championship of Central Illinois among IC, Knox, Monmouth, Blackburn, and Illinois Wesleyan. The baseball-playing *Rambler* journalists were happy: "we can bring the national game, the best of all games, into the prominence which it deserves."[70]

Leadership was provided by older men with baseball experience. Samuel W. Parr had arrived in Jacksonville with a BS from Illinois Industrial University, where he was editor of the student newspaper, valedictorian, and a baseball player. At 28, he became professor of agricultural science and chemistry in 1885, and joined the team.[71] H.W. Johnston, recently made professor of Latin and replaced as principal of Whipple Academy by Joseph Harker, became manager and started playing for the team again. The *Rambler* increased its attention to the team by creating a new section, Base Ball Notes.

The team lost to the "Stars" of Jacksonville, which may have been an all-star collection from the various local teams, by a score of 16–10. IC and ISD played nearly every week, with the College boys winning 4 of 5 games.[72] The summary of IC's 20–5 victory over ISD on October 17 describes a game very different from modern baseball. 17 players reached first base on a total of 20 errors, but there were only two walks. Nat English, the Illinois College catcher, allowed 4 passed balls, but a series of three ISD catchers allowed 15.[73] The power hitters were on the IC nine: Triplett, playing third base, was 3 for 6 with two triples, and Wilson hit one, too. ISD substituted for its shortstop and center fielder after the first few innings and moved several other players around the diamond. The game lasted 2½ hours.

Early Baseball and Journalism in the Midwest

The lack of a schedule within an organized league meant that teams like Illinois College had to constantly seek out games with possible opponents, who were usually local teams. Of the 14 games played in the next spring season in 1886, only one was against a team from out of town, a 18–12 loss against the University of Illinois (renamed in 1885) on Osage Orange Day. The team went 6–8, splitting games with ISD and with the town teams. The *Rambler* reported only half of these games. The best hitters were Professors Johnston and Parr, showing the value of experience, and the newcomer Triplett, who had begun college at age 24. Triplett was a coming star. He threw the baseball 291 feet at Osage Orange, and debuted as a lefty pitcher against the U of I.[74]

In June, students created the Athletic Association of Illinois College, evidence that other sports were being played. The Baseball Association turned over all its property to the Athletic Association in exchange for $50, on the condition that a few people were included in the new committee.

Illinois College baseball team of 1886. Standing, left to right: T.W. Smith, Prof. H.W. Johnston, Prof. S.W. Parr, C.E. Sanders, F.E. Kennedy. Seated, left to right: G.H. Wilson, R.D. Galbreth, Norman Triplett, Edward Capps (Illinois College Archive).

This was the first step in making one powerful organization rather than several weaker ones.

An official 1886 team photo in May illustrates the fluid nature of team membership. Professors Johnston and Parr are flanked by seven players, those who had played more than three games. At least 13 men had participated in the spring. Extra players were needed to cope with the concentrated schedule of games: in May five games were played in two weeks, two on Saturdays and the others scattered during the weekdays. Two team members also played a game for the Jacksonville Stars.[75] The rule that players had to be associated with the College had been agreed upon years before, but was not always followed. Knox College apparently often bent the rule. In fall 1880, William S. Harvey, known for having thrown the first curve ball in Galesburg, who had already graduated in the spring, pitched at the IICOA meeting. In the 1887 tournament, Knox beat IC with a ringer who had no college connection, causing a protest. In the 1890s, Knox hired a pitcher for entire seasons.[76]

A Great Season

The fall 1886 season was a spectacular one for the Illinois College team. New uniforms displayed the Illinois College colors: navy blue shirts and pants, white hats with blue stripes, and socks and belt in white. Their shirts were embroidered with shields and white letters spelling "Illinois." This whole uniform cost $63.[77] The biggest change was putting the sophomore Triplett on the mound. In the first game against the Jacksonville Unions[78] Triplett's cannon balls gave the catcher English some trouble, but hobbled the Unions, who hit 10 balls back to the pitcher for easy outs. Triplett also went 5 for 5 at the plate.[79] He struck out 8 through 6 innings, when the game was called because of darkness with the College team ahead 16–11.

Once the IC catchers, English and Wilson, were able to catch Triplett's fast balls, the team slaughtered its opponents. They beat the Unions four more times by lopsided scores, including once when Brown pitched. Triplett was the big story, but the team was playing excellent ball. He struck out 10 in five innings against the Unions on October 12, and the fielders made no errors against 11 by the Unions. They defeated the ISD Browns 23–2, and an all-star team of Jacksonville players 22–9. At the IICOA, they lost again to IIU, but made a spectacular comeback against Knox. Watkins had allowed Knox to score 18 runs in the first three innings, but Triplett came in and

Early Baseball and Journalism in the Midwest

allowed only one hit over five innings, as the IC hitters rallied to win 26–20.[80] That season Triplett had an incredible batting average of .600. English, Sanders, Watkins and Parr were above .300.

The two months of baseball in spring 1887 have many features typical of the team's first decade, but bring this story of early college baseball and journalism to an end. The IC team was organized enough to implement new winter practice rules: players needed to appear in the gym between 4 and 5 p.m. three times a week.[81] Most of the games were played against the Browns of ISD on Saturdays in April and May, and the teams were evenly matched: two losses 21–18 and 17–16 and two wins 22–11 and 21–18. Blackburn came to Jacksonville for a weekend doubleheader on April 22 and 23, but the games were marred by controversy. Blackburn won Friday's game 18–8. Their pitcher Witt, however, turned out not to be a student. On Saturday, the Blackburn team left the field in the middle of the game, but then returned, as IC won 8–2 behind 11 strikeouts by Triplett.[82] For the first time, the *Rambler* editorial staff included no baseball players.

The most important games were played against the University of Illinois, both connected with institutional field days. On Osage Orange Day, May 13, the visiting University team beat IC 13–6. To prepare for a visit to the U of I campus for their own University Field Day a week later, the IC team scheduled two midweek 4-inning games against ISD. They must have helped, because in Champaign on May 20 the IC team took a 19–10 lead into the bottom of the ninth and pulled out the victory 19–16. The *Rambler* printed an expanded story with play-by-play reporting.[83] Despite another attempt to create an urban league among the cities of central Illinois, which IC supported, better organization of baseball in Illinois remained in the future.

The Beginnings of the National Game

In the earliest years of baseball, the student body of Illinois College could put several complete baseball teams on the field at the same time. In today's mammoth universities that may not seem notable. In 1886, in the middle of this story, Illinois College had 58 students, all male.[84] At any moment, at least half of the men were baseball players, and others had been or would be. Baseball had probably not brought them to Illinois College, and we have no information about their earlier history with the game. But we can conclude that among this select group of professionally minded students, from families mostly comfortably off, baseball was great fun.

STEVE HOCHSTADT and JAMES BRANDON TERRY

In a town of about 10,000, little Illinois College supplied nearly half the men who played baseball in Jacksonville. Since most college men played baseball, the spectrum of talent was very broad. Many players were widely active in college activities and were among the best students. While some excellent players have been mentioned here, few played ball after college. They became doctors and lawyers, academics and businessmen, politicians and teachers. The story of early baseball is mostly about ordinary men, who made errors on the field but created baseball history.

That history was written by early student journalists, who developed baseball reporting by copying models from regular newspapers. Often players themselves, college reporters rooted for their teams and promoted further development of collegiate athletics. In its first decade, baseball in Illinois had not yet emancipated itself from other intercollegiate activities, like field days or oratorical contests, to become a free-standing sport. Despite repeated efforts, no league yet provided structure for competition. That came later in the 19th century, encouraged by avid baseball journalists rooting for their teams and for the national game.

NOTES

1. Ed Ackerley, "A History of Early Knox College Baseball from the 1830's to 1900 and an Examination of Its Corresponding Reflection of Knox College's Worldly Transformation" (BA honors thesis, Knox College, Galesburg, Illinois, May 22, 1998), 13.

2. George B. Kirsch, *Baseball and Cricket: The Creation of American Team Sports 1838-72* (Urbana: University of Illinois Press, 1989), 146.

3. "Hardin Base Ball Club of Jacksonville," Protoball, accessed August 4, 2017, http://protoball.org/Hardin_Base_Ball_Club_of_Jacksonville.

4. Brian McKenna, "Sputtering Towards Respectability: Chicago's Journey to the Big Leagues," in *The National Pastime*, v. 37 (Summer 2015), ed. by Stuart Shea, *North Side, South Side, All Around the Town: Baseball in Chicago*, accessed July 11, 2017, http://sabr.org/research/sputtering-towards-respectability-chicago-s-journey-big-leagues.

5. A long and searchable list of the earliest clubs across the country can be found at MLB, "Earliest Baseball Clubs," accessed July 11, 2017, http://mlb.mlb.com/memorylab/spread_of_baseball/earliest_clubs.jsp. Not every date is reliable: the Jacksonville clubs Union, Hardin, Morgan, and Hercules are given the date 1867.

6. Ackerley, "Early Knox College Baseball," 30.

7. Charles Henry Rammelkamp. *Illinois College: A Centennial History, 1829-1929* (Illinois College: 1928), 279.

8. Linus Child Chandler (1846–1897) was born in Chandlerville, Illinois. His father, Dr. Charles Chandler (1806–1879), founded Chandlerville in 1831 and served as town president. He graduated from Harvard University Law School in 1871, when he entered into practice in Chicago. After the Chicago fire that year, he opened a law office in Chandlerville. In 1872 he was elected States Attorney for Cass County, and served four years. In 1873, he married Sarah Louise Beane (1846–1935), a native of Lisbon, New Hampshire. In 1880 he was elected to the Illinois legislature as a Republican and served two years. He served as Justice of Peace and President of Town Board of Chandlerville. He moved to Cincinnati, and then to Pittsburgh in 1890, where he and a partner sold vinegar. In his final years, he peddled vinegar and sauces of his own making in the streets of Allegheny, and he died at the poor farm.

9. "On This Day: July 27, 1878," accessed August 2, 2017, http://www.nytimes.com/learning/general/onthis day/harp/0727.html; Wikipedia, "College Athletics in the United States," https://

en.wikipedia.org/wiki/College_athletics_in_the_United_States accessed July 11, 2017; "Union College Athletics Heritage," https://www.unionathletics.com/sports/2009/10/14/GEN_1014094343.aspx accessed July 11, 2017.

10. Princeton Tigers, "150 Years—Baseball," accessed July 11, 2017, http://www.goprincetontigers.com/news/2014/11/22/209777562.aspx?path=baseball; Wikipedia, "Yale Bulldogs Baseball," accessed July 11, 2017, https://en.wikipedia.org/wiki/Yale_Bulldogs_baseball; "Early History of Harvard-Yale Baseball," *Harvard Crimson*, December 22, 1888; Penn University Archives and Records Center, "Penn Baseball in the 19th Century: Varsity Team Records, 1867–1900," accessed July 11, 2017, http://www.archives.upenn.edu/histy/features/sports/baseball/1800s/records.html; Wikipedia, "Columbia Lions Baseball," https://en.wikipedia.org/wiki/Columbia_Lions_baseball accessed July 11, 2017.

11. Wesleyan University Special Collections and Archives, "Guide to the Agallian Base Ball Club Records, 1865–1869," accessed July 11, 2017, https://www.wesleyan.edu/libr/schome/FAs/ag1000–43.xml; Bates, "Bates Baseball Year-by-Year Records," accessed July 11, 2017, http://athletics.bates.edu/sports/bsb/YearByYearRecords.

12. MLB, "Earliest Baseball Clubs," accessed July 11, 2017, http://mlb.mlb.com/memorylab/spread_of_baseball/earliest_clubs.jsp; This Game of Games, "Baseball at Shurtleff College," accessed July 11, 2017, http://thisgameofgames.blogspot.com/2009/01/baseball-at-shurtleff-college.html; Pioneer Athletics, accessed July 11, 2017, http://pioneers.grinnell.edu/documents/2012/4/18/Season-by-Season_Overall_Team_Records11.pdf?id=75; Kirsch, *Baseball and Cricket*, 249; Harold Seymour, *Baseball: The People's Game* (New York: Oxford University press, 1990), 139.

13. Ackerley, "Early Knox College Baseball," 30, 39–53.

14. "The Ball and Chess Games Between the Students of Amherst and Williams Colleges," *Pittsfield Sun*, July 7, 1859, accessed July 11, 2017, https://ourgame.mlblogs.com/the-first-intercollegiate-ball-game-1859–2ed5b0930f8b.

15. Ackerley, "Early Knox College Baseball," 19, 57–8.

16. Rammelkamp, *Centennial History*, 272–3.

17. *Rambler*, March 27, 1886, 28–9.

18. *Rambler*, February 1878, 31–2.

19. Thomas Powell Antle was son of Dr. Francis Petree Antle, who became mayor of Petersburg. He graduated from Illinois College with a BS in 1879, where he joined Sigma Pi. He studied medicine at the Eclectic Medical Institute in Cincinnati in 1880, and he pitched for the University of Michigan team in 1882. He practiced medicine in Petersburg. He married Anna Smoot in 1886, and they had a son, William Smoot Antle (1893–1968). He disappeared mysteriously in 1898 and was never found.

20. Biographical information about IC players has been found in the Alumni Records of Illinois College, supplemented by internet searches. The seven biographies I could find for this first team show a cattle rancher, a minister, two college teachers, two doctors, and an insurance broker.

21. *Rambler*, March 1878, 45; May 1878, 70.

22. *Rambler*, May 1878, 61, 71.

Harold Whetstone Johnston (1859–1912) was born in Rushville, Illinois. After graduation from IC as valedictorian in 1879, he became principal of Whipple Academy 1880–1884, and then professor at Illinois College 1885–1895, teaching English and Latin. He was granted the MA in 1882 and an honorary Ph.D. in 1891. He continued to play and coach baseball, and he published an edition of Cicero. He married Eugenia Hinrichsen in 1882, a student at the Jacksonville Female Academy. In 1895, he became chair of the Latin Department at Indiana University until his retirement in 1912. His book *The Private Life of the Romans* was used as a college text for many years. He became chair of the Big Eight Conference and was called the "Dean of Athletics" at Indiana, where a building was named for him.

23. *Rambler*, January 1878, 13.

24. George R. Walker (1857–?) was born in Akron, Ohio. He studied at Western Reserve College in Hudson, OH, and then at Yale University, where he graduated with the highest honors in 1878, was president of his class, and was prominent in athletic activities. He became instructor in English and Latin at Illinois College for two years 1878–1880. He moved to Chicago where he studied law and was admitted to the bar in 1882. He was candidate for judge of the Circuit Court as a Republican in 1902. In 1907, President Theodore Roosevelt appointed him attorney general for the southern District of Indian Territory 1907–1910, and he then was appointed by President Taft to be U.S. At-

torney in Alaska 1910–1914. He returned to Chicago, and in 1917, he was a candidate for judge of the Superior Court of Cook County.

25. *Rambler*, November 1878, 98–9. Shurtleff College was founded in 1827, and eventually became part of the Southern Illinois University system in 1957.

26. *Rambler*, June 5, 1886, 84–5.

27. The IHSA website lists a game in Chicago in 1884 as the first game: Illinois High School Association, "Boys Baseball Chronology," accessed July 11, 2017, https://www.ihsa.org/SportsActivities/BoysBaseball/RecordsHistory.aspx?url=/data/ba/records/index.htm.

28. Rammelkamp, *Centennial History*, 281.

George Wyckoff Brown (1845–1918) was born on a farm in Fulton, Illinois. In 1865, he went to Eastman Business College in Poughkeepsie, New York. In 1866, he co-founded a private writing and bookkeeping school in Abingdon, Illinois, but left in 1866 for Jacksonville. He took the position of teacher of penmanship at the Jacksonville Business College, which had been founded in 1866 by Crampton. In 1876, Brown bought the school and renamed it Brown's Business College. He also taught accounts and penmanship at Illinois College 1871–1878. He married Evelyn Hall Fairbank (1851–) in 1872. In 1880 he was president of the Business Educators' Association and he contributed to the publishing of several textbooks. By 1889, he had acquired schools in Peoria and Decatur, and by 1907, there were 19 Brown's in existence.

29. *Rambler*, February 1879, 2–3.

30. *Rambler*, June 5, 1886, 84–5.

31. *Rambler*, March 14, 1885, 1.

32. Ackerley, "Early Knox College Baseball," 53–4.

33. Rammelkamp, *Centennial History*, 274–82.

34. Ackerley, "Early Knox College Baseball," 67.

35. Ackerley, "Early Knox College Baseball," 53–4.

36. Rammelkamp, *Centennial History*; *Ibid.*, 282.

37. *Rambler*, March 18, 1882, 15; April 1, 1882. Although the school had a variety of names during the 19th century, it will be referred to here by its modern name, the Illinois School for the Deaf or ISD.

38. "Early History of Harvard-Yale Baseball," *Harvard Crimson*, December 22, 1888, accessed July 11, 2017, http://www.thecrimson.com/article/1888/12/22/early-history-of-harvard-yale-baseball-it/; *Rambler*, April 22, 1882, 34.

39. *Rambler*, May 6, 1882, 41. The Athenaeum had been founded by William Davis Sanders and was eventually absorbed into Illinois College. Professor Sanders' sons Clarence and Charles were players.

40. *Rambler*, May 20, 1882, 52.

41. *Rambler*, June 3, 1882, 59.

42. Charles Walter Reynolds (1867–1948) was born in Jacksonville. He attended Whipple Academy and then Illinois College 1882–1883, where he joined Phi Alpha. He then began life as a farmer. He married May Holbrook in 1887, and then moved to Indiana in 1898. He specialized in cattle and sheep, learning his trade as a salesman at the Kansas City, St. Louis, and Chicago stockyards. He raised prize-winning chickens and was secretary of the Indianapolis National Poultry Exposition 1936-1937.

43. *Rambler*, September 30, 1882, 75–6. Bedford Brown (1861–1934) was born in Auburn, Illinois. He attended Whipple Academy 1877–1878, then entered Illinois College. He was president of Phi Alpha, salutatorian of his class, assistant editor of the *Rambler*, member of the Glee Club, president of the College Association, captain of the baseball team, and graduated with a BA in 1884. He went to law school at George Washington University, where he graduated in 1887. He practiced in Hastings, Nebraska, where he married Laura Baily in 1896, daughter of Judge Jacob Baily of Hastings. They moved to Spokane, WA, in the 1890s, where he was a lawyer for Spokane & Eastern Trust Co.

44. *Rambler*, October 21, 1882, 79. James William Dalbey (1863–1908) was born in Logan County, Illinois, and graduated from Springfield schools. At Illinois College, he was president of his class, captain of the baseball team for two years, treasurer and president of Sigma Pi, and financial manager of the *Rambler*. He was class orator at Commencement in 1885, when he earned the BS. He earned the MD from Columbia University in 1889. He became professor of ophthalmology at State University of Iowa until retiring around 1905. He and his wife Fannie M. Dalbey had 3 children.

45. *Rambler*, October 21, 1882, 82; November 4, 1882, 92-3.
46. *Rambler*, October 21, 1882, 80; November 25, 1882, 102.
47. According to Major League Baseball's tabulation of the earliest baseball clubs: "Earliest Baseball Clubs."
48. *Rambler*, September 30, 1882, 69, 75. Allen Gilbert Dunaway (c.1862–1902) was born in Pennsylvania, but his family moved to Virginia, Illinois. He earned the BS from Illinois College in 1884, where he joined Sigma Pi. He studied medicine at the University of Michigan, then graduated from Bellevue Hospital Medical College in 1887. He practiced in Virginia. He married Lou E. Dunaway (c.1872–) in 1898.

Henry William Hand (1860–1938) was born in Fayette, Illinois, and grew up on a farm. He entered Illinois College in 1880, where he was president of Sigma Pi, and graduated in 1884 with a BS. He earned the MD at Bellevue Hospital Medical School in New York in 1890 and became a surgeon. He married Dora N. Foreman in 1886. They moved to San Diego about 1913. He helped plant 40,000 trees in Illinois around 1918. Discouraged by his financial losses in the Depression, he turned to philosophy and religion, and wrote several books about philosophy, attempting to find universal truths from many religions. He also became an expert on India. On his last trip in 1935–1936, he contracted cholera, and never recovered after returning home.

49. *Rambler*, October 21, 1882, 80; November 25, 1882, 102; February 24, 1883, 155; March 24, 1883, 6; April 7, 1883, 16.
50. *Rambler*, April 21, 1883, 24–25.
51. Rammelkamp, *Centennial History*, 306–308.
52. *Rambler*, May 12, 1883, 34.
53. Alfred (1863–1935) and Edward Capps (1866–1950) were born in Jacksonville, grandsons of Joseph Capps (1811–1872), who had established a wool business in Jacksonville in 1839. It became the biggest employer in the city. His son Stephen Reid Capps (1838–1914), father of the two players, had graduated from Illinois College in 1857 and sent all five of his sons there. A daughter, Rhoda Jeanette Capps Rammelkamp (1878–1962), married Charles Rammelkamp, President of Illinois College (1905–1932).
54. *Rambler*, September 29, 1883, 62; October 20, 1883, 70; November 10, 1883, 77–8.
55. *Rambler*, February 16, 1884, 110.
56. *Rambler*, March 29, 1884, 16; April 12, 1884, 26; and April 26, 1884, 34.

Sterling Price Bond (1862–1938) was born in Carlyle, Illinois, where he attended the public schools. He graduated from Illinois College in 1885 with a BA. He studied law and moved to St. Louis in 1888 to practice. In 1893 he was elected for one term as a Democrat to the Missouri legislature. He married Ida Jane Alvord (1858–1922) in 1901.

57. *Rambler*, May 17, 1884, 41.
58. "Box Score (Baseball)," https://en.wikipedia.org/wiki/Box_score_(baseball) accessed July 11, 2017.
59. *Rambler*, May 17, 1884, 43–44.
60. *Rambler*, September 27, 1884, 61; October 11, 1884, 70.
61. *Rambler*, October 25, 1884, 73.
62. Secretary, H.W. Denison '87, Treasurer, W.W. Ross '88, Business Manager, G.H. Wilson '88. *Rambler*, March 14, 1885, 5.
63. *Rambler*, April 4, 1885, 13; April 18, 1885, 19; May 2, 1885, 26.
64. *Rambler*, May 23, 1885, 34–35. Brothers Lafayette Seeberger (1854–1904) and Meyer Seeberger ran Seeberger & Bros., clothier for men and boys on the downtown square.
65. *Rambler*, June 10, 1885, 37.
66. *Rambler*, September 26, 1885, 59.
67. Thomas William Smith (1865–1951) was born in Jacksonville. He attended Whipple Academy 1881–1883, and then entered Illinois College, where he was president of Phi Alpha, was editor of the *Rambler*, and graduated in 1887 as valedictorian. He studied modern languages at Yale for one year, then returned to Illinois College as instructor in languages, rhetoric and elocution. In 1894, he earned a degree from the Union Theological Seminary in New York. He then served as pastor in New York 1894–1914, in East Orange (New Jersey) 1914–1918, at the Presbyterian Church in Jacksonville 1920–1924, in Hibbing (Minnesota) 1925–1936, and in Northville (Minnesota) 1936–1941. His connections to Illinois College were strong. His father graduated in 1852, and his brother and daughter both attended. He served on the Board of Trustees 1907–1930.

68. Rush Denny Galbreth (1866–?) was born in Helena, Montana. At Illinois College, he joined Sigma Pi and graduated with a BA in 1886. He became a stenographer in Denver, and also lived in New York and in Los Angeles. He received a patent for food delivering and ordering apparatus in 1920 in Denver.

69. Norman Triplett (1861–1934) was born in Perry, Illinois, and graduated from Perry High School. He graduated as valedictorian with a BA from Illinois College in 1889, where he joined Sigma Pi. He ran the 100 yards in 10.0 and was called the "most noted college pitcher in the Midwest." He served as superintendent of schools in New Berlin 1889–1891. He taught science at Quincy High School 1894–1897. He earned the MA from Indiana University in 1898, and the Ph.D. from Clark University (Massachusetts) in 1900, and his dissertation on the psychology of magic tricks was published in the *American Journal of Psychology*. He was chair of child study at Kansas State Normal School in Emporia 1901–1931, and Dean of Men 1913–1931. He coached the track team in 1909 and played on the faculty baseball team. He married Laura D. Wickard in 1902.

70. *Rambler*, September 26, 1885, 59.

71. Samuel Wilson Parr (1857–1931) was born in Granville, Illinois. After attending the academy in Granville, he enrolled at Illinois Industrial university (later the University of Illinois), where he played baseball, was active in public speaking, was editor of the student newspaper *The Daily Illini*, first president of the Athletic Association, and graduated as valedictorian with a BS in 1884. He earned an MS at Cornell University in 1885. He was an instructor in agriculture at Illinois College 1884–1885, then professor of agricultural science and chemistry 1885–1891. He coached and played on the baseball team. He married Lucie A. Hall in 1887 and they had two children. He was professor of applied chemistry at the University of Illinois 1891–1926, where he created the University's first curriculum in chemistry. He was a major contributor to coal chemistry, fuel calorimetry and metallurgy, writing 69 articles and holding 8 patents. In 1899, he founded Standard Calorimeter Co., later Parr Instrument Co. He was editor of *Fuel in Science and Practice*. He wrote *The Analysis of Fuel, Gas, Water, and Lubricants*, which became a basic text in industrial chemistry. He served as director of the Illinois State Water Survey 1904–1905 and was a consulting engineer for the U.S. Bureau of Mines. He was elected president of the American Chemical Society in 1928.

72. *Rambler*, September 26, 1885, 59; October 17, 1885, 68; and October 31, 1885, 77.

73. Nathaniel English (1865–?) was born in Mason County, West Virginia, son of James Worth English (1829–1888), who had graduated from Illinois College with a BA in 1848 and was a member of Phi Alpha. He was grandson of Dr. Nathaniel English, one of the founders of the Illinois State Asylum and Hospital for the Insane in Jacksonville. He entered Illinois College in 1883, where he joined Phi Alpha and played baseball. He left after his junior year and went into business in Wichita, KS. He was employed on the Chicago and Alton Railroad as civil engineer and then went West, aiding in the construction of a railroad.

74. *Rambler*, May 15, 1886, 75–6; September 18, 1886, 125.

75. *Rambler*, June 5, 1886, 108–9; September 18, 1886, 125.

76. Ackerley, "Early Knox College Baseball," 68–72, 91–3.

77. Because of campus support for the Union during the Civil War, Illinois College students came to be named "Blueboys," with official colors of blue and white.

78. It is even harder to find out information on players for town teams. The Unions played two brothers, John Kastrup (1869–1942) and Henry Kastrup (1866–1947), both born in neighboring Winchester, Illinois, sons of Peter Kastrup (1832–1918) and Gertrude Tendick (1842–1934), both immigrants from Germany. They were about the same age as the college players.

79. *Rambler*, October 9, 1886, 137–8. The *Rambler*'s box score showed putouts and assists, statistics no longer usually reported in typical box scores. Runs batted in were not yet tabulated, being introduced as a statistic in the early 20th century.

80. *Rambler*, October 9, 1886, 137–8; October 23, 1886, 153–4; November 6, 1886, 167–8.

81. *Rambler*, January 29, 1887, 235.

82. *Rambler*, April 18, 1887, 40–1; May 2, 1887, 54–5; May 16, 1887, 68–71.

83. *Rambler*, June 20, 1887, 104–6.

84. Not relevant to this story, but interesting nevertheless: two of the nation's oldest women's colleges were well-established institutions in Jacksonville: the Jacksonville Female Academy, founded in 1830, and Illinois Female College, founded in 1846.

Binding the (Baseball) Nation
The National Base Ball Club's Tour of 1867

Bob Tholkes

The base ball fever of the immediate post–Civil War years fostered, among other items, a resurgence of tourism by the prominent clubs of the day. The club which took the first big leap in that respect was not, however, one of the presumed contenders in the informal championship competition among members of the National Association of Base Ball Players, but an outsider, well-connected undoubtedly, but still an outsider: the National Club of Washington, D.C. It was that club which, in July of 1867, embarked on the most extensive tour to date: ten games in six cities in 16 days with "western" clubs in Ohio, Kentucky, Indiana, Missouri, and Illinois.

Using multiple primary research sources, this article puts the National's innovative tour, the first by an eastern baseball club to the "west," in the context of 1860s baseball tours, describes the organization of the tour, the club's players and leadership, the results of the games, including the club's startling defeat in Chicago following several one-sided matches, and its effect on the remainder of the club's season and on subsequent tours. The presentation is supplemented by images of the chief personages.

PROLOGUE: BASEBALL IN 1867 consisted of hundreds of independent clubs around the country scheduling their own matches. A loose national organization, the National Association of Base Ball Players (NABBP), set the rules. Getting paid for playing was technically not allowed, but the top clubs waived players' club dues and arranged employment, which could be a sham to some degree. This system did not last long—professionalism was allowed as of the

1869 season, and a loosely-organized league began to operate in 1871. This is the story of a step in that process.

The surge in baseball's popularity during the immediate post–Civil War years fostered a resurgence of the team tourism begun before the war by the prominent independent clubs of the day. The club which took the first big leap in that respect was not one of the powerhouse clubs from Greater New York City or Philadelphia that contended annually for the informal championship among members of the NABBP. It was an outsider—well-connected, but still an outsider: the National Base Ball Club of Washington, D.C. It was the National that in July of 1867 embarked on the most extensive tour to date: ten games in six cities in 16 days with "western" clubs in Ohio, Kentucky, Indiana, Missouri, and Illinois.

Touring in the years before paid admission and gate receipts was an exercise for well-heeled teams. It was practiced first (as with many features of early baseball) by cricket clubs, and then, with the spread in an organized form of their American distant cousins, by baseball clubs that could foot the bill. One of these, the Excelsior Club of Brooklyn, had begun exploring inter-city travel at least by 1859, possibly spurred by the successful tour that year to western New York and Canada of an English all-star team of professional cricketers, the All England Eleven. A transplanted Excelsior member had helped found a baseball club in Buffalo and perhaps influenced the club's choice of destination. The Excelsior in 1860 toured both New York State (Buffalo, Rochester, Albany, and Troy) in July and, later in the season, the mid–Atlantic states (Philadelphia, Baltimore, and Washington, D.C.).

The New York State tour, a series of one-sided victories, proved a springboard for the Excelsior's 1860 championship ambitions. The Excelsior was a highly regarded nine but had not competed for the championship in 1859. That would have required scheduling matches against the defending champion, the Atlantic Club of Brooklyn, with which the Excelsior was not on good terms. The Excelsior acquired three young standouts as new members for 1860, undoubtedly with some form of indirect compensation for their services on the club's ball team. Upon returning from western New York, the Excelsior took the field against the Atlantic, still the defending champions, and drubbed them, 23–4.

Seven years later, the National, who would also be breaking in several new players, would attempt to replay the Excelsior's scenario: Take the rebuilt team on tour to gain cohesion and then return to contend for the championship. In the intervening years, though relatively few first-class players enlisted for anything other than short-term militia duty, the Civil

The National Base Ball Club's Tour of 1867

War slowed the spread of the game, and of touring, because the fighting dried up interclub play in many parts of the country. Nevertheless, intercity visits still occurred during the war—among others, the Athletic Club of Philadelphia commenced annual trips to Greater New York City and to western Pennsylvania in 1862. Greater New York clubs returned the Athletic's visits. The Excelsior visited Boston; and the Atlantic made it to western New York. With the war over, these visits increased in frequency. In 1866, the National, the reigning "champions of the South," were among the tourists. They visited Greater New York, and there absorbed their only defeats of that season.

How long the idea of a national (that is, western) tour in 1867 for the National club had been fermenting in the minds of the club's leadership is apparently not a matter of record. The club president was Col. Frank Jones, a Treasury Department official. Prominent also was Arthur P. Gorman, a former Senate official and future senator who at the time had a federal appointment as revenue collector for the Fifth District, in Maryland, and was president of the NABBP.

Left: Colonel Frank Jones was president of the Washington Nationals of 1867. Born in Boston, he had come to the nation's capital from Brooklyn, where he was with the famous Excelsior Club. His high position in the Treasury Department combined neatly with his knowledge of the best ball players in New York and Brooklyn.

Right: Arthur P. Gorman (National Archives).

Col. Jones had been a member of the Excelsior Club before the war, so the Excelsior's earlier experience may have been a conscious consideration in the decision to make the tour. The club seems to have been undecided on a western tour *vs.* a trip to New England until late in March, when an announcement of the tour appeared in a Cleveland newspaper.[1] The choice was presumably smoothed by the well-connected Gorman's contacts in the target cities, which he had visited during the war.[2]

The Nation's simultaneous effort to expand its stock of ringers from Greater New York City, the baseball capital of the nation, bore notable fruit in April 1867, when George Wright, who had played for two clubs in Greater New York in '66, signed on. He was promptly listed as a clerk in Col. Jones's Treasury Department. At 20 years of age, the future King of Shortstops and baseball Hall of Famer (elected as a pioneer in 1937) was a two-sport phenom, regarded as the best all-around batter and fielder at the most difficult position—catcher—in baseball. Wright was also a superb all-rounder—batting and bowling—in cricket, where he had been employed as a club professional since 1862. Despite his youth, Wright may already be described as opportunistic in the business sense. Like his father, cricket professional Sam Wright, and older brother, Harry, also a cricket and baseball professional, George had apparently already decided to make his living from sports. In addition to playing professionally, Harry had been a sales agent for cricket equipment as far back as 1862. The brothers started a sporting-goods business in New York in 1868, eight years before Albert Spalding founded his. George opened a store on his own in Boston in 1871 after the brothers joined the Boston Red Stockings, and operated it for the rest of his long life.

What induced George to move to a swampy, humid baseball outpost such as Washington is apparently not a matter of record, but the increase on his 1866 compensation presumably was significant, and came with an

George Wright.

The National Base Ball Club's Tour of 1867

Union Grounds, Cincinnati.

opportunity to visit Harry, who had left New York in '66 to move to Cincinnati as a cricket professional. Shortly thereafter, Harry became captain of the Cincinnati Base Ball Club.

Frank Norton, another catcher, had signed on with the National in March from the Excelsiors of Brooklyn. First baseman George Fletcher was added from the same club. Norton was good enough behind the plate so that Wright played second base, perhaps at his own request, except when Norton required relief for the sore hands which were the lot of every barehanded catcher.

Thanks to SABR biographical researcher Peter Morris, we know that four of the remaining National players were Civil War veterans who had settled in the District of Columbia after the end of the fighting and then into government positions: Harry McLean, Eb Smith, Sy Studley and Harry Berthrong. McLean, from New Jersey, and Smith, a Brooklynite, had played in Greater New York, and Studley and Berthrong had learned their baseball in Rochester, New York. George Fox, third baseman and captain (field manager), had grown up in Brooklyn and played for the Eckford Club. Speedballing pitcher Billy Williams and outfielder Val Robinson were District of Columbia natives. Little is known of the last, Edward Parker. Studley at 26 was probably the oldest.[3]

Even the *New York Sunday Mercury*, which reported extensively on baseball, considered in describing the tour in May that the National's ball club was now "probably the strongest in the country."[4]

The club went undefeated against local opposition before departing on the tour, which took them first to Columbus, Ohio, for a game on July

13th, and then to Cincinnati for two games, in which Harry Wright participated as player and umpire. The club then went on to Louisville, Indianapolis, St. Louis (also for two games), and to Chicago for the final three. A Cincinnati newspaper thoughtfully described the club's uniform: "blue caps, blue pantaloons, red belts, and white shirts with a Shakespeare collar bearing an "N" on each side"[5] The party of 25, plus servants, included 11 players, various club officials and members, and influential journalist Henry Chadwick, reporting on the tour for his new weekly, *The Ball Players' Chronicle*, founded only the previous month.[6] "Chad" also acted as correspondent for several New York papers.[7]

Chadwick expected the tour to have the benefits of showing the uncouth westerners a new level of skillful play, and also of gentlemanly deportment, improving, as he put it, "the objectionable features of exciting contests in sections of the country where metropolitan influences have not yet been felt." The *Sunday Mercury* hailed it as "the most noteworthy event in base ball circles since the Fashion Race Course games (in 1858)."[8]

Of the baseball played in most of the games there is little to note. In the National's nine wins, the average margin of victory was 63 runs. They twice exceeded 100 runs scored. Wright had six home runs in the game on an unfenced field in Indianapolis. A few results were even mitigated by games cut short to allow the visitors to attend the inevitable post-game banquet and catch their next train—or, in the case of the trip from Cincinnati to Louisville—the river steamer *General Buell*.[9]

The one-sided results did nothing to prevent the club from being warmly welcomed and entertained at each stop, and admired at most—with the exceptions of Louisville and St. Louis, where the throngs, according to Chadwick, were rude, partisan, and poorly controlled. The National presented to western eyes a jaw-dropping level of skill and athleticism, and the one-sided results only seemed to encourage the desire of the locals to improve their game, an indicator perhaps of the westerners' dogged sportsmanship. Efforts to "play down" to the locals' level by the National also would only have aroused the wrath of local bettors. Playing down would also not have fulfilled the club's goal of preparing for championship competition when it returned to the east.

The club was originally scheduled to play two games in Chicago, on July 26–27, but a third game in the Windy City, with the Forest City Club of Rockford, was added, as the host committee expanded the event to a four-team tournament. This proved one game too many for the National. In the opener on July 25th, played at spacious (if probably odiferous, as it

The National Base Ball Club's Tour of 1867

adjoined the stockyards) Dexter Park Race Course, the Forest City, a team twice beaten by the Excelsior Club of Chicago, the local champion, stunned everyone by defeating the National, 29–23, a result heralded a few years back by MLB historian John Thorn as "The Most Important Game in Baseball History."[10] Initial explanations for the upset centered on intermittent rain (there were two stoppages of play), a wet field and soggy baseball, and the rigors of the schedule. Moreover, it was the National's fourth game in six days, the most recent two played in sweltering conditions in St. Louis. They had already looked wilted in the second of those games. They had then taken a red-eye train on the night of the 23rd to Chicago, and, perhaps overconfident, spent the following day sightseeing instead of resting.[11]

After the loss, and with an additional day to rest, the National rebounded, sizzling the Excelsior of Chicago, 49–4, on July 27, and the Atlantic Club of Chicago, 78–17 on July 29. Outraged local bettors reportedly lost a bundle—variously estimated at $30,000 to $50,000—on the Excelsior game to "outside" sharps, including members of the National's traveling party. They immediately accused the National of laying down in the Forest City game in order to alter its odds against the Excelsior, a notion the local press supported in print.[12]

Forest City.	O	R	National.	O	R
Addy, 2b	2	4	Barker, lf	3	1
King, c	2	4	Williams, p	5	2
Stearns, 1b	3	4	Wright, 2b	1	4
Spalding, p	3	4	Fox, 3b	3	5
Barker, cf	2	4	Studley, rf	2	4
Wheeler, lf	3	4	Fletcher, 1b	2	2
Buckman, 3b	5	1	Smith, ss	3	3
Lighthart, rf	6	1	Berthrong, cf	3	3
Barnes, ss	1	3	Norton, c	5	1
	27	29		27	23

Forest City ....2 8 5 0 1 8 0 1 4—29
National ....3 5 0 3 0 7 3 0 2—23

Passed Balls: King 7, Norton 11. Berthrong 4; Balls called, Spalding 6, Williams 33; Baulks, Spalding 5, Williams 2; Flies missed, Wheeler 1. Wright 1; Foul flies missed, King 1, Stearns, 1. Norton 1; Flies caught, F. C. 4. National 5; Left on bases, F. C. 4. National 5; Out on fouls, F. C. 9, National 3; Wild throws. Addy 2, Spalding 1, Barker 1, Buckman 2, Barnes, 2, total F. C. 8; Williams 1, Fox 3. Smith 1, Norton 1, total Nat. 6; Umpire, J. M. Dietrich of Bloomington club; Scorers, H. T. Munson, Nationals, J. H. Barnes, Forest City.

The Chicagoans' outrage was ridiculed elsewhere, with Chadwick and the other teams played on the tour defending the National's conduct. The National's players were described by its leadership as a gentlemanly collection of government clerks and budding scholars (Williams and Fox were law students) who had been praised for their decorum throughout the tour.

The game was played on July 25, 1867. When the Forest City club from Rockford, Illinois—a "country team"—defeated the mighty Washington Nationals, who had brought in their talent from far and wide, it created an uproar, including claims of "fix." This was the Nationals only loss of their grand tour, in which they won every game by at least 27 runs. But the baseball public did not yet know of the prowess of such future stars as Al Spalding and Ross Barnes.

At a team meeting, the Excelsior of Chicago, at a team meeting, issued the opinion that the National had simply been too tired to play their ordinary game.[13]

Also given credit for Forest City's upset victory—in later years, when he had become famous—was their pitcher, 16-year-old Albert Spalding. Henry Chadwick's game account excoriated the National's batting and fielding, but didn't mention the pitching at all, though he did report that the National in several innings could not get the ball out of the infield. The beaten Excelsior, seeking his services for its team, immediately made Spalding a job offer in Chicago that he could not refuse—how many 16-year-old clerks could make a princely $40 a week?[14] The National meanwhile, its tour over, headed back to the District of Columbia to a warm welcome and a sumptuous banquet.

So far so good, mostly, for the National. The scenario now called for the club, buoyed by its strengthened roster and string of victories, to vanquish its scheduled top-tier eastern opponents and earn a two-out-of-three championship series against the 1866 champions, again the Atlantic of Brooklyn. Then

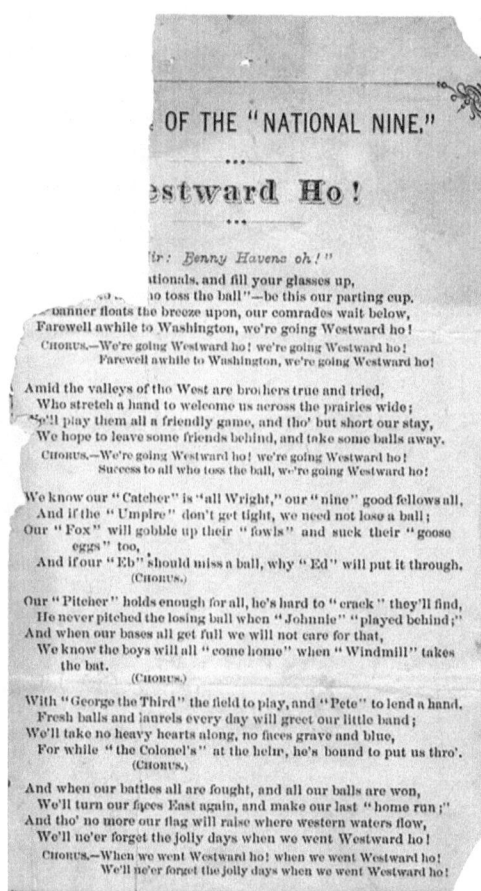

The Washington Nationals' Fight Song, from their great western tour of 1867, with mention of each of their imported heroes. This Steinbrennerian model of team building was something new in baseball. After the Nationals, with George Wright, walloped brother Harry's Cincinnati Red Stockings, the latter went on a buying spree of their own, culminating in the great undefeated club of 1869—starring both Wright brothers!

the wheels fell off. Losses to a championship contender, the Mutual Club of New York, on August 25 in Washington and on October 23 in New York knocked them out of championship contention, and in total they lost five of seven games against eastern clubs. Captain Fox apparently took the rap for this disappointing conclusion to the season. On September 12 the *Washington Evening Star* reported that he had resigned his captaincy and had been replaced by Wright. The club attempted belatedly to fill holes, obtaining two more recruits from Greater New York clubs, including Wright's future teammate on the Cincinnati Red Stockings, pitcher Asa Brainard.

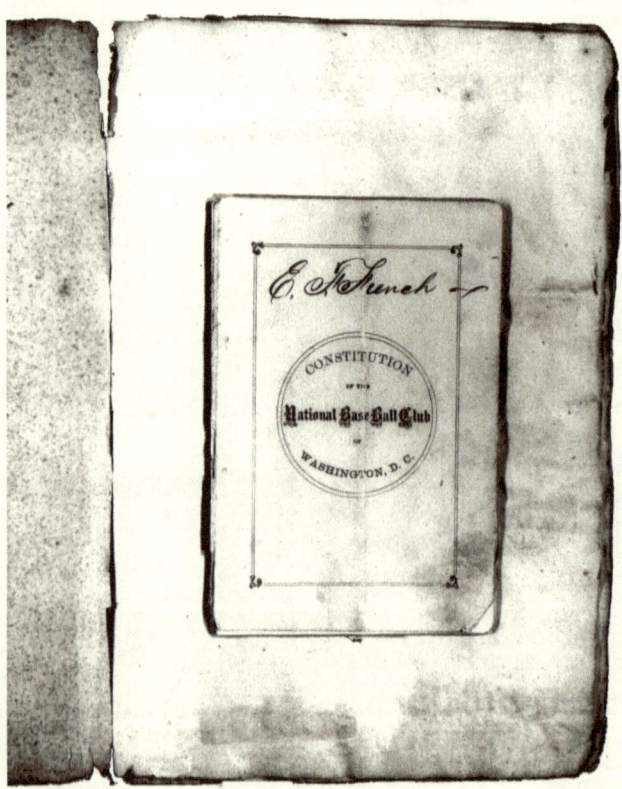

This copy of the Washington Nationals' club constitution was kept by Edmund F. French, a founding member of the club in 1859. More importantly, perhaps, he was a 40-year clerk in the Treasury Department, which offered so many of the no-show jobs by which the imported baseball professionals could be paid under the table. No one was fooled, of course; professional baseball was clearly the future of the game.

The *Washington Daily National Republican* concluded at season's end in November that the National was a "strong individual, but badly disciplined" club.[15] Chadwick, after seeing them lose to teams of lesser individual talent, agreed, and called them "mismanaged," chiefly because they were prone to moving their players from position to position during a game.[16]

From another point of view, what went wrong was simply that the National toured in the wrong direction. While they were astounding the uncouth westerners, the Union of Morrisania (a then-independent town in the Bronx), one of Wright's former clubs and another championship pre-

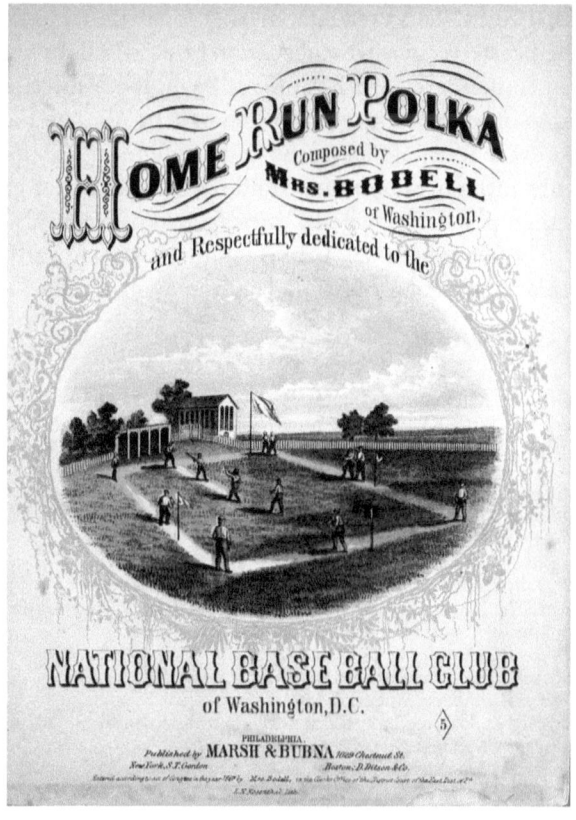

The Home Run Polka was dedicated to the National Base Ball Club of Washington, D.C., in a tradition already well-worn by 1867. Undistinguished polkas, schottisches, and quadrilles, with painfully awkward lyrics, had already been published in honor of the Live Oak of Rochester, the Tri-Mountain of Boston, the Mercantile of Philadelphia, and more.

tender, were re-creating the Excelsior tour of western New York, where the opposing clubs were more experienced. The Union went home, managed to defeat the Atlantic twice, and became the first non–Brooklyn club to hoist the championship whip pennant over its grounds.

If not the springboard to baseball prominence that the National expected, what were the effects of the western tour? The expected stimulative effect on baseball in the west apparently was achieved. Record crowds were attracted everywhere. Despite the National's later lack of success back in the east, the club's displays of skill apparently spurred professionalism in the west. Cincinnati and, later, Chicago both began to recruit easterners for professional clubs. This created a market for national tours in 1868 by less well-heeled eastern clubs who needed to be paid. All three of the prime championship contenders—the Atlantic of Brooklyn, Athletic of Philadelphia, and Union of Morrisania—toured the west in '68. The National's tour also provided evidence that clubs relying on gate receipts, a practice then becoming more and more common, could perhaps do better playing intercity matches than playing repeated games against other locals, even if gate receipts had to be shared. This in turn was a major step toward the concept of a national association of professional clubs playing a round-robin schedule.

Notes

1. *Cleveland Leader*, March 25, 1867, 1.
2. Brian McKenna, "Arthur P. Gorman," https://sabr.org/bioproj/person/1c2a4dc3.
3. Peter Morris, "The Nationals of Washington," *Base Ball Pioneers*, 271ff.
4. *New York Sunday Mercury*, May 12, 1867.
5. *Cincinnati Daily Gazette*, July 16, 1867, 2.
6. *The Ball Players' Chronicle*, July 18, 1867, 1.
7. *Washington Evening Star*, July 12, 1867, 1.
8. *New York Sunday Mercury*, July 7, 1867.
9. *Cincinnati Daily Gazette*, July 17, 1867, 1.
10. John Thorn, "The Most Important Game in Baseball History?" https://sabr.org/gamesproj/game/july-25-1867-most-important-game-baseball-history.
11. *The Ball Players' Chronicle*, August 1, 1867, 1.
12. *The Ball Players' Chronicle*, August 8, 1867, 2.
13. *The Ball Players' Chronicle*, August 8, 1867, 1.
14. Bill McMahon, "Al Spalding," https://sabr.org/bioproj/person/b99355e0.
15. *Washington Daily National Republican*, Nov. 14, 1867
16. *The Ball Players' Chronicle*, October 31, 1867, 1.

The Catch Heard Around the World

Gary Sarnoff

On August 21, 1908, two gentlemen wagered over the possibility of someone catching a baseball dropped from the top tier of the Washington Monument. Not only was one of the men willing to bet in favor of the catch being made, but he knew who could execute the catch.

Gabby Street, the catcher for the Washington Senators, was considered undersized for a major league backstop, but he was the perfect candidate in the opinion of the bettor who wagered in favor. Street was aware that others had attempted the stunt, and that nobody had ever succeeded in making a catch, but believed nevertheless he could make "the catch heard around the world."

"Extra! Extra! Read all about it!" A paperboy shouted the words as he held a copy of the August 21, 1908, afternoon edition of the *Washington Star* for all to see while standing at a street corner near Washington's American League Park prior to the ballgame between the Detroit Tigers and the Washington Nationals. "Did he really do it?" fans wanted to know.[1] The answer was in a six-paragraph article on the front page of the *Washington Star*: "Five-hundred dollars was exchanged when (Gabby) Street performed the unprecedented feat of catching a regulation baseball dropped from the top of the Washington Monument."[2]

Unsuspecting spectators among the 5,000 in attendance at American League Park buzzed with enthusiasm when hearing the news. "Will he be in shape to catch a full game this afternoon?" someone inquired.[3] The response came when Street, dressed in his catcher's gear, trotted to his sta-

The Catch Heard Around the World

tion behind home plate as he and his teammates took the field prior to the top of the first inning. When the man of the hour stepped into the batter's box for his first plate appearance, Street received a thunderous ovation, which baffled the few that had yet to hear the news. Thinking that the applause was due to Street retiring would be base stealers throughout the week, the unaware fans clapped along with those who knew what happened earlier in the day.

As the news spread through the District of Columbia, it also generated excitement. "Fans, near-fans and people who were not fans at all, ate it for dinner, put it under their pillow, slept on it, had it for breakfast at chewed it all over again at business this morning,"[4] is how one local sportswriter described the effect the fear had on the population. Thrilled when hearing the details, some citizens were unable to contain themselves to the point where they had to hear about it from the hero of the day himself. Later that evening, following a 3–1 Washington win, Street's hotel room telephone began to ring off the hook:

> "Hello, o-hello. Is that Mr. Street?"
> "Mr. Charles Street. Delighted to make your acquaintance in this way, Mr. Street."
> "Perhaps you know my son, Mr. Street. He always sits in the right field bleachers and has a loud voice."
> "It was a wonderful catch you made."[5]

Twenty-five-year-old Gabby Street became a member of the Washington Nationals in 1908, when the Nats had purchased him from the San Francisco Seals of the Pacific Coast League. Upon his arrival in Washington, D.C., the team's new catcher visualized a catch at the Washington Monument. "I always wanted to do this since the first time I saw the monument," he said, "but I gave up on the idea when I heard that a law prohibited it."[6]

Street's dream was revived when two members of Washington's prestigious Metropolitan Club arrived at American League Park on the morning of August 21, 1908. They were looking for Street to help settle their $500 bet regarding the possibility of somebody catching a baseball dropped from the top story of the Washington Monument. Washington outfielder and team captain Bob Ganley and starting shortstop George McBride agreed to accompany Street and the two gentlemen to the site to witness the attempt. Before the five men squeezed into the automobile, somebody in the party packed five discolored baseballs from the Washington clubhouse. Gabby Street grabbed his big game-worn catcher's mitt. Biddle and Gibson also had eight additional regulation balls and a seven-foot wooden chute designed to carry the ball beyond the wide-tapering base of the obelisk-shaped landmark.

When the party arrived at the Capital Mall during the late morning, there was a slight southern wind that could alter a baseballs' downward course. The sun was bright; the temperature was in the upper seventies—mild for a summer day during the city's dog days of August. A small gathering of fifteen to twenty—including a cluster of small boys and a few photographers—were present. Preston Gibson, the Metropolitan Club member who had put his money on Street to make the catch, ascended to the top story of the monument with his home-made wooden chute and a basket containing thirteen baseballs. "He was superstitious and said thirteen was his luck number," Street would recall twenty-nine years later.[7] Before Gibson reached his position, Street doffed his sports coat, placed his catcher's mitt on his left hand and positioned himself several feet from the base of the monument. When he looked skyward, the 550-foot landmark appeared so tall that it seemed as if the ball would have to sail through the clouds before coming within sight. "I understand that no one ever before accomplished this trick," Street said.[8] He was also aware that he was not the first to try.

Gabby Street (Library of Congress).

In the mid–1880's, outfielder Paul Hines was the first to attempt the feat. A major league player for twenty seasons (1872–1891), Hines enjoyed three tours with Washington major league clubs during his career. He had retired long before 1908, but he was living in Washington and working on Capitol Hill as a government employee when, in 1906, he described his experience: "(in 1885) A New York man in the business of selling sporting

The Catch Heard Around the World

goods made me an offer of $200 for the ball if I succeeded in catching it. The Monument back then was unfinished, and the scaffolding built around the top used in placing the capstone rose some feet higher than the monument itself."[9]

Hines offered to pay Charles "Pop" Snyder and a few other ballplayers to go to the top of the unfinished obelisk and toss the baseballs, but they were unenthused about the idea of having to stand on a plank that was higher than the Washington Monument itself and declined the offer. Still needing someone to toss the baseballs, Hines employed a monument workman and gave him three new shiny white baseballs.

According to Hines:

> The first one he tossed landed on top of a shed. The second one dropped into the lake. The third one was thrown some distance from where I stood, but I made a run for it and reached for it. The ball just tipped the end of my fingers. Though I had no glove (we didn't wear 'em back then), the ball did not sting my hands as much as many that I had caught in centerfield.
>
> I have no doubt that the feat can be accomplished, but the ball should be thrown out of it, and the ball ought to be black. The balls thrown to me were new, white ones, and it was hard to distinguish them from the white background of the Monument. It isn't easy to catch a ball thrown from so great a height. One must strain his eyes to the utmost in order to catch the ball. When it leaves the top it appears to be no bigger than a pea, but as it gets nearer to the ground, it seems to increase in size to be as large as a football.[10]

Shortly after Hines' brush with destiny, an ordinance was passed prohibiting any attempt to duplicate Hines' effort, with violators subjected to a $500 fine and arrest. This did not discourage members of the Chicago Colts (the team name would later be changed to the Chicago Cubs) from trying in 1894. Leading the illegal endeavor was a man who would later have a major influence on professional baseball in the Nation's capital.

In August of the 1894 season twenty-four-year-old Chicago pitcher Clark Griffith—nicknamed "Old Fox" for his crafty pitching style—and the rest of the Chicago team were in Washington when Arlington, Virginia, chief clerk H.P. Burney insisted that it was not in mortal men to hold fast a ball that dropped from five hundred feet or more in sheer space. Chicago manager Cap Anson, a good friend of Arlington's chief clerk, argued that it could be done and insisted he had a player on his current roster who could make the catch, Colts catcher Pop Schriver. Griffith tossed the first baseball from the north window of the monument, which Schriver did not catch. The second toss was made, and according to the *Washington Post*,

Schriver succeeded, "catching it fair and square."[11] Twelve years later, Griffith denied a catch was made that day:

> I had time to make two throws to Schriver before the monument police hustled up the elevator demanding to know what nonsense was going on.... We beat a hasty retreat before we all got locked up.
>
> Schriver had no chance to catch the first throw, but that was my fault. I tossed it too far and he couldn't reach it. The second toss, I merely dropped out of the monument and the ball carried directly to his mitt, but he couldn't hold it and it plopped out. It wasn't a catch, no matter what the papers say. Schriver was too nervous to hold the ball, and I don't blame him.[12]

Phil Baker, Jim McGuire, Malachi Kittridge, Buck Ewing and Charley "Pop" Snyder were rumored to be the other major league ballplayers who had tried (prior to Street's attempt). Although it is unclear exactly who attempted it and when, one thing was certain—a catch of a baseball dropped from the Washington Monument had yet to be executed.

The Washington Monument baseball debate carried into the twentieth century, with several active ballplayers inquiring about how to take their chances. Then one day a man named John Biddle told his friend, Preston Gibson, that he would wager $500 that it would never be done. "I'll take that bet," replied Gibson. "And I won't have to go far for my man. He's here in town"[13]

The man that Gibson had in mind was Washington's catcher, Gabby Street, known for his ability to handle the Washington Nationals young flame throwing pitching star, Walter Johnson. But while Gibson was most impressed by the catcher's ability to consistently catch Johnson's blazing fastball, Street always maintained that it was no big deal. "He (Walter Johnson) was straight and true with the stuff he threw," Street contended.[14] Gibson, however, saw it differently. If Street could consistently catch Johnson's burners, shouldn't he be the right man to catch a baseball dropped from the Washington Monument? Some baseball fans debated that, for Street was not very big, at 5'11, 180 pounds, was known to be a weak hitter who couldn't hit for power, and was said to not "look strong enough to catch a cold."[15]

Biddle and Gibson were aware of the law that outlawed a repeat of the Paul Hines's stunt, "due to extreme danger involved."[16] With help from the *Washington Post* they were able to get that ban temporarily lifted through permission from the Washington D.C. superintendent of public buildings and grounds. Once the required permit was obtained from Superintendent Colonel Bromwell, the two men proceeded to make all of the arrangements to settle their dispute.

The Catch Heard Around the World

Walter Johnson poses with long-time battery mate Gabby Street.

Preston Gibson stationed himself at the small square window facing south, picking that side to aid Street in having the bright late morning sun at the catcher's back. He made a signal to communicate to Street that he was ready to send the first baseball. He then rolled a ball through the seven-foot wooden chute, which hit the side of the monument, making the first attempt uncatchable.

Another ball was dropped, and then another, and yet still one more. But the problem persisted, with the horsehide continuing to bump against the obelisk or falling too close to the structure. Street also struggled with other problems, such as trying to measure the speed of the ball and fighting the sunlight reflecting off the monument. After ten unsuccessful attempts, Street's two teammates, Bob Ganley and George McBride, suggested that Street should move to the other side of the monument, believing he would have a better chance there of following the baseball's downward flight. True, he would be facing the sun from the north side of the structure, but he wouldn't have to battle the sun beaming against the monument.

As Street strolled over to the other side, Gibson decided to discard the chute since it wasn't working out as he had hoped. When Street was ready,

Gibson heaved baseball number eleven through the window, which sailed too far for Street to make an effort. When the ball landed at full force against the ground's concrete surface, it bounced fifty feet into the air. Gibson tossed another baseball, which Street was successfully able to time. "I could see it very plainly," he would later say. He did manage to get his glove on this one, but was unable to hold it. "I guess I was a bit timid about closing my hands on it, for it struck the end of my mitt," said Street.[17]

Gibson clutched the thirteenth and final baseball from his basket and hurled it. "I was given a signal when it was thrown," said Street, "but I would not see it until it was almost half way down. Then it seemed to me that the ball was wavering."[18] As the ball topped an estimated speed of ninety-five miles per hour and gained three hundred pounds of force,[19] Street prepared to make the catch by extending his arms over his head, like getting ready to catch a foul ball during a ballgame, "only that I held my arms more rigid," he said. "The ball hit my glove with tremendous force, much greater than any pitched ball I have ever caught, and I have caught some pitchers who are given credit for having wonderful speed. Though my mitt is three or four inches thick, the force of the ball benumbed my hand."[20]

The ball plunged into Street's mitt with "a resounding whack"[21] that was audible to Gibson, five hundred feet above and inside the monument. The force of the blow staggered Street and nearly pushed his mitt to the ground, but the Washington catcher held on for an official catch. The gathering crowd had increased during the spectacle to about fifty applauded and cheered. "I couldn't tell whether or not you held on [to the ball]" Preston Gibson told Street after riding the elevator to the ground floor and quickly exiting the monument, "but I knew it was in your glove. The report sounded like a rifle."[22] "I

This is the ball that, when tossed from the top of the Washington Monument on August 1, 1908, would make Charles E. "Gabby" Street famous; he caught it.

Base Ball 10 137

The Catch Heard Around the World

always felt sure that I could catch a ball thrown from the monument if it were possible to gauge it from that height," Street told reporters, "but when I failed to see the first few that were rolled through this groove, I had about concluded it was impossible. However, when the ball was thrown out I noticed that it was easier to gauge. I am satisfied that the task would be much easier on a still day. There was considerable wind blowing when I made the catch and this necessitated the use of many balls."[23]

The account of Street's catch traveled from coast to coast and made the catcher famous. The feat went down in baseball history, where it was considered a monumental event. Nearly six decades later, a sportswriter tabbed it as "The catch heard around the world."[24] The feat also served as an inspiration for others to duplicate or surpass. In 1910, White Sox catcher Billy Sullivan was one of the major league catchers who spoke of emulating the catch. It was said that during each White Sox trip to Washington, Sullivan would gaze at the monument, longingly and speculatively, imagining an attempt to equal the stunt. He finally secured a permit from the Washington superintendent of public buildings and grounds, but kept it a secret. When the White Sox made their last visit to Washington of the 1910 season, Sullivan decided after breakfast one morning that this would be the day. Accompanied by teammates Ed Walsh and Doc White, the three ballplayers journeyed to the monument.

The first ball dropped was catchable, and had Sullivan made the grab he would have gone down in history as the man who caught a baseball at the Washington Monument on the first try. More interested in timing the flight of the ball, Sullivan let it fall to the ground. He managed to make a catch on the eighth, ninth and eleventh tries, then kept one of the baseballs while giving each his two teammates as a souvenir.

During spring training at Daytona Beach in 1915, Brooklyn Dodgers manager Wilbert Robinson made an effort to set the record by catching a baseball tossed from an airplane at a higher distance than the Washington Monument. The idea came about when a female pilot named Ruth Law had scattered golf balls from her plane onto a Daytona golf course. Why not have her drop a baseball at the local ballpark to officially start the spring training season, someone brainstormed? Charles Ebbets, the Dodgers owner, offered to make the catch until the Dodgers team trainer warned that it might not be a good idea for a man of fifty-five years to perform the task. When a single ballplayer failed to step forward, Wilbert Robinson declared, "I could do it myself."[25]

On the morning of the attempt, Miss Law unintentionally left the baseball in her hotel room. She decided that a small grapefruit, taken from the lunch box of one of the ground crewmembers, would be the next best thing. When her plane appeared over the field, Robinson, donning a chest protector and a barrowed catcher's mitt, readied himself to set the record. An object fell through the sky, which Robinson camped under as if it were a foul ball during his playing days when catching for the great Baltimore Orioles teams of the 1890's. When the object hit his mitt, it exploded and knocked him flat on his back. Thinking that the grapefruit juice was blood, the manager yelled for his life: "Help me, lads. I am covered with my own blood," he cried out, while his eyes were clenched shut.[26] His players, paralyzed with laughter, didn't budge. When Robinson realized what had happened, he accepted the misunderstanding as a practical joke and went on about his business. Never knowing the real story, the Dodgers manager hired a new trainer the following season.

A few years later, a corporal of the 819th Aero Squadron named Michael Angelo Bessolo was reported to have caught a baseball dropped from an airplane from a height of over 700 feet. The catch caused Bessolo to stumble and it bruised his hands, but he managed to hold on. The stunt received little publicity, perhaps because it did not involve a major league player. Bessolo was once a catcher at Santa Clara University and was offered a contract to play professional baseball, although his credentials didn't seem to inspire the news writers enough to give his catch the coverage it probably deserved.

In 1924, Babe Ruth, the showman that he was, saw an opportunity to cash in on some publicity by catching a baseball thrown from the roof of New York City's Cohen Theater. The toss was only from a distance of 130 feet, Nevertheless, Ruth had fun performing the act. In 1925, White Sox catcher Ray Schalk caught a baseball dropped from the top of the Chicago's Tribune tower, a distance of 460 feet. In 1939, Cleveland Indians catcher Frank Pytlak and Hank Helf each caught a baseball tossed from Cleveland's Terminal Tower, a distance of 708 feet.

In May 1945, Gabby Street, then a broadcaster for the St. Louis Browns and St. Louis Cardinals, reenacted his 1908 feat during a War Bonds rally when his rookie broadcasting partner, Harry Caray, dropped baseballs from atop the 386-foot St. Louis's Civil Courts building. "I dropped five balls before he caught one," Caray recalled in 1972.[27] Afterward, members of the press asked Street if this was as great an achievement as catching the ball dropped from the Washington Monument. "No," replied Street. "Now if I'd been able to throw the ball back to the top of the building that would have been an accomplishment."[28]

NOTES

1. *Washington Star*, August 21, 1908.
2. *Ibid.*
3. *Washington Star*, August 22, 1908.
4. *Ibid.*
5. *Ibid.*
6. *Washington Post*, August 22, 1908.
7. *Washington Post*, July 25, 1937.
8. *Washington Herald*, August 22, 1908.
9. *Washington Post*, July 1, 1906.
10. *Ibid.*
11. *Washington Post*, August 26, 1894.
12. Shirley Povich, *The Washington Senators: An informal History* (New York: G.P. Putnam, 1954), 19; *Washington Post*, July 1, 1906.
13. *Washington Post*, August 22, 1908.
14. *Washington Post*, July 25, 1937.
15. *Washington Star*, August 21, 1908.
16. *Ibid.*
17. *Washington Post*, August 22, 1908.
18. *Ibid.*
19. Joseph Wancho, *Gabby Street's Monumental Catch: "It Weighed 300 Pounds and Traveled 95 MPH"* (SABR Deadball Era, "The Inside Game," September, 2015, newsletter).
20. *Washington Post*, August 22, 1908.
21. *Ibid.*
22. *Chicago Tribune*, February 7, 1951.
23. *Washington Post*, August 22, 1908.
24. *Washington Post*, January 12, 1964.
25. Jack Kavanagh and Norman Macht, *Uncle Robbie* (Cleveland, Ohio: Society of American Baseball Research [SABR], 1999), 73.
26. Kavanagh and Macht, 74.
27. *Chicago Tribune*, August 13, 1972.
28. *Ibid.*

Baseball and the Yellow Peril
Waseda University's 1905 American Tour
ROBERT K. FITTS

> At the turn of the 20th century, Japan was striving to become a world power. It had defeated China in 1895 and in 1904 declared war on Russia. As its power grew, so did anti–Japanese sentiment in the United States. In the midst of increasing tension, Isao Abe, one of the founding fathers of Japanese baseball and the founder of the socialist movement in Japan, brought his Waseda University baseball team to America in the spring of 1905. His goals were twofold—to teach his players "scientific baseball," and to increase international cooperation and peace through the mutual love of the game. This article focuses on the tour's importance to the development of international baseball and the socio-cultural aspects of Waseda's visit to America. It also reveals how the media depicted the Japanese players, how the tour affected American attitudes toward Japanese, and discusses the tour's role in international diplomacy.

ISOO ABE (PRONOUNCED EE-SOH AH-BAY) was an idealistic man. He spent his life trying to improve Japanese society; championing women's suffrage, unionizing labor, and devising methods to eliminate poverty. He is known as "the Founding Father of Japanese Socialism" and recognized as one of the greatest intellectuals of the late Meiji era (1868–1912). He was also the Founding Father of Japanese baseball and the first to use the game to foster goodwill between two nations.

Born Isoo Okamoto in 1865, Isoo was the second son of a samurai and martial arts teacher from the southern city of Fukuoka.[1] At the age of 14, he enrolled at the Christian Doshisha Seminary in Kyoto where he became both a Christian and a pacifist. Soon after graduating from Doshisha in 1884, he arranged to be adopted by the heirless Abe family, thereby allowing him to be excused from military service as an only son. Now known as Isoo Abe, he returned to Doshisha as an instructor before leaving in August 1891 for the United States to study at the Hartford Seminary in Connecticut.

Abe lived in Connecticut for three years, graduating in June 1894. During this time, he read Edward Bellamy's popular novel *Looking Backward*—a story of a man transported 113 years into the future when America had become a socialist utopia. Deeply moved, Abe became a socialist. Surprisingly, during his three years in the U.S., Abe never watched a baseball game. He would not be introduced to his lifelong passion until he returned to Japan.[2]

In 1894, Abe traveled to Europe and during a brief stop in England read a newspaper article describing track and field event between Oxford and Yale Universities. On July 18, nearly 50,000 people braved the rains and "cold gusty wind" to watch the two universities "struggle for athletic supremacy" at the Queen's Club Grounds in London. The *Los Angeles Herald* reported:

> It is probable that no event of recent years in the history of English athletics has attracted half the interest which centered in today's contests on the grounds of the Queen's club. The champion university team of England was to meet the champion university team of America, and this was sufficient to cause the wildest enthusiasm among all admirers of athletic sports, and among sportsmen generally throughout the British Isle.[3]

The excitement surrounding the contest made Abe realize the potential for international athletics to bring countries closer together. "I was inspired by that news," he wrote. "What a nice idea it is! I hope I can organize such international competitions someday."[4]

Isoo Abe, circa 1908 (author's collection).

Soon after Abe returned home in 1895, a baseball craze swept Japan. American teachers introduced the game in the early 1870s but the game achieved only limited popularity until schoolboys from Daiichi Koto Gakko (The First Higher School), commonly known by its nickname Ichiko, upset an American adult team from Yokohama Country Club in a series of games in 1896. After the Japanese victory, teams sprang up on high school and college campuses across the country. Walking on the Doshisha campus around 1897, Abe saw a baseball game for the first time. He immediately realized that the game not only developed notions of team unity and fair play but was also the ideal sport for Japanese to play against the United States. Baseball, he would come to believe, was a tool for eliminating prejudice and thus would contribute to world peace.[5]

In 1899, Abe joined the faculty at Waseda University (then known as Tokyo Senmon Gakko), teaching economics and political science. Focusing on the growing economic inequalities in Japan as it modernized, he soon became one of the nation's most prominent and prolific social critics. In 1901, he formed Japan's first socialist political party. Advocating disarmament, public ownership of land and industrial rights for workers, it was promptly banned by the government. Despite his intellectual prowess, extensive publications, and role in creating the socialist movement in Japan, today Abe is primarily known as "the father of Japanese baseball."[6]

In 1901 Abe helped create Waseda's baseball club and became the team's manager. Although a poor player and 36 years old, Abe practiced with the students to learn the game. In the evenings, he often lectured the team on his philosophy of sport. For Abe, baseball and the quest for a socialist utopia were intertwined. "He was convinced," writes historian Masako Gavin "that team sports, as exemplified by baseball, were the best way to instill the spirit of fair play and cooperation required of citizens in the coming social order."[7]

Soon after forming the team, Abe met with Waseda's founder Shigenobu Okuma to explain his desire to take the baseball team abroad. "He laughed at me," Abe told the Stanford University newspaper, "and told me that we must first have a team that would win the championship of Japan."[8] With the help of former University of Chicago player Fred Merrifield, who was teaching at Tokyo Gakuin College, Abe trained his team for two years. In 1904, Waseda went undefeated to take the championship. That summer, Abe asked the university administration to send the team abroad, but this timing could hardly be worse.

On February 8, 1904, Japan attacked the Russian navy stationed at Port Arthur in Manchuria starting the Russo-Japanese War. Despite stunning victories at Port Arthur and Liayand, tiny Japan was fighting for her life against the mighty Russian Empire. Japan's economy and military was stretched to its limits as they waited for a Russian counterattack.

To send a group of students across the world to play baseball in the midst of this crisis seemed insane. The Waseda administration promptly rejected Abe's request. Abe, however, was stubborn. He appealed to Okuma, reminding him of their earlier conversation. Harkening back to the Oxford-Yale track and field competition of 1894, Abe argued that the tour would strengthen ties with the United States through the mutual love of sport and fair play. Furthermore, he maintained that Americans would be impressed that Japan was confident enough to sponsor a sporting event in the midst of a major conflict.[9] Okuma, who had served both as Japan's Prime Minister and Foreign Minister, agreed and approved the tour provided that funding could be procured.

Abe later wrote,

> I explained to [the administration] that the money would be raised from the admission fees from our games in the United States. I showed them *Spalding's Baseball Guide* and insisted that the professional baseball game held in New York drew 40,000 fans and the other game in Boston attracted 35,000 spectators. I told them that we could earn at least ¥6000 (about 3000 1905 dollars) per game, if our game drew 10,000 people and we requested our opponent to yield us two-thirds of the total admission fee…. They believed what I said and finally allowed our tour. If I had known that college baseball in the United States was far less popular than professional baseball at that time, I would not have planned our baseball tour.[10]

On April 4, 1905, Abe and his squad of twelve students boarded the S.S. *Korea* in Yokohama and set sail for the U.S. The team traveled in first class, an unheard of expense for students, to underscore the importance of the trip. "The students are representatives of all Japanese universities," Abe told critics.[11]

Abe would later confess that he worried about the team's reception in San Francisco. He had reason for concern. In general, across the United States admiration for Japan was high in 1905. Its stunning success in the war against Russia captivated newspaper readers. It was a classic David vs. Goliath story and the American public loved an underdog. But many Californians did not share this enthusiasm for Japan or its people.

On February 23, nearly two months before the Waseda team arrived in the city, the *San Francisco Chronicle* began what historian Rogers Daniels called "a crusade against the Japanese."[12] It began with the front-page headline in large type, "The Japanese Invasion, The Problem of the Hour for the

ROBERT K. FITTS

The 1905 Waseda team in California (author's collection).

United States." The article laid out a thesis that the paper would expound upon for the next few months:

> In the accompanying article the *Chronicle* begins a careful and conservative exposition of the problem which is no longer to be ignored—the Japanese question. It has been but lightly touched upon heretofore; now it is pressing upon California and upon the entire United States as heavily and contains as much menace as the matter of Chinese immigration ever did if, indeed, it is not more serious, socially, industrially, and from an international standpoint.... The Japanese is no more assimilable than the Chinese and he is no less adaptable in learning quickly how to do the white man's work and how to get the job for himself by offering his labor for less than a white man can live on. Once the war with Russia is over, the brown stream of Japanese immigration is likely to become an inundating torrent and the class of the immigrants is likely to become worse instead of better.[13]

Future headlines read: "Japanese a Menace to American Women," "Brown Men an Evil in the Public Schools," "Brown Peril Assumes National Proportions," and "The Yellow Peril—How the Japanese Crowd Out the White Race."[14] The *Chronicle*'s stories were just the beginning. In early March, the California legislature passed an anti–Japanese resolution calling upon the U.S. Congress to limit Japanese immigration. The resolution's ten points included, "Japanese laborers, by reason of race habits, mode of living, disposition and general characteristics are undesirable."[15]

Agitation continued. On May 14, 1905, in a well-attended meeting in San Francisco, representatives from over a hundred civic and labor organizations formed the

> Japanese and Corean (sic) Exclusion League. Later known as the Asiatic Exclusion League, the organization would remain at the forefront of the anti–Japanese movement until after World War II. From the League's birth, its organizers not only objected to the use of cheap Japanese labor but also to the immigrants on racial grounds.
>
> We cannot assimilate them without injury to ourselves. ... No large community of foreigners, so cocky, with such distinct racial, social and religious prejudices, can abide long in this country without serious friction. ... We cannot compete with a people having a low standard of civilization, living and wages. ... It should be against public policy to permit our women to intermarry with Asiatics.[16]

As anti–Japanese sentiment grew, negative stereotypes for them emerged. They depicted the Japanese as an alien race who were inherently dishonest; deviously clever; and animal-like in their lack of sexual morality and ability to withstand appalling work conditions. They also were portrayed as prideful, clannish, and militaristic with unwavering loyalty to their native country and Emperor. Physically, Japanese were depicted as small, often misshapen, and dirty. These stereotypes pepper the newspaper articles covering Waseda's tour.[17] Not surprising, this stereotype supported the Asiatic Exclusion League's rhetoric and was used not only by the league but also by sympathetic newspaper writers to stem Japanese immigration.

When S.S. *Korea* docked in San Francisco on the morning of April 20th, reporters from most of the city's newspapers gathered to interview and photograph the first foreign team to tour the U.S. At the time most American were unaware that the game was even played in Japan. Printed references to Japanese baseball were few and far between. The *Sporting News*, for example, contained no stories on Japanese baseball prior to 1905. The visitors made a favorable impression on the reporter from the *Call*, although the article's prose makes clear what he thought of most Japanese immigrants. "The Waseda ball team is as compact and sturdy looking an aggregation of athletes as ever graced these shores. The men are far above the average Japanese in height and are possessed of more good looks than falls to the lot of the ordinary Jap."[18]

Although most Japanese Americans now consider the expression "Jap" highly offensive, nearly every newspaper at the time routinely used the term. According to the *Houston Post* in 1906, three-fourths of Americans considered the term to be an acceptable abbreviation of "Japanese."[19] Even then, however, many Japanese, complained that it was usually used as a term of derision. (Despite its offensiveness, I have included the term in numerous quotes throughout this article as it reflects the attitudes of the time.)

The *San Francisco Examiner*, owned by William Randolph Hearst, who would soon be at the forefront of the anti–Japanese immigration movement, ran a story poking fun at the Waseda team. "Our territory has been invaded," wrote E.B. Lenhart. "And what's more—the invaders propose to beat us at our own game." "Down the gangway tripped eleven nervously-active subs of the Mick-a-doo." The article continues with several paragraphs making fun of the ball players' names. For example, "Kyoshin Hashido represents the short stop of the collection. The name suggests that Kyo stops the ball with his shins and that at bat ... he manages the leather into the hash."[20]

The *Chronicle* did not cover the ball club's arrival in the following morning's paper but instead ran an article entitled "More Japs Arrive on the Korea." It reported that "Swarming on the lower decks of the liner Korea, arriving yesterday from the Orient and Hawaii, were 717 Japanese emigrants ... as devoid of Americanism as Hottentots."[21]

Similar negative articles welcomed the team when they went to Los Angeles in mid–May. The *Los Angeles Examiner*, also owned by Hearst, ran an article, photograph and cartoon, under the headline, "Jap Baseball Team is Playing Real Ball."[22] The cartoon depicts five figures in three vignettes. To the left, a single Japanese runs awkwardly above the caption: "Jiu Jitsu Ball." In the center, a Japanese player has thrown a western man to the ground by grabbing and twisting his left leg. The caption reads, "For the Umpire" and a dialogue box depicts the player speaking in nonsensical kanji. On the right, a Japanese pitcher in midst of an impossibly goofy windup pitches to a Native American batter (probably representing their upcoming opponents from the Sherman Institute). The caption reads, "Port Arthur." The cartoons show the Japanese with typical yellowface characteristics—over-sized board faces with gigantic grinning teeth and small, slanted eyes. The players' bodies are shown in ungraceful and even unathletic, comical poses. The message seems clear; the Waseda team is alien—foreign and un–American—and, despite the article's headline, not to be taken seriously.

The accompanying article, under the sub headline "Fellow Japanese All Over Los Angeles Studying Up on Rules and Are Prepared to Root

Waseda University's 1905 American Tour

Cartoon of Waseda players from *Los Angeles Examiner*, May 16, 1905.

Countrymen to Victory," focuses on the alleged meeting of a literary society at the Presbyterian Japanese Mission, where the usual erudite reading had been replaced by a copy of the rules of baseball. Although the event could have occurred and the article is devoid of overt racial slurs, the tone is condescending and belittles the Japanese. At the time, when baseball was not only considered the national game but was also seen as a conduit to American values, not understanding the basic rules was yet another example of how Japanese were unable to assimilate into American society.

On April 21st, the Waseda team traveled to Palo Alto, where they would practice before beginning their baseball schedule with two games against Stanford. The Bay Area papers covered the practices. Nearly all expressed surprise and admiration at the Japanese players' skill, although several of the writers couched their complements in racist prose.

E.B. Lenhart of the *Examiner* managed to provide the greatest praise and most offensive comments. Below the headline "If You Think the Japs Can't Play Ball You'd Better Turn on Your Alarm Clock" and a large photograph of second baseman Kiyoshi Oshikawa, he wrote:

> Some ... [of the Stanford students] are still unwilling to bet that what they saw yesterday morning was a condition and not a theory. You could see intelligent young men gouging their knuckles into their eyes and trying to convince themselves that they were really out of the feathers. ... That flock of brownskins from Waseda University, Japan was the cause of all this commotion. They were out for a little loosing of their joints and those who watched the proceedings got a shock of about three thousand and three volts. We calculated the Japs knew nearly as much about the great American game as a rooster does of laying bricks. That none of us suddenly died of apoplexy must go into history as one of the wonders of the age.
>
> ... These Wah! Wah! Wah! Se-Dah! undergrads frolicked with the regulation swatstick and sphere with the ease and agility your distant cousin, Orang Outang shows when he leaps from a bare limb to one that promises him a succulent mouthful. ... They grabbed grounders, snatched throws, seized flies and generally cavorted around that lot like a bunch of individuals sent here by Satan to make us jump out of our heads to drink unto him.
>
> ... Of truth they were rather tiny, somewhat warp-legged and awkward. But they got there just the same and when they line up against the [Stanford] Cardinal team next Saturday the Occidental young men will have to hustle very hard unless they want to be the subjects of an Oriental trimming. As of this writing, there's no telling how the strangers would loom up in a battle with Uncle Henry's Seals or Johnny McGraw's Giants. But you can stow one fact away for future reference: IF YOU ARE INCLINED TO REGARD THE WASEDA UNIVERSITY BASEBALL TEAM AS A JOKE—Wake up![23]

The *Examiner* continued its bigoted tone when covering the Stanford games. An article supposedly penned by Uknown Imawanda (You Know I'm a Wanda) of Japan but most likely another E.B. Lenhart masterpiece of bigotry, is full of pigeon English and false honorifics as it pokes fun at the Japanese even while praising the team's fielding.[24]

After the opening games against Stanford's varsity, Waseda remained in the Bay Area for another two weeks, playing against Stanford clubs and other local schools. On May 16, they boarded a train for Los Angeles where they played another seven games in just eight days, before returning to Palo Alto with stops in Bakersfield and Fresno. Waseda finished out their tour with a week in the Pacific Northwest before leaving for Japan on June 13 **(Table 1)**. Throughout the tour fans crowded into the ballparks "to see whether the 'Yellow Baseball Peril' was all that it had been cracked up to be."[25] The first game against Stanford drew about 2,500—the largest crowd the Stanford team had ever attracted. The two late-June games in Bakersfield were called "the biggest baseball days of the season" and the event "was instrumental in giving baseball in the city a new lease on life."[26]

Table 1: 1905 Waseda Tour Schedule and Results

April 29	Stanford University 9–Waseda 1
May 2	Stanford University 3–Waseda 1
May 3	Yerba Buena Naval School 11–Waseda 8
May 4	Waseda 5–Encina Club of Stanford University 3
May 5	Waseda 8–Stanford University Faculty 2
May 9	St. Mary's College 16–Waseda 0
May 13	Presidio Army Team 7–Waseda 5
May 14	Vallejo Semi-Pro 14–Waseda 3
May 15	University California, Berkley 5–Waseda 0
May 17	Waseda 5–Los Angeles High School 3
May 18	Occidental College 6–Waseda 5
May 20	Waseda 12–Sherman Institute 7
May 21	Los Angeles Pacific Railroad 5–Waseda 4
May 22	St. Vincent's College 6–Waseda 4
May 23	Pomona College 12–Waseda 4
May 24	Waseda 13–University of Southern California 6
May 27	Bakersfield High School 6–Waseda 5
May 28	Bakersfield High School 5–Waseda 2
May 30	Fresno (California State League) 10–Waseda 3
May 31	Fresno (California State League) 13–Waseda 0
June 6	University of Oregon 3–Waseda 0
June 7	Multnomah Athletic Club 3–Waseda 2
June 9	University of Washington 9–Waseda 2
June 10	University of Washington 4–Waseda 0
June 11	Waseda 2–Seattle Rainiers 1
June 12	Waseda 2–Whitworth College 0

Twice, bigotry left the pages of the newspapers and entered the grandstands. On May 3, the Japanese squad traveled to Yerba Buena Naval base on Goat Island in San Francisco Bay to play against a team of naval students from the training ship U.S.S. *Pensacola*. The game was a slugfest, with ragged fielding, and ended in an 11–8 *Pensacola* victory. Details from the game were not reported in local papers but it seems that the naval students in the bleachers taunted the Japanese—probably with racial slurs. Abe would later write, "The rudeness of the naval school's students not only upset us, but also made the umpire make unfair judgments."[27] Two weeks later, as Waseda won "a sizzling contest" over Los Angeles High School, the *L.A. Examiner* commented that "the howling of the High School rooters was also very unsportmanlike, considering that the Japanese players are from a foreign nation on a friendly visit."[28] The *L.A. Herald* quipped, "here is fresh cause for the anti-Japanese crusade in California. Being 'ruined by ... cheap labor' is not half so humiliating as being beaten by Jap players [in] the 'favorite American game.'"29

Hundreds of Japanese immigrants came to each game. According to the *L.A. Herald*, "many came dozens of miles on bicycles, with a day's provisions in packets; others journeyed by boat or railway."30 Accounts from several games note entire sections filled with Japanese fans suggesting that the bleachers may have been segregated. Several newspapers focused on the Japanese spectators' behavior for large portions of their articles. Their descriptions abound with stereotypes, Pidgin English and racial humor, portraying the Japanese immigrants as ignorant aliens, unable to properly assimilate into American life. In its coverage of the May 17 game against Los Angeles High School, for example, the *L.A. Times* wrote, "A short, fat, greasy-faced Mongolian in the center of a compact bunch of his countrymen rose and began a strange yell. 'Whatta Matta his high school? He's no good,' he shouted and his fellows, greatly to the amusement of the other spectators, took up the refrain."31

The *L.A. Examiner* continued:

> The little crowd of sympathizers could not restrain themselves. They were dancing up and down in their excitement when suddenly a little chap wearing a large Panama raised the hat high in the air and began to yell. That was enough to start the others and the cheer that went up drowned the yell of the high school boys.

Cartoon of Japanese fans from *San Francisco Chronicle*, May 3, 1905.

> True it was a mixed yell, some cheering in Japanese and some in English but the little players on the field waved their hats in response. A second later another run was scored ... and the Japs hugged each other in the exuberance of their joy. So if it happened that your Jap boy dropped eight or ten dishes last night don't be too harsh with him. He was cheering inwardly at every step.[32]

In contrast to their fans' enthusiasm, the Waseda players remained stony-faced, barely uttering a sound on the ball field. Bench jockeying and shouting encouragements to teammates was not a part of the Japanese game. When asked about his players' silence, Abe told a reporter from the *Seattle Daily Times*, "Every player in Japan is expected to observe strict silence during a baseball game and that, more than this, the spectators are requested to be absolutely silent, except for modest a pause with the hands ... [because] the Japanese believe that they can play a better and more scientific game by not speaking during the playing."[33] Even today, Japanese players are relatively quiet on the field.

During the May 18 loss to Occidental College, the American players tried to distract their foreign opponents by bench jockeying, but the Japanese remained unmoved. According to the *L.A. Times:*

> ... the collegians were quite at a loss for a time. They had never before played against such silent foes. They also found that the Japs could not be rattled. They only grinned when joshed and went on chewing gum.... Spaulding, the Presbyterian catcher, started some rapid-fire talk to rattle the man at bat. The Jap never moved an eyelid to the banter, but his friends took it up strong. Spaulding came in for a line of funny talk that put him to the bad, and he found he needed all his wits concentrated on playing ball. It was all in very good nature, and both sides showed a friendly spirit.[34]

Perhaps no game was looked forward to more than the matchup with the Sherman Institute on May 20th. It "marked an epoch in the history of our national game..." wrote the *Sporting Life*, as "the first time a base ball game was played by teams ... from two races that have adopted a sport heretofore distinctively that of the white man."[35]

Founded and operated by the United States Government in 1892, the Sherman Institute was the first "off-reservation" boarding school for Native Americans in California. It educated children from 5 to 20 years old with the explicit goal of assimilating them into white American society. Like many government sponsored Native American schools, the Sherman Institute encouraged the boys to play football and baseball to help instill "American values." The school soon became known for its outstanding football squad and would produce a number of professionals. But its baseball team was weak. To bolster the ream against Waseda, the school recruited local

Native American John Tortes (Chief) Meyers who in 1909 would become the star catcher for John McGraw's New York Giants.

The game began at three o'clock and "the largest crowd of the series gathered at Fiesta Park ... and cheered loud and long."[36] Waseda scored a quick run in the first on an error by the Sherman shortstop Padillo and added three more in both the fourth and sixth innings. Meanwhile, Waseda starter Atsushi Kono shut out the opposition for five innings. "The teams formed a curious contrast," the *L.A. Times* noted. "The Red Men, burly and muscular, seemed to tear through their game. The Brown men, lithe and wiry, slipped around them and out-played them."[37]

In the bottom of the sixth, down 7–0, the Institute fought back, scoring six as Meyers "tried to remove the cover from the ball by knocking it to the score board."[38] But Waseda's slick fielding held the Native Americans. "The little warriors from Waseda dashed around the field, taking down the long drives of the red man with ease and grace that was surprising."[39] The Japanese padded their lead to win the game 12–7. All the newspapers agreed that it was a sensational game "replete with lively hitting, speedy base-running and good and bad fielding."[40]

With the novelty of opponents from different races playing each other, the newspapermen could not resist racial stereotypes, allusions and metaphors in their game descriptions. "Jap Team Scalps Sherman Braves"; "Wiry Japs Wallop Reds"; and "Japs Stop a Break from Reservation" declared the next morning's headlines. Typical was the *L.A. Herald*'s lead: "determined to win against a team which they considered in every way equal in strength to a company of Russian soldiers, nine little Japs from Waseda college across the sea took into camp the scalps of nine of the hardiest braves from the Sherman reservation school of Riverside yesterday afternoon and sent the big bucks crashing back to defeat with a one-sided score of 12 to 7."[41]

Accompanying an article loaded with racial stereotypes and demeaning terminology, the *L.A. Examiner* published a contrasting large montage covering the top of the sports section under the headline "Orientals Win Ball Game from the Aborigines."[42] The centerpiece is a drawing of a Native American and Japanese man in traditional clothing each holding a baseball bat. Unlike previous illustrations, these are not cartoon caricatures but respectful, even if somewhat fanciful, depictions of men from the two ethnic groups. On either side of this centerpiece are the photographs of three players from the respective teams. This illustration is in marked contrast to the *Examiner*'s earlier graphic as it treats the players as named individuals rather than stereotypes. The visiting Japanese were slowly gaining respect.

Waseda University's 1905 American Tour

The game against Sherman would be one of Waseda's few victories. The Japanese won just 7 of their 26 games, but their ability surprised the American opposition and onlookers. After their initial 9–1 loss to Stanford, the *Call* concluded that the team "covered themselves with glory, for they played a much better game than was expected of them."[43] A week later, former Major League star Bill Lange, who umpired a close game against a U.S. army team noted, "The Japs surprised me. ... I had heard they could play the game some, but I had no idea that they were as good as they were."[44]

Waseda impressed nearly all with their base-running and fielding. "They are speedy and fearless base runners," announced the *Fresno Morning Republican*.[45] "Veritable demons," said the *Pacific Commercial Advertiser*, surprising fans with "the manner in which they tore up the earth sliding to the cushions."[46] In the field, they were fast on their feet, handling the ball quickly, playing a "sharp, snappy" game. After a win against the University of Southern California, the *L.A. Times* announced, "they performed like a bunch of leaguers and showed no weakness whatever in the field, handling their chances with mechanical precision of star professionals."[47]

The star of the team was undoubtedly the diminutive pitcher Atsushi

Illustration of Waseda and Sherman Indians from *Los Angeles Examiner*, May 21, 1905.

Kono. With only a 24-inch long arm, he started, and finished, every game on the tour except one. Newspapers dubbed him Iron Man Kono. "He is a speed pitcher with good curves and a change of pace that is puzzling, "noted the Examiner.⁴⁸ He was also "the personification of good nature and wears a perpetual smile of the variety that won't rub off" added the Daily California.⁴⁹ When the Waseda team attended a Pacific Coast League game between L.A. and Tacoma, manager Jim Morley asked Kono to pitch for the Angels while the Waseda team was in town. Abe, realizing that the event would only be a publicity stunt to attract fans to the ballpark, declined on Kono's behalf. If Kono and Abe had agreed to Morey's proposal, Kono would have been the first Japanese, and Asian, to play in Organized Baseball. We are left to wonder if Kono's acceptance would have hastened the debut of Japanese players into the Major leagues by decades.⁵⁰

Waseda pitcher Atsushi Kono (author's collection).

Although the Waseda squad could run, field, and pitch, they were in the words of the *Pacific Commercial Advertiser*, "woefully weak with the willow."⁵¹ Or in the blunter words of the *S.F. Examiner*, they "Hit Like a Team of Spinsters."⁵² Opponents outscored them 250 to 96 and they were shut out in 5 of their 26 games. The players generally made good contact, but were befuddled by curveballs and hard-throwing pitchers. They also lacked power, with most of their hits being "of the scratchy variety."⁵³ In the ten surviving box scores, Waseda players hit a measly buck-ninety-nine (.199) and slugged just .239.

Throughout the games, Waseda impressed spectators with their sportsmanship. Reporters noted that the Japanese refused to argue—even when clearly wronged. In the game against Los Angeles High School, for example, the *Herald* reported, "no matter how rank a decision was, the Japs never made a sound. Once they looked very hard and were evidently thinking a lot when given the short end but never a kick."⁵⁴ Umpire Bill Lange commented, "They didn't kick over my decisions. They were good fellows.... A Presidio player batted the ball along first base line and I called it fair. It was so close that.... I asked ... the catcher if my decision was correct. He ... replied that the ball was fair by about a foot. What American catcher would have made such an admission? Our catchers would have claimed that the ball hit foul five feet."[55] Stories such as this may have helped undermine the stereotype of Japanese dishonesty.

In each city, the team's gentlemanly behavior won over many American fans. After a game against the Pacific Railroad in Santa Monica, the *L.A. Times* concluded "Most of the Americans in the bleachers yesterday seemed to lend their sympathies to the brown men. Their sportsmanlike game seemed to appeal to them."[56] And in Bakersfield, Waseda "played with sufficient vim and vinegar and comported themselves with such uniform courtesy as to win the admiration as well as the sympathy of the grand stand."[57]

Waseda's play and behavior also affected the sports reporters. As the tour progressed, the tone of the newspaper articles covering the games shifted. Gone where the racial slurs, the anti–Japanese jokes, innuendos, and the yellow-face cartoons. Instead, the articles concentrated on baseball, treating the Waseda players as individual ballplayers rather than representations of their race. Abe's team had won respect, and his mission had, in some small part, succeeded.

Of course, the Waseda tour did not bring about Abe's ultimate goal of world peace. Nor did it abate the discrimination against Japanese immigrants. In October 1906, San Francisco voted to segregate Japanese in the public schools, the first of many acts that would culminate with the forced incarceration of 120,000 Japanese Americans during World War II. But the tour did impact American attitudes toward Japanese, provide the impetus for Japanese American baseball, revolutionize the game in Japan, and mark the beginnings of international baseball.

Abe had been correct when he told Waseda's founder Shigenobu Okuma that the tour would strengthen ties with the U.S. though mutual love of sport and fair play. Newspapers across the United States carried articles on Waseda's tour. Nearly all praised the Japanese for successful adopting baseball and emphasized the shared love of the game as a bond between the two nations. Abe was also correct that holding the tour in the midst of the Russo-Japanese War would impress Americans. Just before the team arrived, the *San Francisco Herald* proclaimed, "Japan is a very small country in the Pacific and is now fighting against Russia, one of the biggest countries in the world. However, the Japanese people have shown incredible composure. Recently, the Waseda University baseball team have asked Stanford for a challenge match. What a brave attitude this is!"[58]

Waseda's visit led to the birth of Japanese American baseball. Although Japanese immigrants had created ball clubs as early as 1903 in San Francisco and 1904 in Los Angeles, the Waseda tour introduced the game to large numbers of others in the Japanese community. In 1906 and 1907, Japanese teams sprang up throughout the West Coast. Intrigued by the press coverage of the Waseda games and large attendance, Guy Green, the owner of the famed Nebraska Indians Base Ball Club, created a Japanese team. Guy Green's Japanese Base Ball Club barnstormed across the Mid-West in 1906 playing over 150 games and in the process became the first Japanese professional team on either side of the Pacific. Baseball soon became a social centerpiece for Japanese American communities prior to World War II and during the war helped them survive the indignities of the internment camps.

The tour also helped modernize Japanese baseball. After returning to Japan, Abe and his players introduced new equipment and techniques to their countrymen. The team brought back cleats and modern gloves. Japanese manufactures copied the imports and soon teams across the country had the latest equipment. The players also imported the latest techniques of Scientific Baseball: they taught other teams the hit and run, the art of bunting, the windup, the spitball, and the basics of systematic practice. Team captain Shin Hashido published the book Recent Baseball Techniques, which disseminated scientific baseball throughout Japan.

But most importantly, the tour marked the true beginnings of international baseball. Discounting a disorganized visit by an Australian club in 1897, the Waseda tour was the first foreign team to come to the U.S. Moreover, they played well and drew widespread interest. In 1908 American teams began

Waseda shortstop and team captain Shin Hashido (courtesy National Baseball Hall of Fame and Museum).

annual trips to Asia. Over one hundred teams would travel across the Pacific before 1937. Cuba already had a professional league and the game had spread to Latin America and Hawaii. Thus, soon after the Waseda team left the U.S., baseball diplomacy would be born and newspapers across the country would speculate on when a true World Series would be played.

Acknowledgments

I would like to thank Keiko Kamei for translating the Japanese sources; Santaro Hirofumi Kawakami, the author of *Samurai Baseball*, for sharing sources on the 1905 Waseda tour; Izumo Ishii for helping me contact Mr. Kawakami; Yoichi Nagata for answering numerous questions on Japanese baseball history; Tom Shieber of the National Baseball Hall of Fame and Museum for supplying the photograph of Shin Hashido; and Dennis Snelling for copying newspaper articles at the California State Library.

Notes

1. On Isoo Abe see, Ikuo Abe, "Muscular Christianity in Japan: The Growth of a Hybrid," in *Christianity and the Colonial and Post-Colonial World*, ed. John Macaloon Muscular (London: Taylor and Francis, 2013),14–38; Masko Gavin, "Abe Isoo and Baseball," in *Rethinking Japanese Modernism*, ed. Roy Starrs (Boston: Global Oriental, 2012), 452–470; Masako Gavin, "Poverty and Its Possible Cures: Abe Isoo and Kawakami Hajime," (2007): http://epublications.bond.edu.au/hss_pubs/232; Elise K. Tipton, "In a House Divided: The Japanese Christian Socialist Abe Isoo," in *Nation and Nationalism in Japan*, ed. Sandra Wilson (New York: Routledge, 2002), 81–96.
2. Gavin, "Abe Isoo and Baseball," 458–459.
3. *Los Angeles Herald*, July 17, 1894,1,4.
4. Isoo Abe from *Yakyu to Tomoni Sanjunen* quoted in Ryoichi Shibazaki "Seattle and the Japanese–United States Baseball Connection, 1905–1926" (Master's thesis, University of Washington, 1981), 9.
5. Gavin, "Abe Isoo and Baseball," 457–58; Koichi Kiku, "The Japanese Baseball Spirit and Professional Ideology," in *Japan, Sport, and Society*, eds. Joseph Maguire and Masayoshi Nakayama (New York: Routledge, 2006) 42.
6. Masko Gavin, "National Moral Education: Abe Isoo's Views on Education," *Japanese Studies*, 24, no. 3 (2004): 323-333. 2004; Cyril Powles, "Abe Isoo the Utility Man," in *Pacifism in Japan: The Christian and Socialist Tradition*, ed. Nobuya Bamba and John F. Howes (Kyoto: Minerva, 1978), 143–167.
7. Gavin, "Abe Isoo and Baseball," 464–5.
8. *Stanford Daily*, May 1 1905, 6.
9. Shibazaki, "Seattle and the Japanese," 11–12.
10. Isoo Abe from *Yakyu to Tomoni Sanjunen* quoted in Shibazaki "Seattle and the Japanese," 12.
11. Shibazaki, "Seattle and the Japanese," 13.
12. Roger Daniels, *The Politics of Prejudice* (Berkeley: University of California Press, 1962), 24.
13. "Japanese Invasion: The Problem of the Hour for United States," *San Francisco Chronicle*, February 23, 1905, 1.
14. Daniels, *Politics of Prejudice*, 25.
15. Quoted in Daniels, *Politics of Prejudice*, 27.
16. Quoted in Daniels, *Politics of Prejudice*, 28.
17. John W. Dower, *War Without Mercy: Race & Power in the Pacific War* (New York: Pantheon,

1986); Sidney L. Gulick, *The American Japanese Problem: A Study of the Racial Relations of the East and the West* (New York: Charles Scribner's Sons, 1914); Robert G. Lee, *Orientals: Asian Americans in Popular Culture* (Philadelphia, Temple University Press, 1999); James Maynard, *World War Two, America's Divine Mission & the Formulation of the Japanese "Other": A Study of Wartime Propaganda as a Tactical Weapon and a Euphemism for Racial Discrimination* (Amazon Digital Services, 2014); Dennis Ogawa, *From Japs to Japanese: The Evolution of Japanese-American Stereotypes* (Berkeley: McCutchan, 1971).

18. "Balltossers from Mikado's Realm Cross Ocean to Play Game," *San Francisco Call*, April 21, 1905, 10.
19. "It Makes Them Angry," *Houston Post*, November 23, 1906, 6.
20. "Japs Here to Fight Us on Our Own Soil at Our Own Game," *San Francisco Examiner*, April 21, 1905, 9.
21. "More Japs Arrive on the Korea," *San Francisco Chronicle*, April 21, 1905, 9.
22. "Jap Baseball Team Is Playing Real Ball," *Los Angeles Examiner*, May 16, 1905.
23. E.B. Lenhart, "If You Think the Japs Can't Play Ball You'd Better Turn on Your Alarm Clock," *San Francisco* Examiner, April 23, 1905, 55.
24. Uknown Imawanda, "Japs Hit Like a Team of Spinsters," *San Francisco Examiner*, May 3, 1905, 9.
25. "Japs Are on Deck and Ready for Big Game," *Daily Californian*, May 26, 1905, 3; "Big Game in Progress," *Daily Californian*, May 27, 1905, 6.
26. "Japs Lost Both Games," *Daily Californian*, May 29, 1905, 6.
27. Isoo Abe, "Diary of 1905 Tour," in *Saikin Yakyu Jutsu*, ed. Shin Hashido (Tokyo: Hakubunkan, 1905).
28. "Foreigners Handle Ball Like Veterans," *Los Angeles Examiner*, May 18, 1905.
29. *Los Angeles Herald*, May 6, 1905, 6.
30. "Jap Ball Players Are Defeated," *Los Angeles Herald*, April 30, 1905, 8.
31. "Brown Boys Nettle High," *Los Angeles Times*, May 18, 1905, II3.
32. "Foreigners Handle Ball Like Veterans," *Los Angeles Examiner*, May 18, 1905.
33. *Seattle Daily Times*, June 6, 1905, 14.
34. "Occidentals Get the Japs," *Los Angeles Times*, May 19.1905, II3.
35. "A New Departure," *Sporting Life*, June 10, 1905, 19.
36. "Orientals Win Ball Game from the Aborigines," *Los Angeles Examiner*, May 21, 1905, 41.
37. "Wiry Japs Wallop Reds," *Los Angeles Times*, May 21, 1905, II11.
38. "Jap Team Scalps Sherman Braves," *Los Angeles Herald*, May 21, 1905, 6.
39. *Ibid.*
40. "Orientals Win Ball Game From the Aborigines," *Los Angeles Examiner*, May 21, 1905, 41.
41. "Jap Team Scalps Sherman Braves," *Los Angeles Herald*, May 21, 1905, 6.
42. "Orientals Win Ball Game from the Aborigines," *Los Angeles Examiner*, May 21, 1905, 41.
43. "Mikado's Men Are Active on the Field but Prove Weak at the Bat," *San Francisco Call*, April 30, 1905, 51.
44. *Seattle Daily Times*, May 21, 1905, 18.
45. "Japs Easy Victims," *Fresno Morning Republican*, June 1, 1905.
46. "Waseda vs. Stanford," *Pacific Commercial Advertiser*, May 11, 1905, 6.
47. "Ball Lesson by the Japs," *Los Angeles Times*, May 25, 1905, p.II3.
48. "Orientals Lose to Occidentals," *Los Angeles Examiner, May 19, 1905,* 12.
49. "Japs Are on Deck and Ready for Big Game," *Daily California*, May 26, 1905, 3.
50. Abe, Isoo. "Waseda Daigaku Yakyi Senshu Tobeiki-14," *Tokyo Asahi Shimbun*, June 22, 1905, 3.
51. "Waseda vs. Stanford," *Pacific Commercial Advertiser*, May 11, 1905, 6..
52. Uknown Imawanda, "Japs Hit Like a Team of Spinsters," *San Francisco Examiner*, May 3, 1905, 9.
53. "Waseda vs. Stanford," *Pacific Commercial Advertiser*, May 11, 1905, 6.
54. "Foreigners Handle Ball Like Veterans," *Los Angeles Examiner*, May 18, 1905.
55. *Seattle Daily Times*, May 21, 1905, 18.
56. "Rushin Run Defeats Japs," *Los Angeles Times*, May 22, 1905, I12.
57. "Japs Lost Both Games," *Daily Californian*, May 29, 1905, 6.
58. *San Francisco Herald* quoted in Shibazaki, "Seattle and the Japanese," 28.

A Closer Look at the Pennsylvania Base Ball Club
Peter Morris

The social class of antebellum baseball clubs has often been the source of wild exaggerations and misstatements, even by scholars. In particular, the Eckfords of Brooklyn have often been inaccurately described as a working-class club. Meanwhile, actual working-class clubs, such as the Magnolias of New York City and the Green Mountain Boys of Boston, have been written out of the game's history. This article assesses the validity of another such assertion, David Voigt's description of the pre–Civil War Pennsylvania Club of Philadelphia as one of the era's rare blue-collar clubs, by identifying thirty-two of the club's thirty-four members and reconstructing their lives. The need to review earlier assumptions on this subject in light of the growing amount of digitized nineteenth-century demographic source material is also discussed.

Few subjects have produced more confusion and misinformation than the social class of the members of the earliest baseball clubs. When much of the underlying data proved too difficult to track down, all too often sweeping generalizations and misleading caricatures have been substituted.

Albert G. Spalding was one of the worst culprits, describing pre-war players in general as "gentlemen 'to the manor born'" and the Knickerbockers in particular as a "silk-stocking aggregation" that was "reluctant to accept challenges from shipwrights, boilermakers and other grades of 'greasy mechanics.'"[1] Conversely, the Eckfords of Brooklyn have often been inaccurately described as a working-class club because many of its members were associated with the thriving shipyards located on the East River.[2] In fact, as the distinguished historian Sean Wilentz explains, shipbuilding was one of the two remnants of the artisan tradition that remained largely untouched by industrialization in mid-nineteenth century New York City (food preparation being the other one).[3]

Wilentz's observations suggest the need to bring into this conversation historians with a specialty in the relationship between occupation and social class in the nineteenth-century United States. Unfortunately, the only academic historians to give much attention to these questions have been George B. Kirsch and Melvin Adelman, each of whom studied this topic more than thirty years ago and limited their studies to specific regions (New Jersey/Philadelphia in Kirsch's case; New York City in Adelman's).[4] Adelman's methodology is especially troubling. He correctly draws attention to the caricatured portrayals of clubs like the Knickerbockers and the Eckfords.[5] But his research consisted largely of trying to match the surnames found in box scores to the city directories, an approach that obviously invites inaccuracy even when carried out with great care.[6] Worse, Adelman appears to have been anything but meticulous. Among the relatively few ballplayers he mentions in the text, he refers to Hervey Schriver as Henry Schrivner, Fred Waterman as Fred Waterson, George Flanley as George Flannery, and Alfred Gedney as John Gedney.[7]

One of my hopes when I organized the Pioneer Project was that the carefully documented membership lists of early baseball clubs that it produced would inspire renewed interest in these questions among academics.[8] That has yet to happen, though perhaps one day it will yet occur. Instead, John Thorn's important research on the Magnolia Club—published in this journal, as well as in Thorn's *Baseball in the Garden of Eden* and *Baseball Founders*—has given new urgency to this matter by suggesting that a concerted effort may have been made to write such "sporting-life characters" out of the history of early baseball.[9] Support for this contention can even be found in Spalding's take on the matter. After all, if antebellum ballplayers were in fact mostly "gentlemen 'to the manor born,'" then why did the Knickerbockers keep receiving challenges from clubs made up of "greasy mechanics"?

In this context, the Pennsylvania Base Ball Club takes on new significance. According to Charles Peverelly, this prewar club was one of the participants in a contest on June 26, 1860, that was the first match game played in Philadelphia under the New York rules.[10] This claim has been disputed by Philadelphia baseball historian John Shiffert, however, and since the Pennsylvania Club did not survive the Civil War, the club would appear to be of limited significance.[11] Yet one distinction suggests otherwise: a claim by David Voigt that the Pennsylvania Club was one of the few blue-collar clubs of the era.[12] Unfortunately, the obscurity of the club long prevented verification of Voigt's assertion.

Recently, however, I discovered two articles that made it possible to assess the veracity of Voigt's claim. A brief sketch of the Pennsylvania Club that appeared in *Wilkes' Spirit of the Times* on February 2, 1861, stated that the club had been organized on November 5, 1859, and now boasted forty members. This article also described the club's uniform and provided a list of its officers and the names of three members of its playing nine.[13]

By themselves, these fairly sparse details would not have been of much help, but the Pennsylvania Club came into much clearer perspective as a result of the second article, which appeared in the *Philadelphia Sunday Mercury* on March 2, 1873. Like most articles of the era, this article is not bylined, but it internally identifies its source as George Batties, who had been listed as the club treasurer in the 1861 article. That correspondence supports the article's veracity, as does the fact that it was published only a decade and a half after the club's origin, when plenty of eyewitnesses could easily have come forward to correct any inaccuracies.[14]

The *Sunday Mercury* article described the club's involvement in the allegedly historic game on June 26, 1860, and added that its membership was "composed almost exclusively of printers connected with" a newspaper called the *Pennsylvanian*. It also mentioned that the club practiced two or three times a week in 1858 and 1859 at a diamond at the corner of Columbia and Ridge with two other pioneer clubs, the Equity Club and the Winona Club. At first glance, this latter statement appears to contradict the 1861 article, but this is not necessarily the case. The club (or at least its nucleus) could well have practiced for a couple of years before formally organizing. Intriguingly, in the summer of 1858, the *New York Clipper* had reported that the Typographical Cricket Club had been formed by a group of approximately thirty Philadelphia printers. So the Philadelphia Base Ball Club very likely was made up of mostly the same men, who probably initially focused on cricket but eventually gravitated toward baseball.[15]

An especially important feature of the 1873 *Sunday Mercury* article was that Batties had provided a list of the thirty-seven original club members, making it possible to identify them and verify their backgrounds. Several factors made this work much easier than Melvin Adelman's efforts to match surnames with city directories. First, the availability of city directories, census listings, vital records, and contemporaneous newspaper articles is far greater than was the case three decades ago, and in many cases these sources can be accessed via the Internet. Second, the clue that most of the club members were printers made it much easier to pick out the right man. Third, the article provided far more than just surnames: a first name and middle initial was also given for twenty of the thirty-seven original members. For nine more, a first name alone was provided. For another seven, both initials were given, leaving only one member (T. McCusker) who was identified only by an initial. Finally, eight of the thirty-seven members were identified as deceased, providing yet another valuable clue.

With all of these factors working in my favor, I was able to identify with a high degree of confidence thirty-four of the thirty-seven original members of the Pennsylvania Club, the exceptions being James W. Prentis, James Brogan, and the aforementioned T. McCusker. In the case of the first man, no man by that name of a plausible age could be found in Philadelphia. In the case of the latter two men, there was more than one such candidate, and since none of them were identified as printers, there was no way to be sure which one was the club member.

Of the thirty-four members who could be identified, a remarkable thirty-two were listed as printers (or compositors) at least once in a city directory, census, or obituary (and most were so listed on more than one occasion). Those two exceptions are themselves instructive. One was Charles B. Sharrett, a local grocer and well-known cricket player, whose membership adds weight to the supposition that the Pennsylvania Base Ball Club was closely related to the Typographical Cricket Club. The second was James Derham, a local innkeeper and tavern owner, who likely hosted the club's postgame festivities. That at least was the case with another notable pre–Civil War club of printers, the Franklins of Detroit, whose role of members also included Jeremiah Calnon, the owner of the club's tavern of choice.[16] Even if we assume that Prentis, Brogan, and McCusker, the three unidentified club members, were not printers—a likely, but not inevitable conclusion—we are still left with thirty-two of the thirty-seven club members (86.5 percent) being printers. So a clear picture of the club has begun to emerge that justifies the description of the club as being primarily made up of printers.

My next step was to determine birth dates for as many club members as possible. Exact birth dates for Americans of this era can be very difficult to pin down, but the ages provided for censuses, death certificates, and obituaries are usually close enough for our purposes, especially when several different listings can be compared. Of the thirty-three original Penn-

The Pennsylvania Base Ball Club

sylvania Club members for whom a relatively accurate year of birth could be determined, five were born between 1820 and 1824 (making them in their late 30s when the club was formed), ten were born between 1825 and 1829 (early 30s), eleven between 1830 and 1834 (late 20s), six between 1835 and 1839 (early 20s), and a single outlier who was born in 1813 (late 40s). These ages are less than ideal when looked at strictly from a ballplaying standpoint, suggesting that social aspects of the club were valued more highly than competitive ones. (Indeed, the Pennsylvania Club won only one of its four known match games.) No doubt the younger members earned most of the places in the first nine, with the older members taking part in practices but acting as spectators when match games rolled around.

Based on these ages, one would not expect the Pennsylvania Club to have been long-lived, and that supposition is reinforced by an examination of Civil War service records. At least seven club members were confirmed to have enlisted in the Civil War, and no doubt there were others who did so, especially among those with common names. One club member, Jesse J. Thomas, a printer and medical student, enlisted as a surgeon and was fatally wounded in 1862. Another, William B. McCloy, was taken as a prisoner of war in 1863 and may too have been a casualty of the war, as Batties reported him to be deceased. The Civil War thus cost the Pennsylvania Club a significant number of members, and those members were disproportionately taken from the younger portion of the club, leaving the future bleak.

I also ascertained dates of death for thirty-one club members, though this information was of less direct relevance. Ten members had already died when the list of members was published in 1873 (two of them unbeknownst to Batties). Five more had passed away by 1880, followed by two more during the 1880s and another seven during the 1890s. When William Shields died in 1910, only two known survivors of the original club remained—Jefferson Christman, who died in 1916, and George W. Kugler, who passed away shortly after the conclusion of the 1924 World Series.

All of these hard facts are interesting enough, but how do they help us to approach the far more elusive question of social class? Knowing that such a high percentage of the Pennsylvania Club's members worked as printers is helpful, but the status of the printer during those years was volatile. Sean Wilentz does not include printers among the two examples of New York artisanship that pretty much resisted industrialization, instead considering them as a special case. By 1845, he notes, the *New York Tribune* was reporting that most of the work traditionally performed by printers was now being done by "mere typesetters and not printers or workmen in the strictest sense of the world."[17] With competition growing more and more intense, "every man was compelled to work for what he could obtain."[18]

These discomforting trends were to some extent mitigated by a boom in newspaper publishing that followed the introduction of the telegraph. Rather like the dot.com bubble that occurred a century and a half later, excitement over the new technology led to an unsustainably large number of newspapers popping up in most American cities, only to soon fall victim to the glut of competition. This further increased the predicament of the printer during these years.

The requirements necessary to enter the printing profession were also unusual. Printers had to be highly literate and typically underwent a rigorous apprenticeship, but otherwise there were few barriers to entering the profession. This was reflected in the membership of the Pennsylvania Club.

Due to the importance of literacy, only four original club members were born outside the United States.[19] Aside from that, however, there was considerable diversity in their backgrounds. It seems likely that quite a few—probably a majority—came from families of modest means and looked at the printing profession as an end in itself. But there were some notable exceptions who used it as a stepping-stone. Jesse J. Thomas, for example, doubled as a printer and medical student before dying in the war. Julius Oehlschlager was the son of a German-born professor of languages. Of particular note were Thomas Egan, who moved on from printing to journalism, and Aaron K. Dunkel and William Messer, who became the publishers of, respectively, the *Sunday Republic* and the *Sunday Mercury*. (No wonder the 1873 club history was deemed newsworthy by the *Sunday Mercury*!)

In the end, then, describing the members of the pre-war Pennsylvania Base Ball Club as blue-collar workers is a generalization that conceals at least as much as it reveals. Indeed, in many ways, the club's members were very like the Knickerbockers in pursuing a profession with intriguing opportunities for upward mobility. The subject of the social class of antebellum baseball clubs remains a fluid one in more need than ever of further investigation.

Notes

1. Albert Goodwill Spalding, *America's National Game: Historic Facts Concerning the Beginning, Evolution, Development, and Popularity of Base Ball, with Personal Reminiscences of Its Vicissitudes, Its Victories, and Its Votaries* (1910: reprint, Lincoln: University of Nebraska Press, 1992), 51, 66.

2. Melvin L. Adelman, *A Sporting Time: New York City and the Rise of Modern Athletics, 1820–70* (Urbana: University of Illinois Press, 1986), 325, cites several sources for this myth. See the Eckford Club entry in Peter Morris, William J. Ryczek, Jan Finkel, Leonard Levin, and Richard Malatzky,

ed., *Base Ball Founders: The Clubs, Players and Cities of the Northeast That Established the Game* (Jefferson, NC: McFarland, 2013), and page 168 in particular, for a more thorough discussion of the background of the members of the Eckford Club.

3. Sean Wilentz, *Chants Democratic*, 134–140.

4. George B. Kirsch, "American Cricket: Players and Clubs Before the Civil War," *Journal of Sport History*, Vol. 11, No. 1 (Spring, 1984), 28–50, and George Kirsch, *The Creation of American Team Sports: Baseball and Cricket, 1838-72* (Urbana: University of Illinois Press, 1989); Melvin Adelman, "The Development of Modern Athletics: Sport in New York City, 1820–1870" (Unpublished Ph. D. dissertation, University of Illinois at Urbana-Champaign, 1980), and Melvin L. Adelman, *A Sporting Time*.

5. Melvin L. Adelman, *A Sporting Time*, 123–125, plus the corresponding footnote on page 325.

6. A special appendix in which Adelman describes and defends his methodology appears on pages 287–289.

7. Melvin L. Adelman, *A Sporting Time*, 129, 160, 178, 179.

8. The two books that resulted from the Pioneer Project are Peter Morris, William J. Ryczek, Jan Finkel, Leonard Levin, and Richard Malatzky, ed., *Base Ball Pioneers, 1850-1870: The Clubs and Players Who Spread the Sport Nationwide* (Jefferson, NC: McFarland, 2012) and Peter Morris, William J. Ryczek, Jan Finkel, Leonard Levin, and Richard Malatzky, ed., *Base Ball Founders: The Clubs, Players and Cities of the Northeast That Established the Game* (Jefferson, NC: McFarland, 2013).

9. Peter Morris, William J. Ryczek, Jan Finkel, Leonard Levin, and Richard Malatzky, ed., *Base Ball Founders*, 62.

10. Charles A. Peverelly, *The Book of American Pastimes: Containing a History of the Principal Base Ball, Cricket, Rowing, and Yachting Clubs of the United States* (New York: n.p., 1866), 486–488.

11. John Shiffert, *Base Ball in Philadelphia: A History of the Early Game, 1831-1900* (Jefferson, NC: McFarland, 2006) 21–26.

12. Proceedings from Philadelphia's Baseball History, 8.

13. *Wilkes' Spirit of the Times*, February 2, 186.

14. *Philadelphia Sunday Mercury*, March 2, 1873. My thanks to Robert Tholkes and Richard Hershberger for scanning this article for me.

15. *New York Clipper*, August 14, 1858, 133, citing the *Philadelphia Journal*; noted on 42 of George B. Kirsch, "American Cricket: Players and Clubs Before the Civil War."

16. Peter Morris, *Baseball Fever: Early Baseball in Michigan* (Ann Arbor: University of Michigan Press, 2003), 25–26.

17. *New York Tribune*, September 15, 1845; quoted in Sean Wilentz, *Chants Democratic*, 129.

18. *New York Tribune*, September 11 and 15, 1845; quoted in Sean Wilentz, *Chants Democratic*, 130.

19. Three were born in Ireland and one in Newfoundland.

"The American Ideal of Manly Beauty"
Isaac Broome's Base Ball Vase, 1875–76

JAMES E. BRUNSON III

Isaac Broom's Base Ball Vase, *designed by Etruria Pottery for the Philadelphia Centennial Exhibition of 1876, was inspired by the formation of the National Base Ball League. As an item of mass-produced statuary aimed at middle-class audiences, the piece attracted a great deal of attention—and reinforced prevailing notions of class, gender, and race. In this article, rather than focus primarily on the formal elements of* Base Ball Vase, *I explore how it participated in the cultural discourse surrounding white racial masculinity.*

BASE BALL VASE, A SCULPTURAL object designed by Trenton, New Jersey's Etruria Pottery specifically for the Philadelphia Centennial Exhibition of 1876, is arguably the most famous work of Isaac Broome. A portrait painter, sculptor, fresco artist, and writer, Broome (pronounced "Vroome") produced a series of objects in Parian ware, sculptural imitations of white marble, both in surface and tint. Among them were two covered baseball vases that flanked their display in the ceramics area of the Manufacturer's Building. Their nationalistic spirit, inspired by the formation of the National Base Ball League, attracted so much attention that one of the vases was moved to the Art Gallery of Memorial Hall a month after the fair opened. In 1887, the company owner, John Hart Brewer, gave one of them to the National League of Professional Baseball Players to serve as a pennant trophy. *Base Ball Vase* is the first work of American ceramic to be officially classified as art.[1]

Isaac Broome's Base Ball Vase, 1875–76

When Brewer hired Broome in 1873, the 38-year-old immigrant from Quebec had already established his reputation. In 1851, Broome studied wood and stone carving with his neighbor, the sculptor Hugh A. Cannon, who had trained and exhibited at the Pennsylvania Academy of Fine Arts. Broome was a student there by 1856, when he was issued a permit to copy a painting. In 1858, his name appears in the Academy's life-class register and in the antique-class register of 1859. He participated in annual exhibitions from 1859 through 1869 and in 1876, 1878, 1903, and 1906. Between 1855 and 1856 Broome worked on the statues designed by Thomas Crawford for the east pediment of the United States Capitol. Between 1857 and 1858, Broome traveled to Italy, France, and England. While abroad, he visited museums and collected art for American patrons. He maintained a studio in Rome, translating into marble several busts of Americans. In Italy, he studied Greek and Etruscan pottery, which inspired an interest in ceramics that remained through-

Artist Isaac Broome. *Base Ball Vase.* Parian (marble imitation). 1876. Detroit Institute of Arts. *Base Ball Vase* is the first work of American ceramic to be officially classified as art. Broome's statuary, created for the parlor, offered a representation of the refined beauty of the white male body.

out his life. After his return to the United States in 1860, he was made an associate of the Pennsylvania Academy and, the following year, elected an academician. In 1865, Broome moved to Pittsburgh and established himself as a manufacturer of terracotta objects. In 1871, he attempted to open a terracotta works in Brooklyn, New York, but was forced to abandon the venture when the board of health ruled his kilns a fire hazard.[2]

In 1863, Trenton had seven pottery works, among them William Bloor,

Joseph Ott, and Thomas Booth's Etruria Pottery. Ott had owned a livery stable with William P. Brewer, and Booth had been in the stationery business. Ott and Booth provided the financial resources necessary to erect a new pottery works. According to the historian James Mitchell, Ott's livery stable had been valued at $9,900 and Booth's business had been valued at $10,000. Bloor, a potter from Staffordshire, England, came to the United States in 1842. He had a thorough knowledge of and experience with porcelain. The combination of economic resources and practical knowledge of pottery production allowed the new firm to build a factory and start production. Within a year the ownership of the new business changed. In 1864, Booth retired and sold his interest to Garret Schenk Burroughs. In 1865, Burroughs sold his share to John Hart Brewer, the son of William P. Brewer, Ott's former partner in the livery business. The pottery artisan-craftsman community elected John Hart Brewer to state assemblyman in 1875 and, in 1880, elevated him to congressman. Brewer, a descendant of a Declaration of Independence signatory, was an ideal standard bearer for the pottery trade. Prominent men, Ott and Brewer were uncle and nephew, respectively. In 1871 the peripatetic Bloor left the partnership, and Ott and Brewer carried on the Etruria Works.[3]

My fascination with Isaac Broome derives from an interest in his baseball representations during the postbellum Gilded Age, a period of economic ascendency in the Unites States following the Civil War. In material terms, *Baseball Vase* dovetails neatly with baseball trophies (badges, bats, and balls made of wood, gold and silver), objects that embodied what the social critic Thorstein Veblen called symbols of "conspicuous consumption" and "sumptuary display."[4] Veblen coined these terms to define the cultural behavior of the country's new and expanding leisure class. Historian Regina Lee Blaszczyk demonstrates that this self-conscious pursuit of beautifully-decorated objects represented the cultural delineation of material refinement and difference—indeed, the democratization of difference. Broome represented the highly-paid labor aristocracy, artisan-craftsmen who used their creativity, skills, embellishing technologies, and understanding of fashion to satisfy the consumer's physical and psychological needs.[5]

Broome's work merits attention for another reason: rather than just viewing it as a rarefied high-art object, this paper explores how it participated in a cultural discourse of white racial masculinity. By discourse, I mean an organizing set of beliefs and social practices that build, modify, and naturalize constructs such as gender and race. I will argue that it is within this framework that *Base Ball Vase* takes part in the construction of

Isaac Broome's Base Ball Vase, 1875–76

white racial masculinity by serving as both a material expression of, and a site for, gendering/racializing beliefs and practices. My idea is not new. Art historian Elizabeth Johns explains: "As the nineteenth century saw the rise of self-made and widely admired men in all disciplines of activity who optimistically aspired to the moral discipline of their predecessors, a host of portrait painters arose to document and honor their achievements." Art historian Martin Berger examines the sports paintings of Thomas Eakins, zeroing in on how the artist fashioned manhood for his white, middle-class contemporaries. Eakins's *Base Ball Players Practicing* (1875), a contemporary of *Base Ball Vase*, offers a heroic portrait of the white ballplayers of the Philadelphia Athletics.[6]

Heroic portraits were foundational to many baseball representations, and the foundation of binary definitions that reinforced notions of class, gender, and race. Eakins created several paintings devoted to hunting, sailing, rowing, and baseball. While he also painted the black male body, Eakins was intensely interested in the refined beauty of the white male body. Broome also engaged in heroic portraiture—his design and production of decorative objects wares extended a sense of male control over domestic interior spaces. His baseball objects created for the parlor, fashionable white goods, were styled, as literary critic Bridget T. Heneghan has demonstrated, "racially 'white'—because white goods were the popular elite products and markers of upper- or middle-class refinement and because respectable, middle-class, or sentimental characters of a literary nature were allowed a fictive white skin."[7]

Taking my lead from Heneghan's studies of material culture, I view Broome's marble-like objects not as "monoliths of whiteness" but as "a fictive white skin." His "white things" permit me to focus on the material object as a constituent agent of these ideas, zeroing in on visual moments of social construction. Skin color is the easiest cue for racial stereotyping and those Parian sculptures that confuse the beholder's understanding of the visible differences between white skin and white marble-like forms. So where does this leave blackness? Is it a symbol of the non-white Parian racial other (Broome's *Bust of Cleopatra* and *Pair of Vases* are exemplary, but they are beyond the scope of this paper), black, mulatto, quadroon, or octoroon? Or is it an emblem of class struggle, color defining the greatest distance from wealth and privilege? As iconologist and art historian W.J.T. Mitchell argues, blackness and whiteness are not colors at all. Yet they designate the 19th century baseball color line, the veil between the races that W.E.B. DuBois announced in 1903 as the problem of the 20th century. *Base*

Ball Vase can symbolize a beautiful form fashioned into a prized objet d'art, personify the national body, or simply, the triumph of baseball as the National Pastime.[8]

Manly Beauty: An Aesthetic of Whiteness and Racial Formation

> Porcelain—the most seductive of all ceramics in its whiteness, translucency, smoothness and steely hardness since T'ang potters invented it in ancient China—proved as challenging to Americans as it was to Europeans from the 18th century on.[9]

Base Ball Vase, its subject matter in particular, is uniquely American. One may read the white sculpted object vertically, horizontally, or in the round. It comprises at least four distinct registers. From its circular pedestal rises a gradually tapering vase, a fluted column that doubles as baseball bat. The lowest register is encircled with baseballs, sculpted in low relief. The middle register—the narrowest portion of the vase (or bat handle), depending on one's point of view—is covered in low relief with a series of shelved bats held in place by a thick band or leather strap. Just above this register, also in low relief, is a series of figures engaged in batting, running and catching. Finally, the uppermost register is covered with a wreath of laurel leaves. Surmounting the smoothly rendered spheroid dome, half of a baseball, is an American eagle.

Batter, pitcher, and catcher: three hierarchic, sculpted in-the-round figures dominate the space around the vase. Lean and lanky, the wiry ballplayers are self-absorbed. Looking intently over his right shoulder and resting the weight of his body on the outward-stretched bent left leg, the left-handed batters' twisted upper torso leans aggressively inward. The catcher, hands clasping a ball, gazes into space. Leaning slightly forward, his squared shoulders balance the profiled head. The pitcher braces to hurl the ball: his upraised right hand and bent right leg bear the brunt of his body's next movement. These figures display a gritty naturalism. Snug-fitting baseball caps, curly hair bulging beneath, look soft and pliable: the bill of the batter's cap, for instance, twists skyward. The uniforms, their materiality, detail not only the folds and crinkling of the fabric, but the laced shoes as well. Knee breeches and stockings wrap around muscles, exposing tightly formed buttocks and leg muscles. Long-sleeve blouses,

Isaac Broome's Base Ball Vase, 1875–76

rolled up past the elbow, reveal strained muscles and bulging biceps. These cream-colored figures display manly vigor as they contest one another, at least in the mind's eye, with a physicality that transforms gesture into a well-understood baseball drama.

When Rita Reif reviewed "American Porcelain: 1770–1920," an exhibition held at the Metropolitan Museum of Art in 1989, the *New York Times* reporter probably had Broome's triumphant baseball vases in mind. She called them "show-stoppers."[10] For Reif, Isaac Broome had transcended his predecessors, both ancient and modern. Mesmerized by their "marble-like whiteness," she described the "all-white vessels" as "a tour de force of porcelain manufacturing."[11] The bat-shaped sculptures were analogous to ice-cream cones—each with an eagle instead of a cherry topping the scoop of vanilla. Alice Cooney Frelinghuysen, curator of the exhibition, believed differently. *Base Ball Vase* was flamboyant, if not gaudy; its form loosely classical, altered and overlaid with an explicit patriotic theme. The artist used the "art of carving" to create "dramatic shadows in the porcelain's chaste surface."[12] Still, Frelinghuysen attributes their "marble-like whiteness," their smooth surface and luster, to Broome's invention of "an improved porcelain or parian kiln," giving "equal distribution and perfect regulation of heat."[13]

Frelinghuysen's description of the medium, particularly the historical relation of Parian manufacture to aesthetic ideas, is illuminating: The word "Parian," which quickly became the medium's generic name, as coined by the Minton firm to suggest Paros, derives from the Greek isle that furnished much of the stone used in the classical Greek period. Parian was probably first made in the United States in the mid–1840s, at the Bennington factory, of Vermont, run by Christopher Webber Fenton and Julius Norton. Parian has a higher proportion of feldspar than conventional porcelain and, when fired, the increased amount of feldspar causes the finished body to be more highly vitrified; in short, it possesses a color verging on ivory and having a marble like texture that is smoother than that of biscuit (unglazed) porcelain. *Base Ball Vase* was formed by slip-casting—that is, by pouring liquefied clay into a plaster-of-paris mold that absorbed the water from the slip while retaining the fine details from Broome's sculpted forms. Some of the relief ornamentation and the three-dimensional figures would be molded and fired separately and then attached to the columnar vase. *Broome's Base Ball Vase*, like most Parian ware, was left in its natural, creamy white state.[14]

Art critics, past and present, have expressed fascination with porcelain's creamy whiteness. The postbellum Gilded Age art critic Jennie Young identified specimens from the New York and Trenton potteries as very pure and translucent, substantiating fully the right of the ware to the distinctive names of American porcelain, semi-china, and ivory porcelain. Regarding Broome's sculpted forms, Young observed: "The most noteworthy attempt to combine artistic work with the manufacture of white ware was made three years ago by Ott & Brewer the present Etruria Company."[15] Art critic F.E. Fryatt described *Base Ball Vase* as ivory porcelain, the same body produced in a dozen other Trenton factories. Fryatt pointed out that they "possess the dense, fine-grained, semi-vitreous biscuit, and exquisite glazes that make them equal in appearance and superior in durability to French and English china."[16]

Between 1871 and 1876, the Etruria Pottery Company produced both cream-colored earthenware and white graniteware. Why? For upper- and middle-class consumers, white things radiated refinement, order, discipline. But in doing so, they also radiated race. White aesthetic objects flooded antebellum households (tableware, bric-a-brac, statuary) and landscapes (buildings, gravestones), according to Heneghan, and they created essentially a conservative message: exploitation and miscegenation in slavery were ignorable; the wage slavery of emerging industrialism was justifiable; the stricter delineation of gender roles channeled greater power to disenfranchised women; and all of these were mitigated by the sanctified otherworldly sphere of the home. As the most expensive available, the whitest items—white paint, marble, porcelain, parian—distinguished the wealthy (On the other hand, archaeological digs from antebellum slave sites reveal that slaves were more often issued dark, undecorated and coarse earthenwares.) Ceramic manufacture, for instance, was paralleled by a movement towards even whiter dishes; pearl-ware eclipsed cream ware; cream-colored ware improved upon yellow ware; and white ware arrived between 1820 and 1830. This whitening process transformed tableware into specialized common sets; these sets increased in specialization, elaborateness, and number of vessels. "Things were the building blocks of antebellum culture," Heneghan states, "and white things helped to build the binary definitions that supported notions of class, gender, and race."[17]

The ties that bound Ott, Brewer and Broome extended beyond the search for national themes and the production of Parian wares. They capitalized on the production and consumption of decorative art pottery that had exclusive white masculine meanings. They embodied the currents of the time; they entered the Centennial exhibition well aware of baseball's growing importance. In 1876, one journalist wrote: "The Centennial year in base-ball is what the fraternity calls a red hot one." Impressed by Otto & Brewer's modeler, the art critic Charles Wyllys Elliott noted that Broome, Pygmalion-like, "made some base-ball players which are full of life and spirit." The words artistic and aesthetic penetrated the national pastime— the figure of the baseballist became a beautiful objet d'art, and yet endorsed as manly, the conspicuous detail of Broome's Parian sculptures constituting a feminine subtext that affected his contemporaries understanding of them. Fryatt viewed the baseballists occupying the circular pedestal at the foot of each vase stand as "three lithe, graceful figures, full of action, and embodying the American ideal of manly beauty." Jennie Young agreed, calling *Base Ball Vase* a thorough American ideal of physical beauty, embodying muscular ability rather than ponderous strength. Thus the Philadelphia Centennial Exposition of 1876 was the catalyst for the aesthetic movement, and *Base Ball Vase* embraced the country's vogue for the decorative arts.[18]

Broome's *Base Ball Vase* dovetails neatly with growing demand for American decorative art in general and Parian sculpture in particular. Aside from the busts and silhouettes of famous American statesmen, one English firm manufactured copies of Hiram Powers' *The Greek Slave* (1844). Hiram's marble sculpture portrays a Greek girl captured by the Turks and put up for sale in a Middle Eastern slave market. One of the country's most popular antebellum statues, *The Greek Slave*, was produced in vast numbers. The Parian medium brought miniature copies of the work into the parlors of America's expanding middle-class. As the literary writer Henry James quipped, "so undressed, yet so refined, in sugar-white alabaster, exposed under little glass covers in such American homes as could bring themselves to think such things right." Such objects, writes Heneghan "worked to make race—and slavery—into a condition of color that seemed natural but not personal: white things, their ownership and proper management, constituted racial whiteness, and skin became simply another thing."[19]

Art historian Susanne Ebbinghaus has shown that traditional histories of marble statues are wrong: the ancient Greeks painted marble statuary. The ideal of unpainted sculpture took shape in Renaissance Rome, inspired by the finds of early collections of marble statues, such as discovered by the Laocoon Group in 1506. These sculptural artifacts were denuded of their painted surfaces by prolonged exposure to the elements, burying conditions, and a good scrub upon recovery. "With the works of Michelangelo," adds Ebbinghaus "white marble sculpture was established as the noblest of arts. It was greatly admired in the neoclassical period of the eighteenth and nineteenth centuries, when ancient Greek sculpture was regarded as the ultimate expression of 'noble simplicity and quiet grandeur,' to use the famous phrase for the German art historian Johann Joachim Winckelmann." Hiram Powers, William Wetmore Story and Edmonia Lewis—19th century American sculptors—rejected pigment as dangerous and sensual, argues art historian Charmaine A. Nelson, adhering to white marble and abandoning the racialization of the black body by skin color. Isaac Broome would have been familiar with the work of these famed sculptors, including Lewis, who was a black woman.[20]

One art critic cared little for Broome's elongated, elastic-looking ballplayers. Elliott felt that they didn't resemble the neoclassical forms of his contemporaries. For Elliott, "We cannot admire even what was considered to be the best among the American work exhibited. This was a gang of baseball players. No fault was to be found with the material, but the modeling was all pulled out, attenuated, and sure wire drawn human figures were impossible."[21]

What is the source for Broome's "sure wire drawn" ballplayers? I want to suggest that Broome found inspiration in the work of the contemporary artist David Gilmour Blythe (1815–1865). They shared artistic and ideological views. Blythe and Broome came out of an artisan tradition. Both enjoyed artistic freedom and maintained their independence. They may have thought themselves as outsiders, artists determined to maintain control over their labor. In Pittsburgh, Broome met and became friends with Blythe who had schooled himself in popular comic art and political caricature; Blythe also appropriated images from past and present prints, illustrations, and cartoons. His elongated and twisted human forms—staged in realistic, urban scenes—captivated audiences. He displayed his works in the window of a print dealer, his friend John Jones Gillespie. His exhibits at Gillespie's Gallery included a double portrait of Broome and himself standing before the firm's doorway. Both Blythe and Broome spent many hours at Gillespie's.[22]

Broome was not the only baseball enthusiast familiar with America's art colony in Italy. John McNamee, former New York City alderman and Sheriff, pursued an art career as sculptor in marble. After visiting various art centers in Europe, he settled in Florence and remained there for the rest of his life. McNamee, a stonecutter by trade, was also a baseball enthusiast: in 1873, the first idea to engage his attention was the modeling of a baseball player in the act of receiving a badly delivered ball. According to a critic who saw the completed clay figure: "The subject of *The First Base* is poised upon the left foot with the right touching the base, and the body bent forward with every muscle strong to the utmost tension in anticipation of the coming ball." Another critic called it amateurish, but strong and manly. In 1878, McNamee modeled another version. It represented "Mr. McNamee's more mature thought and conscientious study." While the stonecutter-turned-sculptor had planned to transform the baseball figure into a high art object, *The First Base* was never attempted in marble.[23]

If *Base Ball Vase* figured among high art objects, other baseball trophies took on more popular forms in the 1870s. Baseball patrons (silver and goldsmiths) created awards and trophies. Baseball tournaments expanded middle-class forms of desire by transforming trophies into things; conspicuous and sumptuous things that acquired more than one name, more than one identity. They were worn and/or displayed. In 1867, the Detroit baseball tournament honored players with gold and silver things, blue and red silk field flags, wine sets, and greenbacks. Of course, these cultural practices were hardly uncommon. Yet the emerging reverence for gold and the decline in the prestige and, ultimately, the acceptance of silver bears contemplation: silver ice pitchers, silver mounted balls, silver mounted opera glasses, silver tea-sets, silver tobacco boxes, silver star badges competed for acceptance with gold-mounted rosewood bats, regulation-size gold balls, gold badges of baseball design, and gold-mounted opera glasses. *Base Ball Vase* would make Broome the finest of all American artists in the Parian porcelain medium.[24]

Trenton Potters and Baseballists

Why did John Hart Brewer, of the Etruria Pottery Company, hire Isaac Broome? English competition is one answer. Between the 1850s and 1870s, the domestic pottery business was marked with the stigma of inferiority. It was generally held that imported goods, English in particular, were inherently better, whatever their quality. According to labor historian Marc J. Stern, competition from English goods forced Trenton's potters to acknowledge the poor quality of their wares by 1876 and to improve product lines. Even so, both English and American firms produced Parian ware which was less expensive than bronze and more durable than plaster. The Minton and Company of England, as stated, made copies of works of art by American artists, reproducing smaller versions of Hiram Powers' *Greek Slave* (1848). The Centennial encouraged the passion for accumulation and ornament by exposing nearly ten million people who toured the fair to an astonishing array of new technologies and consumer products. For Ott & Brewer, Broome's designs and sculptural forms would emphasize American themes: political luminaries (George Washington, Benjamin Franklin, Abraham Lincoln, Rutherford B. Hayes, and Robert Fulton), newsboys, and baseball players figured prominently. The passion for pottery and porcelain touched the lives of men and women, rich and poor, city dwellers and rural folk. The display of decorated objects in an office, firehouse, clubhouse, restaurant, barbershop or private home helped to define social status.[25]

Another answer is Broome's extensive experience. Trenton pottery production was well-established, with English-born and local entrepreneurs, often in partnerships, employing thousands of workers. Etruria Pottery relied on foreign-born laborers to re-create England's production system. William Bloor, a talented English pottery operative, remained especially crucial to pottery-making's highly divided, skill-intensive trade. Broome's employment "was an unusual undertaking as the models for pottery and porcelain were usually created by unnamed artisan modelers who never signed their work."[26] Broome's talent and technical skill embodied the desire of Ott and Brewer to produce eminent American porcelain objects.

Many cultures—ancient and modern—trace their mythological origins to image-making. In the Judeo-Christian tradition, God fashions the first man from a lump of clay, and the result was a kind of defiant self-portrait, since God took himself as model and formed Adam (or Adam and Eve together) in his image. Art historian W.J. T. Mitchell explains:

> Man is both the sculpted object and the sculpting agent, both created as and creator of sculpted images. God introduces man and other creatures into the world by means of the art of sculpture. Then man brings sculpture (and gods) into the world by creating material images of himself and other creatures. The dangerous moment, of course, is always the moment of animation, when the sculpted object takes on "a life of its own."[27]

Trenton potters belonged to an exclusive brotherhood. The owners were master potters, part of an Anglo-American network, who both worked in and managed their own shops. Prior to 1880 almost all pottery workers in Trenton were white, Christian, and of Western European origin or descent. From the beginning Englishmen and their sons controlled skilled work. Irish workers initially held less-skilled, and more physically-taxing and dangerous jobs. They remained subject to the oversight of foremen, mostly English-born. Self-motivated work, the discipline of pottery workers, and the ability to earn a living from it were so central to masculine

Isaac Broome's Base Ball Vase, 1875–76

class mobility that they were, at times, regulated against by their employers. New Jersey potters pursued a visible, regulated, self-motivated wage labor that distinguished not only the male worker, but also the white worker. Prior to 1860, women and girls formed only a small portion of Trenton's pottery labor force; however, the growth in decoration spurred the rise of the industry. Interestingly, one visitor to Broome's studio observed his three daughters working, who were surprisingly "artists of fine ability." According to Stern, Trenton potteries excluded blacks from the trade: an 1890 census reported only six black workers.[28]

Trenton claymen formed ethnic lodges, fraternal orders, social clubs, and baseball clubs. The city's first recorded ball game occurred, July 4, 1867, between the Trenton Atlantics and the Philadelphia Athletics. (The visitors won, 66 to 8. Apparently, the ball club improved. In 1871, the Trentons won fifty-one out of fifty-four games.) Baseball enjoyed a strong working-class following in the Trenton potteries. Between the 1860s and 1870s, pottery workers formed ball clubs. The Pottery League was comprised of many good teams. Given the fact that Broome's son, Roebling Ericson Broome, modeled for *Base Ball Vase*, I suspect that he played for one of the ball clubs. Casual competition evolved into a formal organization that was subjected to close discipline: Cook, Equitable, Delaware, Greenville, Enterprise and Ott & Brewer's potteries had teams. John Hart Brewer, a baseballist, captained his firm's nine. Only bona-fide workmen of the respective establishments played. No salaries were paid but a division of gate receipts brought pocket money to the players. Initially, games occurred only on Saturdays when firms shut down at 4 p.m.; later, three games a week were played.[29]

Broome's role as art director for Etruria Pottery became frustrating. He complained that the firm wasted resources on expensive experiments, and that American potters were not particularly creative. Broome criticized "American potters for their poor taste, lack of foresight, and other crimes against common sense and industrial art."[30] The company blamed the inferior performance of potters on exorbitant wages and material costs. In 1877, he left Ott and Brewer and took charge of Trenton's newly established design school.

Broome's human and animal forms embrace an ancient, intractable, and conservative medium, yet they remained capable of being refashioned, altered and sculpted. According to Mitchell, "Sculpture especially that modeled on the human body, is not only the first but also the most dangerous of the arts. It impiously elevates the human image to the status of god, reifies mortal men into immortal idols, and degrades spirit into dead matter. Sometimes it seems as if sculpture achieves its truest vocation not when it is erected but when it is pulled down."[31]

Birds (Not) of a Feather: The Personification of the National Pastime

Base Ball Vase commemorates the nation's centennial anniversary. I imagine the cream-colored trophy as a primordial habitat that gives birth to our National Game and national symbol, the North American Eagle. The bottom register portrays a leather-bound rack of baseball bats that mimics a marshy thicket of reeds. There is a quiet, though vigilant feel to this eagle perched high above the action on the ground. Its summit is half a baseball, rendered naturalistically, down to the stitching, and defined in low relief. It watches over the men, as if they were eaglets. It displays massive thighs and sharp talons; the ballplayer's sinewy bodies—taunt and muscled—mimic the eagle's physical characteristics. If its wings convey serenity and calm, the gesturing arms and legs of the players mimic the predatory nature of flight and aggression. *Base Ball Vase* embodies the nation's sense of conspicuous wealth, refinement, self-mastery, and whiteness.

Base Ball Vase helps to imagine how the centrality of animals is deeply linked with motives of domination. As Mitchell argues, animals stand for all forms of social otherness: race, class, and gender are frequently figured in images of subhuman brutishness, bestial appetite, and mechanical servility. Literary critic John Berger adds: "If the first metaphor was animal, it was because the essential relation between man and animal was metaphoric. Within that relation what the two terms—man and animal—shared in common revealed what differentiated them. And vice versa." Historically, baseball representations have embraced animals both as team icons and emblems of male virility. Animal and human thus converged on the baseball landscape, a sports medium in which the dialectics of stereotype and individual found metaphoric expression. But how did the metaphor of the North American Eagle function? At a minimum, the eagle represented the dominion of humanity over nature, figured in animal-versus-human; at a maximum, the eagle embodied the dominion of one nation/race/gender over another, expressed by the figure "man-as-animal."[32]

Birds possess an almost magical relation with human beings. As the historian Philip M. Isaacson explains, the eagle was the first flexible U.S.

emblem to be officially sanctioned (the earliest symbol was a woman). Its formal origins are European, though motifs derived from diverse ancient and modern sources, tempered by strong North American vernacular attitudes. Its evolution reveals naturalistic and emblematic forms. The scrawny emblematic figure has its wings spread outward; the naturalistic incorporates a "dropped-wing bird."[33]

The eagle was not a conventional American icon prior to the revolution. In adopting it, the Continental Congress reached into older, ancient traditions: Sumerian and Egyptian. Let us take, for example, the Great Seal of the United States. The United States, following the tradition of English ancestors, decided to create a great seal for the new nation, and thus incorporated into is design elements of masonry, numerology and ancient Egyptian symbolism. Between 1776 and 1782, committee representation consisting of Benjamin Franklin, Thomas Jefferson, John Adams, Pierre Du Simitiere (a French consultant), and William Barton (chief artistic consultant), incorporated design elements for a two-sided seal that included visual images and language. The obverse depicted the American eagle, with an escutcheon, or shield, on its breast. It holds an olive branch of 13 leaves and 13 olives in its right talon, and 13 arrows in its left. It faces the olive branch to symbolize a desire for peace, but it is always prepared for war. In its beak is a scroll inscribed *E pluribus unum*, which translates as One (nation) out of *many* (states).[34]

Broome's eagle begins as a "drooping-wing bird." Isaacson calls the form a descendant of the German eagle, one sculpted by many Pennsylvania-German artists. This Teutonic statuary is supported (or perches on) a half-ball. The German eagle is also called a lectern eagle because it is often frontally disposed and supported by great wooden orbs. Ordered feathering is another chief characteristic: "[It shows a] Gothic passion for systematic order and a rigidly controlled scheme of feathers. They are fashioned in precise layers, each one painstakingly articulated...." During his years in Pennsylvania, Broome became familiar with this distinct form. *Base Ball Vase* provides a double revelation and reassurance—that human representations are true, accurate, and natural (Broome's eagle agrees and comprehends them on its own accord), and that human power over others is secured by mastery of representations (Broome's eagle is forced to agree, not of its own accord, but automatically).[35]

The man-as-animal scenario associated with *Base Ball Vase* is directed at the work itself as much as the beholder. The *Harper's Weekly* illustrator Frank Bellow engaged in this mode of pictorial expression in which man-as-animal images mapped the terrain of white male anxiety and fear. Bellow parodied Allan Poe's poem "The Raven," transforming emancipation and blacks into a man-bird hybrid. Neither animal nor human, this monstrosity embodies and projects hatred, guilt and fear. Bellow's black bird was antithetical to the American eagle: the former embodied enslavement; the latter, freedom. Politically, Poe had identified with the southern plantation aristocracy. Enslaved blacks were subhuman, he thought, too degraded and brutal to be entrusted with freedom. According to art historian Sarah Burns: "He shared in its paternalistic justification of slavery and condemned abolitionists as rabid and dangerous fanatics." Burns uses the phrase "gothic art of haunting" to frame "a constellation of themes and moods: horror, fear mystery, strangeness, fantasy, perversion, monstrosity, insanity."[36]

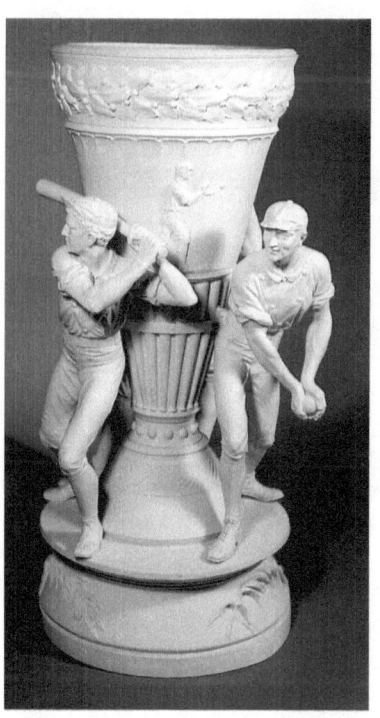

As Mitchell has elaborated, animals are figures in scenes of visual exchange. Bellow's *The Bird of Freedom and the Black Bird* (1863) depicts the American Bald Eagle and the black man-bird hybrid greeting one another, following President Abraham Lincoln's signing of the Emancipation Proclamation. Congratulating the "black bird," the eagle says: "A happy new year to you." Both figures extend clawed feet, mimicking a handshake. Both figures have dropped wings. Bellow employed the "Gothic passion for systematic order." Bird feathers are given the impression that the cartoonist carefully articulated them. Similarities end here: the eagle is clearly taller, his talons are thick and muscular, and despite the relative shading, which gives the eagle form, it is relatively white. On the other hand, the hybrid figure has a human head and bird torso. It possesses curly hair, a flattened nose, and thick, beefsteak lips. Both funny and frightening,

Artist Isaac Broome. *Base Ball Vase.* Parian (marble imitation). 1876. Detroit Institute of Arts. This detail focuses on the model, Broome's son, who worked (along with his three daughters) at his Etruria Pottery studio in Trenton, New Jersey.

the black bird resonates as a minstrel image. The black bird's spindly legs and pathetically-thin claws, it seems, might be crushed under the weight of the eagle's "handshake."

Bellow's pastoral scenario, a barnyard, contains other birds: directly between the central figures is a bird weathervane, the figure's beak wide-open as if singing; to the far right, another bird, with outstretched wings, head skywards, celebrates the scene as well. The habitat, dominated by barnyard fowl, is innocent enough. Another Bellow cartoon, however, depicts a newly-emancipated black standing proudly before an astonished array of barnyard animals and snobbishly declaring his freedom: "Ugh! Get out. I ain't one 'ob you no more. *I'se a Man, I is*. The message is clear: "cutting his old associates," he is no longer chattel.

The sporting press circulated racialized animal epithets of black base-ballists. When the St. Louis Black Stockings made their first professional tour in 1883, the *National Police Gazette* called them "mokes," a term applied to broken-down horses or jackasses. Following their victory over the Cleveland Blue Stockings, another black aggregation, the sportswriter dubbed the Black Stockings, "the champion coon club of the west." After the St. Louis Grand Avenues, a white club, defeated them, the reporter wrote that the "St. Louis Blackbirds" were polished up to the Queen's taste.[37]

Professional baseball and the political struggle for black civil rights emerged almost simultaneously in the 1860s, when they developed into powerful agents of social action and expression. Critics of the Fifteenth Amendment complained that the combination of sports and civil rights had transformed the American citizen of African descent into a creature of legislative enactment. They argued that organized baseball and the green diamond belonged to the domain of white men. For a number of reasons, sportswriters represented the black baseballist with contempt. By playing the national pastime, black players stepped outside their class position by indulging in leisure activities reserved for white men. Additionally, on pseudo-scientific anatomical grounds, their tender shins couldn't withstand the red hot grounders. Sports journalists dubbed political appendages of the National Pastime: "amendments" or 15th amendment-club slingers. Of course, these fallacies didn't hold water.[38]

The representation of the black man as blackbird, an anti-national symbol—given Bellow's imagery—penetrated representations of the Philadelphia Centennial Exposition of 1876. An ominous cartoon depicts an enormous blackbird sitting atop an equally enormous egg: the white egg has hatched, and from its cracked shell emerges an eaglet. It is ominous because of what it portends. Practically rendered in silhouette, the blackbird, in this instance not a man-bird hybrid, casts a large shadow against the amorphous white background. Across the egg's cracked surface is the word "centennial." Has the blackbird protected and kept the egg warm for the past two hundred years? Or is it a predator, simply waiting to attack its prey? Striding forward, the eaglet smugly—note the furrowed brow and twisted smile—declares: "I've had a deal of trouble, but this repays me for it." This cartoon offers an intriguing counter response to Broome's *Base Ball Vase*.

Like *Base Ball Vase*, the egg as a "white thing" embodies conspicuous consumption and sumptuary display, aptly characterized in terms of refinement and excessiveness: the gargantuan egg as a beautiful form has been fashioned into a prized objet d'art, two hundred years of nation formation personified in the pint-sized, but dandified bird. The well-dressed eaglet,

Artist Frank Bellow. *The Bird of Freedom and the Black Bird*. Illustration. *Harper's Weekly*. January, 1863. Bellow's black bird, which prefigures *Base Ball Vase*, was the antithesis of the American eagle: the former embodied enslavement; the latter, freedom.

statesman-like in appearance, confidently sports a white high-collared and ruffled blouse, black swallow-tail jacket, white pants, and black boots. Combining black and white tonalities and angular forms, the artist depiction of the eaglet's jacket mimics bird wings. While this cartoon may be incidentally a statement on white racial mastery, it is impossible not to see it as a veiled expression of racial fear and personal despair.[39]

What did the baseball sporting fraternity think of the Centennial? How did they rate Broome's *Base Ball Vase*? The *Chicago Tribune* offers one answer. Its Centennial reporter writes: "A statue of a base-ball player sculpt for the Centennial Exhibition was rejected. It had four straight fingers, and a sound thumb on each hand, and its nose wasn't bent a particle, and no court-plaster on the ears. Wonder the fraud was admitted." This amusing account was, it seems, a response to the Parian sculpture. After all, given the physical demands of the game—"red hot grounders," bruised ears, broken noses, and gnarled hands—no player resembled those that Broome submitted for the American public's approval. The joke, such as it was, hinged on the idea that *Base Ball Vase* was too beautiful. Baseball, a violently tough and manly sport was not something for display in Victorian parlors, the domain of upper- and middle-class women.[40]

Ott & Brewer's mass production of Broome's baseball sculptures seemly counters this argument. When the Etruria Pottery Company put Parian objects on a display at the American Institute Fair at New York City in 1877, their exhibit included two interesting baseball figurines. They depict American youth playing an American sport. These Parians show young white males, dressed not in uniforms, but in everyday attire. One portrays a pitcher and, the other, a batter. Both boys have their pant legs rolled to the knees. The pitcher wears a bowler hat; the batter sports a floppy hat. While these Parians helped to transform the national game into a democratic form, and helped to naturalize baseball as a refined subject matter that might appeal to the aesthetic tastes of upper- and middle-class consumers, they also expanded the market for creamy-white objects with national themes deemed virtuous enough to decorate the American home.

"In Broome's realization of John Hart Brewer's imaginative concept," writes Frelinghuysen, "he utilized subject matter that despite the contemporary and immensely popular theme, incorporated several elements of classical derivation." Unfortunately, the American ceramic objects shown at the Centennial did not attract the attention that pottery makers had hoped for, nor did they receive particularly favorable reviews in the newspapers and periodicals of the day. No evidence exists for how many baseball

"I'VE HAD A DEAL OF TROUBLE, BUT THIS REPAYS ME FOR IT!"

Artist Frank Bellow. *I've Had a Deal of Trouble, But This Repays Me for It*. Illustration. *Harper's Weekly*, July 1876. Bellow's youthful eaglet embodies Gilded Age conspicuous consumption and sumptuary display, at the expense of the laboring black bird.

objects of Parian were produced or sold by the Etruria Pottery Company. Broome's figures are described in a company broadside as "taken from life or the best photographs to be obtained." This broadside includes five singular baseball figures, those of the *Base Ball Vase* and the young baseballists.[41]

I want to conclude with a meditation that offers a comparative study of imagery in ancient and modern settings. When the Israelites asked Aaron to make them a golden calf, they provided him with gold jewelry, the most valuable materials they possessed. When Moses discovers the abomination, he demanded that Aaron explain the making of the idol. Aaron's brother says that he merely threw the Israelites' gold jewelry into the fire "and the calf came out," as if it were a self-created automaton. The idea that images have a kind of social or psychological power of their own is, writes Mitchell, "the reigning cliché of contemporary visual culture." Not unlike the Israelites and Aaron who created a calf to "'go before them' as a leader, predecessor, and ancestor that has begotten them as a people," Ott & Brewer and Broome offered *Base Ball Vase* as a self-consciously produced object

Isaac Broome's Base Ball Vase, 1875–76

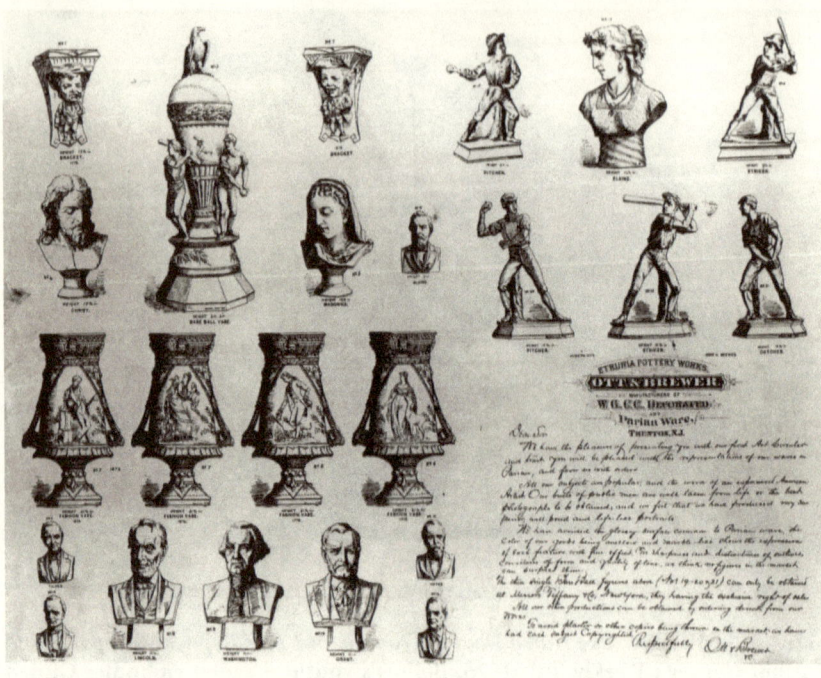

Base Ball 10

of national origins: the American Bald Eagle as American totemic symbol. In *Base Ball Vase*, race and gender mark the boundary between the faithful and the pagans, the chosen people and the gentiles. It is the worship given to the statue's white racial masculinity, not the making of the parian sculpture, at least in my reading, that seems to be an abomination. (God instructs Moses to destroy the idol and to kill all his brethren who have been involved in this most hateful offense: the creation of an image that is offensive to God. The modern equivalent is the destruction of Saddam Hussein's bronze statue by the Iraqi people.) "Image-making, like thinking for yourself" Mitchell portends, "is a dangerously god-like activity."[42]

NOTES

1. "The Centennial Awards," *New York Times*, September 28, 1876; Edwin Atlee Barber, *The Pottery Porcelain of the United States* (New York: G.P. Putnam's Sons, 1893), 220–224; Ellen Paul Denker, "Parian Porcelain Statuary: American Sculptors and the Introduction of Art in American Ceramics," *Ceramics in America 2002*, edited by Robert Hunter (Milwaukee, WI: Chipstone, 2002), 62–79.
2. Susan James-Gadzinski and Mary Mullen Cunningham, *American Sculpture in the Museum of American Art of the Pennsylvania Academy of the Fine Arts* (Seattle and London: University of Washington Press, 1997), 82.
3. James Mitchell, "Ott & Brewer: Etruria in America," *Winterthur Portfolio* 7. 1972, 217–228.
4. Thorstein Veblen, *The Theory of the Leisure Class* (Oxford: Oxford University Press, 2009), 51–52.
5. Regina Lee Blaszczyk, "The Aesthetic Movement: China Decorators, Consumer Demand, and Technological Change in the American Pottery Industry, 1865–1900," *Winterthur Portfolio*, 29 (2/3), 1994, 122.
6. Michel Foucault, *The Archaeology of Knowledge and the Discourse of Language* (New York: Pantheon Books, 1972), 215–37; Martin Berger, *Man Made: Thomas Eakins and the Construction of Gilded Age Manhood* (Berkeley: University of California Press, 2000), 1–5; Elizabeth Johns, *Thomas Eakins: The Hero of Modern Life* (Princeton, N.J.: Princeton University Press, 1983), 24.
7. Allen Guttman, *The Erotic in Sports* (New York: Columbia University Press, 1996), 64; Bridget T. Heneghan, *Whitewashing America; Material Culture and Race in the Antebellum Imagination* (Jackson: University Press of Mississippi Press, 2003), xx–xxi.
8. Alice Cooney Frelinghuysen, *American Porcelain: 1770–1920* (New York: The Metropolitan Museum of Art, 1989), 170–73.
9. Blaszczyk, "The Aesthetic Movement," *Winterthur Portfolio*, 122.

Opposite, above: Artist Isaac Broome. *Art Objects.* Parian (marble imitation). 1877. Alice Cooney Frelinghuysen. *American Porcelain: 1770–1920.* New York: The Metropolitan Museum of Art, 1989. When the Etruria Pottery Company put Parian objects on a display at the American Institute Fair at New York City in 1877, the exhibit included two baseball figurines. They depict two young white males, dressed not in uniforms, but in everyday attire.

Opposite, bottom: Artist Isaac Broome. *Art Objects.* Catalogue Broadside. 1876. Alice Cooney Frelinghuysen. *American Porcelain: 1770–1920.* New York: The Metropolitan Museum of Art, 1989. Broome's figures are described in a company broadside as "taken from life or the best photographs to be obtained." This broadside includes five singular baseball figures, those of the *Base Ball Vase* and young baseballists.

Isaac Broome's Base Ball Vase, 1875-76

10. Rita Reif, "Antiques: Here's the Pitch, Made of Porcelain," *New York Times*, April 9, 1989.
11. Reif, "Antiques: Here's the Pitch, Made of Porcelain," *New York Times*, April 9, 1989.
12. Frelinghuysen, *American Porcelain: 1770-1920*, 3.
13. *Ibid.*, 67.
14. *Ibid.*, 29.
15. Jennie J. Young, "The Ceramic Art in America," *The Atlantic Monthly*, 44 (265), November 1879, 595.
16. Young, "The Ceramic Art in America," *The Atlantic Monthly*, 595; F.E. Fryatt. "Pottery in the United States," *Harper's New Monthly Magazine*, 62 (369) February 1881, 366-67.
17. Heneghan, *Whitewashing America*, ix-xv, 7-11.
18. "Ball and Bat," *Brooklyn Daily Eagle*, June 14, 1876; Charles Wyllys Elliott, "Pottery at the Centennial," *The Atlantic Monthly*, 38 (229), Nov. 1876, 577; Fryatt, "Pottery in the United States," *Harper's New Monthly Magazine*, 366; Jennie J. Young, *The Ceramic Art* (New York: Harper & Brothers, 1878); Berger, *Man Made*, 41.
19. "Hiram Powers," *Brooklyn Daily Eagle*, July 23, 1873; Oliver Larkin, *Art and Life in America* (New York: Holt, Rinehart and Winston, 1960), 180-181; Heneghan, *Whitewashing America*, 7-11; Frelinghuysen, *American Porcelain: 1770-1920*, 29.
20. Susanne Ebbinghaus, *Gods in Color: Painted Sculpture of Classical Antiquity*. Arthur M. Sackler Museum, September 22, 2007-January 20, 2008; Charmaine Nelson, "Hiram Powers's America: Shackles, Slaves, and the Racial Limits of Nineteenth-Century Identity," *Canadian Review of American Studies* 34 (2), 2004, 167-183.
21. Charles Wyllys Elliott, *Pottery and Porcelain from the Earliest Times Down to the Philadelphia Exhibition of 1876* (New York: D. Appleton & Co., 1878).
22. Sarah Burns, *Painting The Dark Side: Art and the Gothic Imagination in Nineteenth Century America* (Berkeley: University of California Press, 2004), 46; Rina C. Younger, *Industry in Art: Pittsburgh, 1812 to 1920* (Pittsburgh: University of Pittsburgh Press, 2006).
23. "Fine Arts: John McNamee—First Base," *Brooklyn Daily Eagle*, March 6, 1873; "Sculpture: John McNamee and His Works," *Brooklyn Daily Eagle*, January 6, 1878; "Obituary Record—John McNamee," *New York Times*, August 22, 1895.
24. "Base Ball: Contest for the Silver Ball," *Brooklyn Daily Eagle*, October 22, 1861; "Close of the Detroit Tournament," *Chicago Times*, August 21, 1867; "The Base Ball Tournament," *Chicago Inter-Ocean*, August 15, 1874; "Base Ball," *St. Louis Republican*, April 25, 1876; "Saratoga Notes," *New York Globe*, August 11, 1883.
25. "Trenton Potters," *New York Times*, March 29, 1873; "Plaster Casts; The Image Vender and His Wares," *New York Times*, April 5, 1874; Heneghan, *Whitewashing America*, 29-34; Mitchell, "Ott & Brewer: Etruria in America," *Winterthur Portfolio*, 221; Blaszkyk, "The Aesthetic Movement," *Winterthur Portfolio*, 126; Stern, *The Pottery Industry of Trenton*, 24.
26. Mitchell, "Ott & Brewer: Etruria in America," *Winterthur Portfolio*, 221.
27. W.J.T. Mitchell, *What Do Pictures Want?* (Chicago: University of Chicago Press, 2005), 245-6.
28. Heneghan, *Whitewashing America*, 48; Marc J. Stern, *The Pottery Industry of Trenton* (New Brunswick, New Jersey: Rutgers University Press, 1994); Frelinghuysen, *American Porcelain: 1770-1920*, 35.
29. "Base-Ball," *New York Times*, November 2, 1870; "Base-Ball; The New Jersey Base Ball Convention," *New York Times*, November 10, 1870; "Base-Ball," *New York Times*, June 17, 1871; "Sports and Pastimes," *Brooklyn Daily Eagle*, Aug. 17, 1871; "Base Ball," *Brooklyn Daily Eagle*, June 22, 1875; "Rutgers College," *New York Times*, June 23, 1875; By Mail and Telegraph," *The Times*, July 2, 1875; "Base-Ball," *New York Times*, August 8, 1875; "Notes," *Brooklyn Daily Eagle*, May 19, 1873; "Twenty-Four to Five," *Trenton (NJ) True American*, May 21, 1886; "Ball Playing Extraordinary," *Trenton True American*, June 17, 1886.
30. Regina Lee Blaszcyzk, *Imagining Consumers: Design and Innovation from Wedgwood to Corning* (Baltimore: Johns Hopkins University Press, 2002), 80.
31. Mitchell, *What Do Pictures Want?*, 248-250.
32. *John Berger, Selected Essays*, edited by Geoff Dyer (New York: Pantheon Books, 2001), 59-273; W.J.T. Mitchell, *Picture Theory* (Chicago: University of Chicago Press, 1994), 333-335.
33. Philip M. Isaacson, *The American Eagle* (Boston: New York Graphic Society, 1975), 1-10.
34. Isaacson, *The American Eagle*, 107-110.

35. *Ibid.*, 108–131.
36. Burns, *Painting the Dark Side*, xix, 111–113.
37. "The National Game," *National Police Gazette*, May 12, 1883; "The National Game," *National Police Gazette*, June 2, 1883; "The National Game," *National Police Gazette*, June 9, 1883.
38. "The Sporting World," *Chicago Tribune*, August 24, 1870; "The Green Diamond," *St. Louis Globe-Democrat*, July 10, 1876. The exact dates demarcating Reconstruction are not universally agreed upon. The American historian Eric Foner frames the period between 1863 and 1877. This period begins with the Emancipation Proclamation and ends with southern "Redemption" and "home rule," the equivalent to white rule. Other historians point to 1883 as the end of Reconstruction, the year that the United States Supreme Court declared the Civil Rights Act of 1875 unconstitutional.
39. Burns, *Painting the Dark Side*, 118.
40. "Base Hits," *Chicago Tribune*, May 14, 1876.
41. Frelinghuysen, *American Porcelain: 1770–1920*, 35, 42–3; 166.
42. Mitchell, *What Do Pictures Want?*, 31–2, 246.

Never on a Sunday

Baseball's Battles with the Blue Laws in Rochester

ALAN COHEN

Baseball on Sunday was illegal in many states during the late 19th and early 20th centuries. New York statutes barring Sunday baseball were often challenged and proponents and opponents of Sunday baseball waged their wars in many locations, one of which was Rochester, New York. There team ownership scheduled Sunday games in the small community of Irondequoit to escape enforcement of the law by Rochester authorities. Moves to legalize Sunday play in the summers of 1890 (American Association) and 1897 (Eastern League) met with resistance from local religious authorities. The period from April through July in 1897 was especially replete with ballplaying, interrupted games, arrests, legal maneuvering, lawsuits, and trials dominating the headlines, culminating in the Rochester Brownies moving to Montreal in July 1897. Not until 1919 would there be legal Sunday baseball in New York.

IN THE NINETEENTH CENTURY municipalities throughout the country were uncomfortable with baseball being played on what was, to most Americans, the Sabbath, a day set aside for rest and worship. Laws restricted play on Sundays in both the major and minor leagues. The goal of this article is to show how legislation, clergy, organized baseball, and other interests during a national debate on the issue clashed head on in one city, Rochester, New York, over restrictions on Sunday play, and how they addressed these issues.

The National League totally banned baseball on Sundays when it was formed in 1876. It did not back off this position until 1892, when it became the only major league after the demise of the American Association. On December 17, 1891, National League owners met in Indianapolis after the Association's demise to agree upon basic principles for the constitution of a 12-team National League that included four former American Association clubs. Regarding Sunday play, they announced that "the league will not openly declare in favor of Sunday games, no such games being on the schedule, but it will connive (secretly allow) at Sunday base-ball by permitting those towns which desire to play Sunday games to do so and count the same (as) championship contests."[1] Of the former American Association clubs now playing in the NL, Louisville, St. Louis, Baltimore and Washington, Sunday baseball was allowed in Louisville and St. Louis during their American Association years. While in the American Association, Baltimore did not play Sunday baseball at home, but did play Sunday baseball on the road. Washington was only in the American Association in 1884 and 1891 (having spent 1886–89 in the National League). Washington like Baltimore, did not play Sunday baseball at home, and did so on the road only when it belonged to the American Association. Sunday baseball in the National League was thus played in Cincinnati, St. Louis and Louisville in 1892. Cincinnati had left the National League after the 1880 season over the subject of Sunday baseball, and in 1882 was one of the founding teams in the American Association. They migrated back to the National League in 1890.

Early in 1893, National League President Nick Young reiterated the league's ruling on the issue of Sabbath play, stating, "Playing baseball on Sunday must be regulated by the communities in which the clubs composing our organization have their existence, but I do not think that the people of the east will ever look with favor upon such a proposition."[2] But even with the National League's allowance for Sunday baseball, not all cities elected to permit it. Chicago did so in 1893, but seven cities (eight teams) continued not to have Sunday baseball. At this time, only Baltimore, Washington, and Cleveland played Sunday games on the road.[3]

Clashes between clergy and baseball over the issue of Sunday play also occurred outside the major cities. One of the bitterest confrontations took place in the Rochester, New York, in 1890. That season, there were three major leagues—the advent of the Players League resulted in defections of some American Association teams and Rochester joined the American Association. During the season Rochester's Sunday American Association games were played at Windsor Beach in the Town of Irondequoit, outside the Rochester city limits, locations less likely to stir opposition than if the

Baseball's Battles with the Blue Laws in Rochester

club had played Sunday games at Culver Field, its home park in Rochester. But that did not stop the authorities from interfering. On July 20, 1890, a game was interrupted after the second inning when the Irondequoit Town Justice of the Peace and twelve members of the Law and Order League of the Town of Irondequoit sought to have the players arrested for playing baseball on Sunday in violation of New York State law. A ruckus ensued and blows were exchanged among the fans. Justice Coy did not have a warrant and he departed when assured that the parties would appear before him at the office of W. Martin Jones the next morning.[4] Immediately after the game, club officials pragmatically arranged to have players from Rochester and Columbus indicted and brought before a different judge, Justice Baird, who was more sympathetic to Sunday baseball. Baird released the players. They promised to appear before Justice Baird at a later date, effectively pre-empting the efforts of Justice Coy and his associates.[5]

Rochester's stay at the major-league level ended after the 1890 season, but the travails over Sunday baseball consumed that city again in 1897 when the city was in the Eastern League, and the team was known as the Rochester Brownies.

It was not uncommon to see legislation (widely known as the Sunday Blue Laws) providing for the arrest of those playing baseball on Sunday. Such was the case in certain areas of New York State, including Rochester. In early 1897, the New York State Assembly passed the Wilcox Bill that made the playing of baseball on Sundays a misdemeanor punishable by a modest fine. Proponents of Sunday baseball favored this legislation as it

---

CONVICTION FOR SUNDAY BALL PLAYING.

Rochester, July 2.—Sunday baseball has been killed for the rest of the season in Rochester. A crusade against Sunday ball was begun recently by Law and Order people. The owners of the Rochester Eastern League team, together with the manager and nine players, were indicted by the last Grand Jury for Sabbath-breaking. Gannon, the pitcher, was convicted to-day on the charge. The case will be appealed by the club owners. The other cases will go over until fall. Pending the appeal, the owners have agreed to discontinue Sunday games.

From the *New York Tribune*, July 3, 1897, 2.

would have been an improvement over the more stringent laws then in place. However, the proposed legislation did not get the necessary three-quarters approval in the State Assembly, the vote being 53–44. Thus, the legislation was defeated, and there was no legal Sunday Baseball in Rochester that year.[6]

James Buckley, president of the Rochester team, was dismayed by the turn of events. He had hoped to have his team play Sunday baseball at Riverside Park in Irondequoit, as they had in 1896, but the locals were of a mind to urge prosecution of Buckley for violating the Sunday Blue Laws. A letter from the Young People's Society of Christian Endeavor (Y.P. S.C. E.) said as much. Buckley's reaction was included in the Rochester newspaper in April 1897:

> There was no harm in Sunday ball at Riverside last year. The crowd was quiet and orderly and there were some very nice people at the games and no objectionable ones that I know of. It is the day when the shop people can go to the game. That they do is evident. They (the nice people) certainly knew enough to decide between right and wrong and I don't think the game is of such a subtle, alluring and dangerous nature that it would attract them against their conscientious scruples.[7]

The dialogue on the issue in Rochester's leading daily newspaper, the *Democrat and Chronicle*, was balanced. Reverend Frederick L. Anderson of the Second Baptist Church was one of the people supporting enforcement of the ban. These words are from a letter that was published in the paper on April 17:

> I see it announced in the press that the local management proposes having a game of baseball played next Sunday (April 18). Such a game will be a clear violation of the law of the state and, as a law-abiding citizen, I desire to enter my public protest. The law against Sunday baseball is not an ancient enactment, time-worn and out of date, but a law that is being enforced in this commonwealth every year. It is the living expression of the sentiment of all the best people in the state which these men propose to defy next Sunday. It makes no difference what our (local enforcement) officials think of the wisdom of our laws. They are not to legislate for us. They have no right or authority to pick and choose, to enforce one law and not another.[8]

So, what happened on April 18? A game was scheduled that afternoon between the Buffalo and Rochester Eastern League entries. A good crowd was on hand, estimated at 2,000. Articles in the *Democrat and Chronicle* described both the ball game and the interplay between clergy, police, ownership and players. The newspaper reported that, "There was not one of the spectators who was not pleased with the exhibition given by both teams.

It may truly be said that the players of both teams put up a remarkable game for this early in the season."⁹ Rochester batted first. They threatened, putting runners at second and third, but did not score. At this point, the game had its first interruption."

Present at the game was a Constable Bronson who was determined that there would be no baseball played on that day. The game originally scheduled to begin at 3:30 p.m. got underway at 4:00 p.m., the delay being caused by a prolong conversation between the local constables and the team managers as to whether they were actually going to play the game. The fans were instructed by umpire O'Loughlin to be quiet throughout the proceedings. Nevertheless, after the first half-inning, Constable Bronson took to the mound, and stopped play. Shortly thereafter, the local clergy, led by Reverend Charles Merrill, were on the scene and demanded that the constable arrest the offending ballplayers. The constable did not make any arrests.[10]

Play resumed and exciting plays defined the bottom of the first inning. With one out, Chummy Gray of Buffalo launched a long drive but was gunned down by left fielder Billy Bottenus as he went for a triple. Aided by a single, a misjudged popup and a stolen base, Buffalo put runners on second and third. Jim Field stepped to the plate but no sooner had he done so than Constable Koehler made his presence known. Play was again interrupted while police, team owners, and citizens (including Reverend Merrill and local businessmen David Heffer, Henry Kellogg, and M.W. Jackson) discussed how to proceed. Play resumed again after another 15-minute delay and Field was retired on a ground ball.

The game proceeded with much in the way of threats and little in the way of scoring. Buffalo finally broke through with two runs in the bottom half of the fifth inning. Bill Urquhart scored on Larry Gilboy's single and Gilboy would later score from first when right fielder Henry Lynch dropped a fly ball of the bat of Wise. Rochester halved the lead with a run in the top of the sixth inning. Lynch singled, stole second, and eventually scored on an out by Charlie Dooley, making the score 2–1 going into the seventh inning.

All of this was overshadowed by the events of the top of the seventh. A throwing error by shortstop Suter Sullivan and an RBI single by Dan Shannon gave Rochester a 3–2 lead. Rochester scored two more runs in the inning, the final tally coming on a double steal, making the score 5–2. As noted, Buffalo had taken a 2–1 lead into the frame.

So much for baseball on that day. When play had been delayed in the bottom of the first inning when Constable Koehler interrupted the festivities, David Heffer, one of the townsfolk supportive of the clergy's position against Sunday baseball, decided to head to the sheriff's office. He commandeered a passing vehicle.[11] By the time Heffer returned with the sheriff, play had resumed and the game was midway through the seventh inning. After the top of the seventh the players observed that Sheriff Schroff had entered the ballpark, accompanied by the citizens comprising the "Sunday Baseball Committee." Noticing this, one of the players hid the baseball under his sweater and the teams refrained from taking their positions on the field. Thus the sheriff witnessed no actual playing of baseball and did not make any arrests. The sheriff, per the *Democrat and Chronicle*, "allowed that he would be obliged to arrest the players if he saw them playing and so both teams were called from the field."[12] Play was suspended at that point, the score reverted to the tally through six innings, Buffalo was declared the winner, and the battle for Sunday baseball would be resumed at a later date.[13]

Over the course of the next months the debate would rage. Although ministers such as Reverend Merrill were decidedly against Sunday Baseball, they did have clerical opposition. Father Thomas Hendrick of St. Bridget's Catholic Church said, "I think it is an excellent thing. I'd rather have my people go there, for there is no beer sold there. You can say that I wonder at the people of Irondequoit trying to stop ball playing on Sunday and letting the sale of beer go on at the Sea Breeze and Summerville. It seems to me to be straining at a gnat and swallowing a camel; for there are none of these evils at Riverside Park. I think the opposition nonsensical."[14]

On Saturday evening, April 24, the local Republican Party met and came out strongly for Sunday baseball. But the men of the cloth were not about to give up the fight. On Sunday, April 25, at the First Universalist Church, Reverend L.H. Squires' sermon topic was "Sunday Amusement" He told his flock that, "The persuasion of my mind is that professional Sunday baseball playing conducted as a business is an evil to the community." He went on to call the owners a "greedy lot only interested in money." Further, he said, "This inevitable tendency of Sunday amusements to run down character is plainly evident." He took Buffalo to task for allowing Sunday baseball and categorized that city as "one of the most immoral cities on the continent." He concluded by saying, "We need not go to ball games on Sunday if others do. We can respect the Sabbath, cultivate our moral and spiritual natures, improve our tie to better results and hold up our standard of life and character for what it is worth to the world."[15]

Baseball's Battles with the Blue Laws in Rochester

At the center of all this controversy was the actual and somewhat inconsistent wording in New York's Penal Code. "All shooting, hunting, fishing, playing, horse racing, gaming, or other public sport, exercises or shows upon the first day of the week and all noise disturbing the peace of the day are prohibited." There is nothing, of course, inconsistent here, but a note follows this wording, and this note became the crux of the matter. "Note—Playing ball on private grounds, with the consent of the owner, there being no noise or disturbance, is not an offence under this section"

The "Big Three," as the three saloon keepers who owned the Rochester Brownies collectively were called, were not about to stop Sunday baseball. On Sunday May 16, another confrontation took place. The owners, apparently wary of the clergy, resolved to bar them from entering the ballpark. Buckley and Englert, two of the so-called Big Three, stopped the ministers when they arrived and said, "These are private grounds. We believe you have come here to create a disturbance. You have said that you would break up the game. You cannot come in."[16]

The leader of the clerical group was Reverend Charles A. Merrill, who resolved to take legal action against the team's officials. On May 22, he did just that. He contended that "the defendant, without lawful reason arbitrarily and unlawfully refused to admit the plaintiff (Merrill) to said place of amusement and excluded him therefrom and thereby denied to the plaintiff the full and equal enjoyment of the accommodations, advantages, facilities, and privileges of said place of amusement." He was a determined man. After filing papers, his resolve was intact. He went on to say: "I am no prophet. I am only a preacher. I do not know whether or not an attempt will be made to stop the game (on May 23). A plan of action may be determined upon before (Saturday) night, but at present I cannot tell what will be done. Anyway, I think the baseball people know that they have not long to live."[17] The lawsuit against the team would be heard at a later date.

As the month of May wore on in Rochester, those opposed to Sunday ball continued to meet and strategize. They flooded the newspapers with letters predicting all sorts of gloom and doom should Sunday baseball be allowed to continue. One such letter came from Wilber F. Crafts of the Reform Bureau of Washington, D.C., who noted that "the great majority of Sabbath breakers desecrate the day not through selfishness, but thoughtlessness." Dr. Crafts called those judges who refused to enforce the existing law petty. He took issue with those judges who "discovered (after reading the law) that it is only when Sunday games disturb the neighbors that they are illegal. The decision is as revolting in its grammar as its law." He held that Sunday ball games were clearly criminal under the four counts of State Law, specifically dealing with labor, amusements, noise, and traffic.[18]

On May 28, a letter in support of Sunday baseball appeared in the *Democrat and Chronicle*. The writer in part asked, "Why is the attack (by the opponents of Sunday baseball) directed exclusively at the wholesome and clean game of baseball at Riverside Park, where no intoxicating liquor can be obtained, where a few thousand people can rest and breathe fresh air and pass the time pleasantly, with no harm to the physical and moral being, and with real invigoration of body and mind?"[19]

As if the field was not already crowded with proponents and opponents of Sunday baseball, another actor appeared in the area in late May when the Women's Christian Temperance Union (W.C.T.U.) convened and put forth a series of resolutions, one of which dealt with Sunday baseball. The W.C.T.U. "is in sympathy with the efforts of the clergy of the Y.M.C.A. to prevent the Sunday baseball games, and (it is further resolved) that as the claims of the holy Sabbath are more and more forgotten and its blessings more and more needed, parents restrain their children from all forms of desecration on the Lord's day."[20]

The protests continued into June, with the Young People's Society of Christian Endeavor (Y.P.S.C.E.) or Christian Endeavorers, as they were also known, leading the charge. The Y.P.S.C.E. convened on June 2. Four days prior to the convention, the Monroe County Law and Order League (sometimes called the Citizens, Committee), a group composed largely of many the ministers of the Evangelical churches and a few businessmen, issued a newsletter attacking Sunday baseball.[21] During a meeting on June 2, Reverend F.P. Arthur posed the question "how many of the Christian Endeavorers here tonight are opposed to Sunday baseball?" The 1,200 in attendance rose virtually in unison to make their feelings on the subject known. Reverend Merrill, who in addition to his pastoral duties served as head of the Law and Order League, then spoke briefly, posing three largely rhetorical questions: "Is the penal code of the Empire State a book of mythology? Are the officers of Monroe County counterfeits? Is patriotism waning?" His next battles would be in front of the local magistrates.[22]

At this point in the controversy no less than four cases were in play at the same time. One needed a scorecard to keep them in perspective. The first case involved the game played on April 18, where the constables and sheriff refused to act. The Big Three (Buckley, Englert, and Charles Leimgruber) along with their players were arrested on Saturday morning June 5. With determination, the Big Three maintained:

Baseball's Battles with the Blue Laws in Rochester

> We are glad that the arrests have been made, as only in that way could the question of Sunday baseball playing be decided in this county. The players will be bailed out and will play this afternoon and also with Springfield tomorrow afternoon at Riverside park. There can be no question that the greater number of the people of Monroe County are in favor of Sunday baseball, and if the people want Sunday ball, they will have it.[23]

The magistrate, Justice Porter, heard arguments as to whether a crime had been committed and announced that he would render his decision the following Wednesday, June 9. The ballplayers were released on bail and did not miss either of the weekend games. When arguments were heard the Justice decided in favor of the saloon owners and players. He ruled, "I cannot see that any serious violation of the section of the code under which this charge is brought has been committed. I so discharge the prisoners."[24]

Also in June, a second case made its way into the courts. This was an action against Rochester club president Buckley and members of his team. The case stemmed from arrests made when a game was played on June 13. The trial was held on June 28 and the jury found Mr. Buckley innocent, a bit of a surprise as the judge's instructions to the jury essentially called for a guilty verdict. The jury apparently gave credence to Attorney Hallock's defense that Buckley did not actually engage in the game but was a bystander. What was even more surprising about the verdict was that, at that time, yet another case was headed in quite the opposite direction, with every appearance that another action would result in a favorable ruling for the opponents of Sunday baseball.[25]

The whole matter was effectively trumped by other proceedings (cases three and four if you are counting) involving the convening of a grand jury to handle the incidents of May 16, when the Law and Order League was blocked when trying to enter Riverside Park. Two distinct cases arose out of these incidents. The first one involved Sabbath-breaking by the ballplayers. That was the case heard by the Grand Jury. The Grand Jury issued indictments for Sabbath-breaking against the three owners and 11 of the players on June 14.[26] The second case involved a civil suit brought by the clergy against the ownership of the team.

Meanwhile, the Rochester team was slumping on the ballfield—through the games of June 18, the Brownies were in seventh place with an 18–23 record and trailed first place Syracuse by nine and a half games. But in the courtroom, attorneys for the owners and players sought to have the indictments against the owners and players thrown out, to no avail. Judge

Sutherland in his ruling on June 20 stated that "Contests of this description are forbidden by words so plain and unmistakable as to leave interpretation no office to perform. It is useless to argue that some of these things (as outlined in the statute) are in fact harmless and should be permitted to be done in a quiet and orderly manner so as not to actually disturb the peace of the day. The law makes no such discrimination."[27]

At long last, jury selection began in the first case involving the May 16 game, that against James Gannon. Gannon, a pitcher, was 23 years old and would forge a 7–20 record in 1897. On July 2, the jury returned a guilty verdict on the charge of playing baseball on Sunday. There could have been more than 50 additional trials, one for each of those indicted, but that did not happen. Judge Sutherland informed the owners of the team and their owner that, in the event the team discontinued playing on Sundays, no actions would be taken against the remaining players. The opponents of Sunday baseball in Rochester had won the day.[28] More bad news for the Rochester squad came on July 16 when the Riverside ballpark was consumed by flames. By then the owner decided to sell the ball club to interests in Montreal. The team was rechristened the Montreal Royals and played their first home game in Montreal on July 23.

The final case concerning Sunday baseball in Rochester in 1897 was a civil suit stemming from the incidents on May 16, and involved legal action taken by the clergymen against the team for being denied entry into the ballpark. The case dragged on into the autumn months, and the action was ultimately dropped as there really was no need to carry on. With the team having moved, there was no possibility of Sunday baseball in Rochester, and the banning of Sunday baseball was really what the suit was about.

Postscript

Although the war over Sunday baseball was over in Rochester, confrontations continued in many major-league cities into the twentieth century. As the new century dawned, so did a new league. In 1901 Sunday baseball was played in Chicago, Detroit, and Milwaukee, all in the fledgling American League. Milwaukee moved to St. Louis in 1902, where play on the Sabbath was allowed for both teams in that city, the new Browns and established National League Cardinals. At the time the Cardinals and the Chicago Cubs were the only National League teams playing Sunday baseball. Thus, in all, only six of the sixteen major league clubs played Sunday home games in 1902 and 1903.

It would be more than 30 years before Sunday baseball was adopted in all major-league cities, largely due to inconsistent attitudes from police and courts, and legislatures. Many fans were receptive to Sunday play, but in many cities determined and influential groups of ministers stood fast and, in most major-league venues, won the day for worship.

The Brooklyn Superbas of the National League flew in the face of New York State law (the same law that had been invoked in Rochester in 1897) and started playing on Sundays in 1904, opening the gates of Washington Park for seven Sundays in all through June 26, with more than one trip to the courthouse. After three years of legal skirmishing, however, Brooklyn owner Charles Ebbets stopped Sunday play after the game of June 17, 1906. Aside from two games used to benefit charitable causes, there was no Sunday baseball again in New York City until 1917, when Sunday games were scheduled to raise needed war relief funds. Each of the three local teams hosted events, but they were not without the usual controversy.

The experience of the New York Giants at the Polo Grounds on August 17, 1917 symbolizes the craziness over the issue. On that date, a game was scheduled to benefit New York's Regiment, the Fighting 69th. After marching around the ballpark, the soldiers headed off to the center field bleachers and were on the receiving end of tosses from former Giants pitcher and present Cincinnati manager Christy Mathewson. A baseball signed by President Woodrow Wilson was presented to the regiment's chaplain to be taken to France and auctioned off for the benefit of French children who had been orphaned by the war. In the game itself, Cincinnati shut out the Giants 5–0 as Cincinnati pitcher Fred Toney scattered five hits.[29]

Although the game concert was held for a good cause, the idea of Sunday baseball still did not sit well with many opponents. On August 20, arrest warrants were issued for the teams' managers John McGraw and Christy Mathewson. Magistrate Frothingham of the Washington Heights Court in upper Manhattan issued the summons after being asked to do so by Detective McGovern of Inspector Ryan's unit. When the New York Giants hosted the Cincinnati Reds on August 17, 1917, it was McGovern's contention that the game was not an exhibition, but a regularly scheduled game and, as such was in violation of Section 2145 of the Penal Code.[30] This section outlawed activity that interfered with or interrupted the "repose and religious liberty of the community" on the Sabbath. Matthewson and McGraw appeared before Justice F.X. McQuade on August 21, and the charges were dismissed.[31]

The end of the First World War brought about a change in the attitude of the New York State legislature and the State law was changed to allow for Sunday baseball in 1919. The Giants and Dodgers had their first legal Sunday home games on May 4, and the New York Yankees had their first legal Sunday home game on May 11.

By then, the barriers had also fallen in Cleveland (1911) and Washington (1918). As the first two decades of the 20th century ended, the last two states holding out against Sunday baseball were those cradles of democracy, Massachusetts and Pennsylvania.

Sources

In addition to the sources shown in the notes, the author used Baseball-Reference.com and DeMotte, Charles. *Bat, Ball, and Bible: Baseball and Sunday Observance in New York*. Dulles, Virginia, Potomac Books, 2013.

NOTES

1. "The Twelve Club League," *Baltimore Sun*, December 18, 1891, 1.
2. "Nick Young on Sunday Ball: The Sentiment of the Community Must Settle Such Matters," *Pittsburgh Press*, January 8, 1893, 6.
3. Charlie Bevis, *Sunday Baseball: The Major Leagues Struggle to Play Baseball on the Lord's Day, 1876-1934* (Jefferson, NC: McFarland, 2003), 104.
4. Bevis, 88.
5. "Sunday Baseball Row: The Rochester-Columbus Players Arrested at Windsor Beach, N.Y.," *The News (Frederick, Maryland)*, July 21, 1890, 1.
6. "Was Cleverly Constructed: Fate of the Sunday Baseball Bill Sealed," *Democrat and Chronicle*, April 7, 1897, 1.
7. "No Sunday Ball in Rochester: The Wilcox Bill Fails to Become a Law," *Democrat and Chronicle*, April 7, 1897, 15.
8. "Sunday Ball Playing: Officers Will Violate Their Oath If They Permit It," *Democrat and Chronicle*, April 17, 1897, 7.
9. "Brownies Lost to the Bisons—But They Made More Runs Than the Visitors," *Democrat and Chronicle*, April 19, 1897, 14.
10. "Sunday Baseball: A Test Case Made of the Matter," *Democrat and Chronicle*, April 19, 1897, 15.
11. Ibid.
12. "Brownies Lost to the Bisons—But They Made More Runs Than the Visitors," *Democrat and Chronicle*, April 19, 1897, 14.
13. "Sunday Baseball: A Test Case Made of the Matter," *Democrat and Chronicle*, April 19, 1897, 15.
14. Ibid.
15. "Observance of Sunday: Ministers Preach on the Desecration of the Day," *Democrat and Chronicle*, April 26, 1897, 5.
16. "Were Turned Back from the Gates: Clergymen Were Not Allowed at Yesterday's Ball Game," *Democrat and Chronicle*, May 17, 1897, 10.
17. "Sunday Baseball—An Action Commenced by Rev. Charles A. Merrill," *Democrat and Chronicle*, May 23, 1897, 13.
18. "Sunday Baseball—Other Desecrations and Evils to Follow in Its Wake," *Democrat and Chronicle*, May 27, 1897, 8.

Baseball's Battles with the Blue Laws in Rochester

19. Sunday Baseball—"Why Should Only One Provision of the Law Be Enforced?" *Democrat and Chronicle*, May 28, 1897, 8.

20. "WCTU Convention—Interesting Meeting at Spencerport Yesterday," *Democrat and Chronicle*, May 28, 1897, 12.

21. "For and Against Sunday Baseball—A Red Hot Contest Now on Between Both Sides," *Democrat and Chronicle*, May 29, 1897, 13.

22. "An Opinion on Sunday Ball—The Christian Endeavorers Are Unanimous in Sentiment," *Democrat and Chronicle*, June 2, 1897, 5.

23. "Their Case Adjourned—Ball Tossers Had to Face the Police Justice at Irondequoit," *Democrat and Chronicle*, June 6, 1897, 13.

24. "Ball Players Were Discharged—Result of Their Trial at Irondequoit Yesterday," *Democrat and Chronicle*, June 10, 1897, 11.

25. *Democrat and Chronicle*, June 29, 1897, 17.

26. "Indictments Found by the Grand Jury—Rochester Sunday Baseball Players Will Be Tried," *Democrat and Chronicle*, June 17, 1897, 10.

27. "Their Demurrers Were Overruled—Judge Sutherland Says Baseball Indictments Must Stand," *Democrat and Chronicle*, June 20, 1897, 12.

28. "Gannon was Convicted—Sunday Observance Law Was Vindicated," *Democrat and Chronicle*, July 3, 1897, 11.

29. *New York Times*, August 20, 1917, 10.

30. "M'Graw and Matty Summoned to Court: Police Charge Sunday Benefit Game for 69th Was Part of National League Schedule," *New York Times*, August 21, 1917, 3.

31. *New York Times*, August 22, 1917, 13.

Book Reviews

Recounting the Brotherhood War

The Great Baseball Revolt: The Rise and Fall of the 1890 Players League.
Robert B. Ross. Lincoln: University of Nebraska Press, 2016, 10 illus., 288 pages.

John M. Ward, Robert Ross states in the introduction to *The Great Baseball Revolt*, was "one of the National League's stars since his debut in 1877" (p. xviii). Ward first played professionally in 1877, but not in the National League until 1878. It is never a good sign when the first factual error occurs with the pages still numbered in Roman numerals, but this mistake is more embarrassing than important. What matters is whether this is an outlier or a portent. Sadly, it turns out to be the latter.

Viewed one way, the Players League is unique in baseball history. The players organized a union, the Brotherhood, and organized their own league rather than undertaking the traditional labor action of a strike or its baseball variant, the collective holdout. This is akin to steel workers unionizing and building their own foundry.

Viewed from another direction, the Players League is less remarkable. The players lacked the financial resources to build modern ballparks and pay high salaries. (We might wonder, by way of counterfactual, whether if they had settled for the primitive ballparks and lower salaries of ten years earlier, they might have reached a different outcome.) The players therefore brought in outside owners. These money men were motivated by some combination of profit-seeking and enthusiasm for the game. The players subsequently discovered that the new owners had no particular attachment to the players' cause.

The Players League was neither the first nor the last time an upstart league was attempted. It was the third of five challenges to the baseball establishment between 1882 and 1915, not counting the numerous attempts that never got off the ground. The pattern of these five baseball wars is clear. The successes, the American Association in 1882 and the American League in 1901–1903, faced but a single established major league. The other failures, the Union Association in 1884 and the Federal League in 1914–1915, faced two established major leagues. The Players League faced both the National League and the American Association. This ordinarily would not bode well. The difference in 1890 was the mass defection of players to the new league. Rather than scrambling to get top players to sign, as had the Union Association and the Federal League, the players were in from the start. Would this be enough to break the pattern? Would these players give the new league instant standing? From the perspective of the new owners, the access to these top players was the reason to gamble on a new league. The price the owners paid was that the players demanded and were given a place at the counsel table, with representative membership in the league's governance.

From the perspective of the ownership of both leagues, the ensuing war followed the usual path. Rising salaries and competition for spectators meant that nobody made money, and most lost quite a bit. Eventually negotiations opened for a new accommodation, with the established league probing for fault lines within the upstart. This fault line typically has been between wealthier and poorer clubs, with the wealthier being bought off and the poorer left out in the cold. In the case of the Players League the fault line was within the alliance of convenience between the money men and the players. The Players' League financiers were offered entry into the National League, without any pesky provisions giving authority to the hired help. At that point the Players League was doomed.

The interesting questions about the Players League—anything beyond mere chronicle—are really about its context. What went on in the 1880s that led to the players taking such radical action? Ross implicitly recognizes this, devoting three chapters to events prior to the founding of the league. (Of the remaining chapters, one discusses the preparations for the season, one the 1890 season, and one the collapse in the post-season. There also is one brief chapter, only tangentially related, about non-player workers such as the construction workers who built the ballparks.) The critical early chapters are very weak. For this earlier period Ross relies heavily on secondary sources, not always chosen wisely. For the late 1880s he turns more to primary sources, but haphazardly, and with major gaps. The result is an endless series of errors and omissions.

A representative example is the transfer of John Ward from Providence to New York in 1882. The most important of the Brotherhood's grievances was the system of player sales, by which the reserve rights to a player could be transferred from one club to another without his consent. The Brotherhood made no complaint about the reserve system itself. Quite the contrary: the Brotherhood consistently affirmed the reserve system as necessary for the financial health of baseball. The sales system was a different matter. The image of a white man being auctioned off like a slave was deeply offensive, and the sometimes spectacular prices paid reeked of exploitation. The reserve system had been first enacted in the fall of 1879. The sales system was newer, first enacted in the fall of 1885. Its implications were not immediately obvious, but became clear within a few years as it was fully implemented.

This timing of the sales system goes a long ways toward explaining why the Players League occurred when it did. This explanation is unavailable to Ross because he thinks the sales system was in place all along. He writes of John Ward's move following the 1882 season from Providence to New York that "clubs controlled the movement of players from one team to another regardless of whether the players liked it" (page 59). This is incorrect. The player sales system did not yet exist in 1882. Not only was Ward not sold to New York, he was a free agent. Providence had not reserved him. It may seem incredible that Providence would overlook him this way, but the reserve system at that time was restricted to but five players on a team. Ward had made his name as a pitcher, but the club had Charles Radbourn as its starting pitcher. Ward was making the transition to position player, but in 1882 had only the sixth best batting average on the club. With only five slots available, Ward did not make the cut, and so was able to sell his services to New York. This episode is not, as Ross portrays it, formative of the future labor organizer, but an example of the freedom the players later lost.

Ross discusses the Brotherhood's stance on the reserve system but dismisses it as their only "ostensibly" accepting it. He is led to this conclusion by his conflating of the reserve system with player sales. He argues (p. 70) that:

> While the prereservation years featured players moving from one team to another more or less at will, full reservation without the ability to buy or sell players would have kept them in place but made it impossible for owners to control the flow of players from one team to another. The effects, in terms of the inability to change an unsuccessful team or sell off more-expensive players when times were tight, would have been nearly as debilitating as the free movement of players without reservation.

In reality, player transactions occurred frequently in the early reserve period, before the sales system. The way it worked was as a three-way negotiation. The club acquiring the player negotiated a payment to his old club to release him, while also negotiating terms with the player for him to sign with the new club. The player could refuse to go, or he could negotiate a higher salary. He had control of his fate. This is the system the Brotherhood wanted.

Ross' discussion of the four years between the Brotherhood's formation and the decision to form the Players League is at times perfunctory and other times discursive, with clear signs of haphazard research. We are told (p.72) that "Although rumors had persisted throughout the summer of 1886, the brotherhood did not publicize its existence until November 11..." This overlooks a front-page article in the *Sporting Life* of August 4, headlined "A Big Surprise. A Ball Players' Union Fully Organized," complete with an interview of Ward. The Brotherhood's first victory was its meeting with the League in November of 1887, when it forced the League to recognize it and accept it as a negotiating partner, and negotiated the new player contract. Ross merely touches on this meeting and mischaracterizes the circumstances around it, for example stating (p. 78) that the Brotherhood had "sent a model of its proposed contract to the league in late October 1887." They had done no such thing, as was widely discussed at the time. Had they tipped off the League to the contents of their proposed contract, the League could have acceded to some portion of the demands without formally recognizing the Brotherhood. This would have given the League the moral high ground for being so reasonable as to accept the changes, thereby undermining support for the Brotherhood. Rather than giving away the game, the Brotherhood delegates meeting with the League kept their contractual demands close to the vest, forcing the League first to formally recognize the Brotherhood. And so on, with errors and misconceptions large and small.

The second half of the book, covering the year from late 1889 through late 1890, is better. It provides a good chronology of events. The extended discussion (pp. 126–133) of the securing of ballparks and the issues surrounding this challenge is very good. A reader looking for a chronicle of the events of 1890, not seeking any deeper analysis, would be satisfied.

The Brotherhood only made the decision to form the Players League after a long series of acts of bad faith on the part of the National League. There was nothing inevitable about the matter. The reader seeking to understand how and why it came about will have to look elsewhere.

—Richard Hershberger

Can a Team's Long-Term Fortunes Change in One Series?

The Cubs and the A's of 1910: One Dynasty Ends, Another Begins. Richard Bressler. Jefferson, NC: McFarland, 2016, 26 illus., 196 pages.

Although an otherwise unremarkable year in baseball, some think that 1910 was the true last deadball season. The cork-centered ball was introduced in 1911 (or, as the author of this book points out, at the 1910 World Series, something that almost no one knew at the time and would be a huge story if it happened today). That "lively" ball raised batting averages and home run totals for the next couple of years. But in 1910, as had long been the case, offense was down. The year did not see close pennant races, being the only season between 1901 and 1928 when both leagues were won by more than 10 games. So why write a book about 1910? The significance, according to author Richard Bressler in his book, "The Cubs and the A's of 1910: One Dynasty Ends, Another Begins," is that it was the tipping point between the great Cubs teams of the late 1900s and the great Athletics teams of the early 1910s.

What then is a dynasty? Bressler does not define a dynasty, and oddly does not appear to use the term anywhere except in the book's subtitle. Instead he uses the phrase, "changing of the guard," and says that happens when "an upcoming person or team defeats a multiple title holder." The Cubs had won the World Series twice by this point, in 1907 and 1908, and set a record for the best five-year period in history, but they were not necessarily a dynasty. I do not think there is a widely-accepted definition of dynasty, although a Google search suggests that three titles in five years is a requirement. This the Cubs did not accomplish.

The book begins by retelling the history of the Philadelphia Athletics prior to the 1910 season. The first half of the chapter is simply a retelling of the Connie Mack story. A look at the references in the back of the book show it is a summary of the excellent Norman Macht book on Mack. Bressler begins with Mack's birth, and tells of his family and childhood, subjects that would be interesting in a Mack book but do not necessarily belong in a book about 1910. Yes, Mack was the dominating force and his story is intertwined with the history of the A's, but we get far too much information about him and far too little about how the team was put together. Of interest in a book like this would have been more about each of the players on the 1910 Athletics, and a much more detailed review of the recent seasons and improvement of the team. From 1907 to 1909 the A's won 88–68–95 games each season. The discussion of reasons for the poor 1908 showing (essentially, injuries and the trial of younger players) is relegated by the author to a single paragraph, when it could in fact be seen as a pivotal season in the history of the 1910 team, with Mack deciding to reboot his team at that point.

The Cubs were not as dominated by one man as the A's were, so Bressler does a better job of reviewing them. They were, as he points out, one of the best teams in history, if not perhaps a dynasty. If one were to count championships, the early Cubs won just two World Series. However, after Frank Chance took over the team from the ailing Frank Selee in 1905, the Cubs went on a remarkable run of success. They had the best single, two-year, three-year season records, all the way up to having the best 10 consecutive seasons in baseball history, from 1904 to 1913. Just as with the A's chapter, however, we get relatively spotty coverage of the team's recent history, as the author chooses to highlight the winning seasons and ignore the less successful ones. Bressler gives the most coverage to 1905, when Chance took the reins, somewhat less to 1908, and not much to other seasons. The 1909 season, which one would think would get a lot of discussion in a book about 1910, is covered in one paragraph at the end of the chapter. In addition, getting a comprehensive picture of the origins of the 1910 teams is not easily done in this format, which mentions various players in passing and assumes the reader knows they were on the 1910 team. Perhaps a table somewhere telling us where and how each player on the two teams was acquired could have made things clearer.

After these introductory chapters, we move into a month-by-month recap of the 1910 season, with detailed discussion of each team's schedule. The author explicitly states at the start of the book that he is focusing on these two teams. This does give the reader a feeling of wanting to know more about the rest of the league. Other books, such as *Crazy '08* by Cait Murphy, do a better job of weaving narratives of several teams together and giving a wider picture of baseball at the time. Here, though, we get occasional asides about other teams and players, which at times feels more like reading a calendar than reading a story. There are places where those asides are simply inserted into the middle of a paragraph, and that divergence leads to confusion. One example is when a paragraph begins by talking about a series against Cleveland, goes off on a tangent to give us a summary of the career of Cleveland pitcher Addie Joss, then returns to the Cleveland series without a pause. Breaking these asides into multiple paragraphs would have aided comprehension throughout the book. As it is, the inescapable feeling is that the author wrote the game-by-game summary, then, needing a higher word count, went back and inserted anecdotes about players that had been mentioned.

He then turns to the 1910 World Series, the point at which the Cubs and Athletics came together for the only time. This is perhaps the best part of the book, giving interesting detail about the series and the machinations of Mack and Chance. During the World Series today there is much discussion on how the two teams match up, how the managers will play off against each other, decisions on the rotation and so on. Reading this chapter shows it has always been this way: writers telling us stories about how the teams are doing whatever they can to get the slightest edge, even down to Mack getting his players to promise not to drink during the World Series. This would be another big story if it happened today.

The one thing that does not appear to be covered is the premise of the book—that this series was a turning point between the two teams, the rise of the A's and the fall of the Cubs. It is hard to imagine that one series could affect the teams so much, and the author does not try to make it so. What would be interesting would be to know whether the Cubs were so devastated by their loss in the Series that they fell apart, like the A's did after losing the 1914 World Series (when they fell to the bottom of the league for a decade, albeit for off field reasons. Bressler points out that Mack tore the team apart when the economics of the game changed for Philadelphia). Instead, the Cubs just faded away from the heights, losing more games than the season before for the next six seasons. Indeed, the real turning point for the Cubs may have been the firing of Chance as manager after the 1912 season. But we get little about that. Because the two leagues were so separate at this point, any true impact on the Cubs would come from teams within their own league. Yet there is little mention of other National League teams, such as the Giants, who rose to win the next three NL pennants and knock the Cubs off their perch.

Winning the 1910 World Series was also not a spur to the A's to become a great team, since they already had been very good for several years. In the period from 1901–14, the A's finished either first or second in nine of those seasons, including their three World Series victories between 1910 and 1913. This was not a team getting lucky. Bressler points out that each league expected their champion to win the World Series. Although the betting favored the Cubs in 1910, there was plenty of support for the A's. Mack had a plan from the beginning and he stuck to it, getting his team to be contenders year after year until the financial aspects of baseball moved away from him.

My biggest criticism of the book is probably the reference section. The author has gone through daily newspapers from the two cities—Chicago and Philadelphia—which is the source of the information about the schedules of the two teams. He uses just one newspaper from each city, however: the *Chicago Tribune* and the *Philadelphia Daily Bulletin*. This leaves out many other perspectives from a time when each city had multiple newspapers. It also disregards views of the two teams from other cities around the league. In a few cases, Bressler references Wikipedia, something that would be rejected by a high school teacher as a source. He also lists the Hall of Fame file for a large number of players as a source, and in the bibliography, he says these "consist of newspaper and magazine articles, some unattributed."

Having read widely on this era, I found little that was new. One thing I learned was that the *Chicago Tribune* switched their Cubs and White Sox reporters in mid-season each year, an interesting change of perspective that might be worth an article by itself. Other books, like the Macht book on Connie Mack, or *The Chalmers Race* by Rick Huhn, present more new information. If I were to summarize this book, it would be as a synopsis of baseball writing about the early 1900s, with a game-by-game summary of 1910 included. If the author had left out the part about 1910, and instead gone into more detail on the players and teams of the early 1900s, this book could be the bones of a very good summary of the first decade of the twentieth century in baseball. As it is, after finishing this book the reader has the definite feeling of wanting more.

—Steve West

Baseball and World War I

From the Dugout to the Trenches: Baseball During the Great War. Jim Leeke. Lincoln: University of Nebraska Press, 2017, 32 illus., 238 pages.

Three years after the assassination of Franz Ferdinand triggered World War I, on April 2, 1917, President Woodrow Wilson Addressed a joint session of Congress to ask for a declaration of War against Germany. Even though elected on a platform of: "He kept us out of war," Wilson had reached the realization that war was inevitable because of Germany's reinstatement of unrestricted submarine warfare and the machinations it used to attempt to bring Mexico into the conflict with the United States. Congress passed the declaration of war on April 4, 1917, just a few days before the beginning of the 1917 baseball season.

Jim Leeke, the author of this comprehensive work about World War I and its effect on baseball in the United States, can be considered the expert on this subject. This is his third book on the era, the first two being *Ballplayers in the Great War: Newspaper Accounts of Major Leaguers in World War I Military Service* and *Nine Innings for the King: The Day Wartime London Stopped for Baseball, July 4, 1918*. Both of these books were published by McFarland. The two books mentioned above, along with the book being reviewed, are the sum total of those listed in Amazon under the subject Baseball and World War I. This is in marked contrast to the books and Web sites extant for baseball and World War II.

Leeke has had a varied career both as a writer and in the general field of communications. He is the author of several Civil War history and naval history books in addition to a mystery novel. He has also authored several biographies for the SABR BioProject.

As the author of several books as well as numerous book reviews for *Library Journal*, I was always cautioned not to criticize a book as "not the book I would have written." This is certainly not the case for *From the Dugouts to the Trenches*. This is exactly the book I would have written had I the knowledge of the topic that Leeke obviously has. He has a pleasing, informal writing style that take the reader along for a journey through baseball and the "Great War." (Little did we know that this was not the "War to End All Wars.") The work is a combination of well-written narrative along with the notes and source citations that will please the academic reader and allow the tracing of sources. The wayward academic in me would rather see footnotes than endnotes but that has become prohibitively expensive for most publishers.

Leeke's book consists of eleven chapters and an epilogue that actually carries the story of the War and baseball from early spring 1917 until after the Armistice in November 1918. A short introduction illustrates that baseball owners were well-aware of the possibility of war and the book uses the contrasting views of Col T.L. Huston, co-owner of the Yankees, and Harry Frazee of the Red Sox, as to the effect war would have on baseball. Huston generally believed that war would have a great effect on baseball while Frazee believed the opposite. As Leeke points out, both were correct but at different times.

Chapter One, "Sergeants," is much more than that as it lays the groundwork for the declaration of war. After Col. Huston and the Yankees originated the idea of requesting military personnel to direct his team in drill and ceremonies, many major league teams requested military personnel also be assigned to their teams to direct them in these two tasks. The Yankees led the way in this and the American League far outshone the National in this endeavor. The depth of the author's research is evident in the chapter with much information about the military personnel assigned to the teams and how the teams responded.

Chapter Two deals with the increase in the size of the military and some of the early effects enlistment and the Selective Service System (the "draft") had on baseball. In reality, the time required to get the system in place militated against huge numbers of players entering the military, voluntary enlistments notwithstanding. There was, however, a certain lack of interest in baseball as evidenced by drops in attendance by fans that had implications for the business side of the game. The author points out that there had not been an agreement reached that the baseball game could continue in wartime. Using primary sources Leeke discusses in detail the deleterious effect the early days of the War had on the minor leagues. In 1917, as well as in 1918, the combination of fan apathy and the loss of players were devastating to minor league baseball.

Chapters Three, Four, and Five, "Buildup," "Winter," and "Spring," are to this reviewer three of the best chapters in the book. During the 1917 season players in both the major and minor leagues faced several choices that would affect them. They could enlist, as did many—particularly those players who desired to become commissioned officers. They could wait to be drafted (or perhaps not, depending on local draft boards). Finally, they could obtain a draft exempt job in a war-related or farm-related industry. I believe an analogy could be drawn comparing war-related industries such as shipyards with players joining National Guard or Reserve units during the Vietnam War to avoid serving in the active military. The shipyards competed vigorously for players and a case can be made that the quality of baseball in the shipyard leagues rivalled MLB. In Chapters Three and Four the author uses several interesting vignettes to illustrate how players made their decisions. He discusses the case of Eddie Grant, a former major league player who retired and became a lawyer in New York, and also the case of Fred Toney, who was the only major league player charged (and convicted) of being a draft dodger.

The winter of 1917–1918 raised many questions about the future of baseball during the War. Players were being drafted and were now enlisting in large numbers. The author does a good job of discussing the issue of the future of baseball during the conflict, cogently stating that the opinions of the "magnates of baseball ranged from that of Ban Johnson, who felt the major leagues should shut down for the duration, to other owners and administrators who wanted to wait and see what would happen."

The spring of 1918 was a great period of doubt for baseball. Players continued to join the military and there was concern that there might not be enough players to even begin the 1918 season. Leeke is strong here, chronologically following the progress of the different teams as they prepared for the season. In the end the decision was made to open the 1918 season and see what would follow. There were enough players but little did the owners know that the future of baseball would soon be out of their hands.

The concluding five chapters of the book provide much meat as relates to the future of baseball. Through the early months of 1918 the author describes the confusion that existed among owners as to whether there would be a 1918 baseball season. Leeke describes the seasons beginning as planned but the uncertainty ended on May 23, 1918, when Provost Marshal General Enoch Crowder issued new draft regulations that were called the "work or fight" rule. Leeke efficiently and concisely describes the effect: able-bodied men either had to join the military or had to take a war-related job by July 1, 1918.

The effect of the "work or fight" decision was devastating to organized baseball. All minor leagues shut down by the end of July except the International League. Major league attendance dropped to its lowest level since 1902. Organized baseball appealed Crowder's ruling to Secretary of War Newton Baker. The owners maintained that ballplayers should be exempt from work or fight because baseball was essential to keeping civilian morale high and that baseball players made up a very small part of the draft pool. During World War II Washington owner Clark Griffith successfully urged Judge Landis to send a letter to President Roosevelt asking that baseball continue for the same reasons. Even though Landis and FDR were on the opposite sides of the political spectrum, FDR approved baseball continuing, though players would be exempt from the draft.

The author goes into much needed detail here to explain this and the resulting two-month delay of "work or fight" with a further delay for the World Series. After the completion of the World Series baseball would essentially be shut down for the duration.

Chapter Eight, "Calibers," is another excellent chapter. Leeke discusses in great detail the decisions players made based on "work or fight." This, however, brought the wrath of fans down on those who made that choice, particularly Joe Jackson. This period was one of intense patriotism and the author recounts instances of fans turning against players who were judged not to be patriotic enough. (As an aside, this reviewer's great-uncle, who played for the Pirates in 1914 and 1915, was accused of being draft dodger for taking a job judged not patriotic enough. In this case he was working as an insurance and real estate agent.).

To me, Chapter Nine, the discussion of the 1918 World Series, is the best in the book. But it is one that raises the most questions. At the risk of asking for the book I want rather than the book the author wrote, I could easily see twice as many pages or even an entire book addressing this quirky series. The World Series began September 4 and was low-scoring throughout, as the Red Sox won their last World Series of the 20th century over the Cubs. What made the Series quirky? The Cubs played in Comiskey Park rather than their own home park. Attendance was very low and the fans appeared disinterested. Because of low revenue the players threatened a strike before the fourth game and a drunken Ban Johnson maudlinly appealed to their patriotism to get them to play. Finally, there were strong indications that the Series was fixed. Gambling was endemic in baseball and allegations have also been made that the 1914 and 1917 World Series were influenced by gamblers. As I said, the author has provided a great chapter but what a fascinating book could be written about the 1918 World Series.

Chapters Ten and Eleven fulfill two goals: first, to discuss in some detail the wartime experiences of many major league players and, second, to talk about what had to be considered the sudden armistice that ended the War on November 11, 1918. The wartime experiences of the players are of particular note. Those interested in more of this should consult Leeke's book *Ballplayers in the Great War*. The author makes no claim that all players in the military were in combat but does a good job showing their variety of assignments. I again cannot help but compare this to the Vietnam War, when no active major leaguer was in combat. The author does a fine job of discussing the heroism of Eddie Grant and his role in the rescue of the "Lost Battalion."

As mentioned, the November 1918 armistice came as a bit of a surprise. Many felt the War would last until at least 1920 and perhaps longer, but the addition of 4,000,000 American troops pushed the balance to the Allies and ended the fight. As Leeke describes, many of the players had been in the military barely one year when they began coming home in the winter of 1918–1919. The author correctly points out that this relatively short time away from the game did not have the negative effect on careers that World War II did when some players were away from the game as many as five seasons.

The epilogue is very good. Leeke points out that the number of players involved in the military was really a small part of the 4,000,000 men in the AEF. He points out that about 250 major league players, about 500 minor league players, and some Negro League players served. This included 27 future Hall of Fame members. Of this number, eight current or former major league players were killed, along with 17 minor league players, and three Negro League players.

It is this reviewer's hope that Leeke's work about baseball and World War I will encourage further and deeper research about several topics. I have already mentioned the 1918 World Series, but the Reach and Spalding Guides have insufficient information about industrial baseball. In sum, this is an excellent book, well researched and well written. I highly recommend it. Unfortunately, in retrospect, this was not the "War to End All Wars."

—Bill Scheeren

Not the League You Might Think

The League That Failed. David Quentin Voigt. Lanham, MD: Scarecrow, 1998, 23 illus., 322 pages.

The League That Failed, by the now late David Voigt and which I once assumed was about the 19th century major league, the American Association (AA, 1882–1891), is actually about the National League (NL). Well, almost. It is in fact about the NL and a portion of its former 19th-century rival, the AA, which consolidated into a single "Big League" (1892–1900). For those nine seasons, this new baseball circuit nearly exclusively referred to as the "National League" was rarely referred to by its official name, the "National League and American Association of Professional Base Ball Clubs." This "Big League" was comprised of the eight NL teams that were left standing at the conclusion of the 1891 season (one year after the collapse of the Players League of 1890) and four surviving clubs from the failed AA. Collectively these clubs remained a twelve-team circuit through 1899 before consolidation into a very durable eight member NL which lasted, unchanged, through the mid–20th century. In this review, I will use "Big League" as the author does, to refer to the book's principle subject.

Voigt begins this work with a very efficient 32 page first chapter, "Prelude to the Big League," on the history of baseball from 1845 up to 1892 (the start of the "Big League"). He draws on what was the most recent understanding of that early history—prior to the book's 1998 publication. Therefore, it is a 95-percent accurate history by current standards. Today, we realize, having the advantage of newer research, that Voigt gives a little too much credit to the NY Knickerbockers in general and Alexander Cartwright specifically as being the originators of the New York Game, ignoring the Knickerbockers' early contemporary clubs and some of Cartwright's fellow club members and other early pioneers. But all in all, Chapter 1 (including,

Figure 1-1, "The Evolving Game: Some rules Changes, 1845–1903," pages 24–25) makes for an essential read for the non-baseball historian and a pleasant refresher for those already versed on the 19th-century game.

From there, Voigt breaks from a traditional chronology by assigning five additional chapters [2–6] to specific aspects of professional baseball's highest level of play for the relevant time period. Those chapters are respectively devoted to: each season's campaign including post season play; the Big League's players; the League's owners; "Auxiliaries and Fans"; and, finally, how the Big League provided the groundwork for what followed—the modern 20th-century dual major league structure.

On beginning to read Chapter 2, "Big League Campaigns 1892–1900," a season by season moderate detailing of regular and post season play, I immediately began to think of *The League That Failed* as a potential reference work for future researchers. It includes on-field results, business dealings, and rule changes of each annual campaign that are readily accessible sources for specific seasons within this span of 19th-century play.

Occasionally, Voigt takes opportunities to break from his discussion of each season to create an "aside," amplifying a specific phenomena occurring during the period such as "The Takeoff of the Baltimore Orioles," "John McGraw and Rowdy Play" and "Syndicate Baseball" (where owners own multiple teams within the same league), to name a few. There are also a few topics that run throughout the chapter, such as the problem of not having an interleague championship series, salary reductions for players and growing on-field violence and dirty play. The chapter closes with the 1900 season and offers a particularly detailed account of the Big League's consolidation from twelve teams to eight, subsequently allowing the NL to not only become more competitive but to also escape the grip of syndicate baseball that was an encroaching ownership model within the Big League.

Chapter 3, "The Big Leaguers," provides much more than the chapter title suggests. Yes, Voigt takes the time to highlight many of the prominent players of the decade, including the use of several charts detailing individual performance categories, players from the decade who later became Hall of Fame selections, and players whom Voigt termed "Passovers" who might still be, in his opinion, Hall of Fame worthy (foreshadowing SABR's Overlooked 19th Century Baseball Legends Project by a decade). But he also delves into salary structures and resistance to these structures, and rules governing player behavior on and off the field. He additionally touches on the effects on game attendance resulting from the economic panic of 1893 and the Spanish American War.

The real meat in this chapter, however, is Voigt's discussions of how the evolution of hitting, pitching and fielding during the decade was an essential bridge from everything that came before it to the game that is so familiar to us today. He presents revealing statistics and makes a very convincing argument that the 1893 adoption of the modern pitching distance, the steady improvement of fielding gloves, and several rule changes all combined to turn baseball into its recognizable modern version.

For good measure, Voigt discusses here the lives of Big Leaguers on and off the field both during and after their careers and touches of issues that are often overlooked such as policies and treatment surrounding injuries, off season and post playing careers, and education levels. He provides a number of anecdotes about how some players' lives turned out to be successful and others' tragic, truly humanizing what, otherwise, are often just names in an encyclopedia or modern data base today.

Chapter 4, "Big League Tycoons," is a true reflection of not only how the triumphant Big League owners (survivors of previous "baseball wars") viewed themselves, but how they were described in the press and how the public came to view them. The frequency of use of the term, "Base Ball Magnate" reached its pinnacle during this decade, but the title also became one of opprobrium, as did monopolies, trusts, syndicates and other terms implying greed and power during the 1890s.

It becomes increasingly obvious to the reader that these magnates, given their egos and drive for greater individual profits, were mostly on a course to self-destruct singularly (as some did) and collectively in their efforts to maintain a successful major league monopoly. Voigt offers many examples of plans and schemes that went awry and the growing public resentment toward the heavy handedness of most owners.

It is a credit to Voigt that he does not turn the chapter into a free-for-all bashing of the magnates. He also sizes up both the economic and social factors of the decade that played a significant role in the Big League's struggle and eventual failure. Most history savvy readers will immediately recognize the Panic of 1893 and the Spanish American War as reasons for there being a negative impact on public interest and game attendance, however, the author also details the rise of competing spectator and participation sports and other new recreations and entertainments that were being pursued by the decade's more leisure conscious population.

For the owners, it was a league that started in debt and ended that way, with few real money-making seasons. Ironically, the most profitable clubs were not necessarily the best teams or ones from the largest cities.

In Chapter 5, titled, "Big League Auxiliaries and Fans," Voigt presents his well-documented observations about the rise and development of baseball's bench managers and the plight of baseball's umpires through statistical data, in contemporary newspaper reports, and official league correspondence.

In regard to the shift in prominence from team captains to bench mangers in civilian clothes, the author points out the impact of the 1891 rule allowing for unlimited substitutions as a key factor. Voigt contends, this rule was the cause of non-playing managers becoming the chief on-field decision makers and being held more responsible for their teams' success or failings. He offers interesting career demographics on the pool of individuals who managed at the time, including several player-mangers. In addition to providing a well-presented analysis of how managers faired in terms of success or failure, Voigt summarizes the managerial careers of the most prominent, although, not necessarily the most successful mangers, of the Big League decade.

Here also lies the discussion of umpiring and umpires of the period—statistically the worst time for them in baseball's long history—by virtue of the large number of persons called upon to umpire across the Big League's nine seasons, coupled with the brevity of most of those "careers." Voigt describes the general plight of major league umpires, with the 1897 season becoming particularly extreme in this regard. Combined with his statistical analysis and characterization of umpiring in the 1890s, there is an abundance of umpiring anecdotes bordering on an "R" (Restricted) rating for "GV" (Graphic Violence).

Another, topic that Voigt includes in this next to final chapter is the baseball press. Although there is perhaps much more that could have been stated here, there is ample discussion of the conflict faced by baseball writers of the period; on one hand, their love of the game and on the other hand, writing about magnate-driven baseball filled with on field violence, dirty play, umpire baiting and a dwindling and more abusive fan base. Although, there were some writers who survived the period to reached acclaim in their chosen profession, most others became frustrated and demoralized and left the baseball reporting world.

The chapter wraps up with discussions centered around the fans, the fan base, and ball parks. Voigt gives short shrift to the ball park discussion, mainly sticking to park capacities, wooden ball parks prone to fires, and the reluctance of the magnates to invest in larger and safer structures, Voigt offers an acceptable rationale, given the larger economic conditions of the times.

As for the fans, much of what Voigt offers this late in the book is somewhat redundant to factors and descriptions he offers in previous chapters. He does present here in greater detail, however, the socio-economic conditions of the period, population demographics, household income data, and other factors all impacting negatively upon the Big League's chances for success, despite its major league monopoly.

The author concludes the book with a brief chapter fittingly titled, "Beyond the Big League," which gives a more than adequate account of how the Big League lost its major league monopoly, eventually giving way to the modern duopoly of the National League/American League structure. Voigt also offers evidence of an emerging but unsuccessful attempt from the long defunct AA to reconstitute itself as a major league rival of the NL at the same time that the AL was progressing with the identical goal in mind.

I found Voigt's discussion of this turn of the 20th-century attempt by the AA to re-establish itself as a major league most interesting, whetting this reader's appetite to learn more about this now obscure chapter in the struggle of league dominance. This observation in turn leads to my greatest, though not severe, criticism: *The League That Failed* contains no direct citation notes. The author does provide an extensive appendix offering a chapter by chapter detailed list of "primary" and "secondary" sources mostly comprised of books and articles, and to a lesser extent, annual baseball guides, sporting weeklies and contemporary newspapers, all by title only. Now, to satisfy my newly acquired appetite to learn more about that aborted AA attempt to rise again, I will have to work for my supper. Maybe that's not a bad thing—after all, David Q. Voigt was primarily an educator and it is an educator's principle goal to inspire learning in his students.

I recommend this book particularly to readers who have at least a basic knowledge of 19th century baseball history.

—Peter Mancuso

About the Contributors

James E. **Brunson** III is an art historian who specializes in American modernism. His articles have been published in *NINE*, and *Base Ball*. He is the author of *The Early Image of Black Baseball* (2009) and the forthcoming *Black Baseball: 1858–1900*. He is retired from Northern Illinois University.

Alan **Cohen** has been a member of the Society for American Baseball Research since 2011, serves as vice president–treasurer of the Connecticut Smoky Joe Wood Chapter, and is the datacaster (stringer) for the Hartford Yard Goats. He has written more than 35 biographies for SABR's Bio-Project, and has contributed to several SABR books.

Robert K. **Fitts** is the award-winning author of four books on Japanese baseball. His articles have appeared in numerous magazines and websites, including *Nine, The Baseball Research Journal*, the *National Pastime, Sports Collectors Digest,* and on MLB.com.

Thomas W. **Gilbert** is the author of numerous baseball books, including *Roberto Clemente* and *Playing First*. A long-time resident of Greenpoint, Brooklyn, he is active in local politics and lives on the site of the 1850s playing grounds of the Eckford Base Ball Club.

Richard **Hershberger** is a leading fact-finder in the field. His research interests include the social and organizational history of U.S. baseball from the eighteenth century to 1880. He is a regular contributor to *Base Ball* and has a forthcoming book on the evolution of the rules of baseball.

Steve **Hochstadt** is an emeritus professor of history at Illinois College. He earned a Ph.D. in history at Brown University, taught 27 years at Bates College and 10 years at Illinois College. He has published books on migration in Germany, the Holocaust, Jewish refugees in Shanghai, and Illinois College history.

About the Contributors

Bill **Lamb** is the editor of *The Inside Game,* the quarterly newsletter for the SABR Deadball Era Committtee, and the author of *Black Sox in the Courtroom*. A retired New Jersey prosecutor, he lives in Meredith, New Hampshire.

Peter **Mancuso** chairs SABR's Nineteenth Century Committee. While his research has been most drawn to Staten Islanders associated with the 19th-century major leagues, he seeks opportunities to promote the study of all of 19th-century baseball.

Justin **Mckinney** is an archivist and baseball historian based in Ottawa, Ontario, Canada. He has been an active member of the SABR Biographical Research and Pictorial History Committees. He writes about baseball history online at his blog, http:/medium.com/@baseballobscura, and is in the early stages of writing a book on the Union Association.

John **McMurray** is chair of SABR's Deadball Era Committee and its Oral History Committee. In 2016, he received the SABR Analytics Conference Research Award for Historical Analysis/Commentary. His baseball writing has been published in the *New York Times, The Baseball Research Journal, Baseball Digest,* and other publications.

Eric **Miklich** is the historian of the Vintage Base Ball Association and coauthor, with David Nemec, of *Forfeits and Successfully Protested Games in Major League Baseball.* He lives in North Babylon, New York.

Peter **Morris** is a two-time winner of the Seymour Medal for best baseball book of the year and was an inaugural winner of the Henry Chadwick Award for lifetime achievement in baseball research. A former national and international Scrabble champion, he lives in Haslett, Michigan

Gary **Sarnoff** is the author of two books, *The Wrecking Crew of '33* and *The First Yankees Dynasty.* He has presented his research at both the SABR national convention and the Jerry Malloy Negro League Conference. He lives in Arlington, Virginia.

Bill **Scheeren** is a retired educator and Vietnam veteran. He holds a Ph.D. from the University of Pittsburgh in information science. He is the author of three college textbooks and is an adjunct instructor at both the University of Phoenix and St. Vincent College in Latrobe, Pennsylvania.

James Brandon **Terry** graduated from high school in Cedar Bluff, Alabama, where he played football and threw the shot. He graduated from Illinois College in 2016 with a BA in history. He works in Clarksville, Tennessee, and hopes to become a history teacher.

About the Contributors

Bob **Tholkes** is a past contributor to *Base Ball,* as well as to a number of SABR publications. He is also a charter member of the society's Halsey Hall Chapter (Minnesota) and editor of its Origins Committee newsletter. He resides in Minneapolis.

John **Thorn** is the official historian of Major League Baseball, as well as the founding editor of *Base Ball*. He has written *The Hidden Game of Baseball* (with Pete Palmer), *Baseball in the Garden of Eden* and, since 1974, many other books.

Steve **West**'s love of math attracted him to baseball when it arrived in his native New Zealand via ESPN in 1990. He moved to Dallas in 1998, where he also fell in love with the Rangers. He joined the Society for American Baseball Research in 2006 and has written a number of biographies for the SABR Bio-Project. He is editing a SABR book on the 1972 Rangers.

Index

Numbers in **_bold italics_** indicate pages with illustrations

Abe, Isoo 141, **_142_**, 143–144, 146, 156–157
Adams, Doc (Dr. Daniel L.) 70–**_72_**, 74, 76, 78, 82
admission fees 84, 87, 89–92
Alma College 86
Amateurism 84, 95, 100
American National Game of Base Ball 21, **_22_**, 23, 27, 30
Anderson, John 17n12
Anderson (Indiana) club 52
Anson, Cap 134
Antle, T.P. 107, 116n19
Armour, Bill 55
Atlantic Base Ball Club of Brooklyn (Atlantics) 21, 24–**_25_**, 28–35, 37, 40–44, 79
attendance 90, 92
Aurora (Illinois) club 50

Baker, Frank 1, 10–**_14_**
Baldwin, Kid 64, 69n29
Ball, David 63, 68n20
Ball, Neal 11–14, 20n76
The Ballplayers' Chronicle 125
Baltic (New York) club 32
Baseball in the Garden of Eden 23
Baseball Magazine 9, 15, 19n55
Baseball Writers Association of America 6
Battle Creek (Michigan) Crickets 56
Beecher, Henry Ward 77
Bell, Dr. William H. 79–**_80_**, 82
Bement, George W. 53
Benefit match 90–91
Bennett, Charlie 2
Bessolo, Michael Angelo 139
Biddle, John 135
Birch, Frank Lincoln 106
Birmingham, Joe 2, 11–14, 20n76
Blackburn College 105
Blanding, Fred 13–14, 20n76
Blue Grass League 56
Bogart, Henry 77
Bond, Sterling Price 118n56
boxing 70, 73–75
Bradley, Bill 17n12

Brainard, Rev. 67
Bromwell, Col. 135
Brooklyn Daily Eagle 77–78
Brooklyn Grays 63
Broome, Isaac 167–189
Brown, Bedford 106, 117n43
Brown, George W. 103, 117n28
Brown, John 53
Burns, Tommy 56
Butcher, Hank 13–14

Cammeyer, William 88–89, 91
Canadian League 46
Capitoline grounds 42
Capps, Edward 107, 110, 112, 118n53
Caray, Harry 139
Carroll Park (Brooklyn) 77–79
Castle, Dr. Marion 5, 17n20/24
Central Association 57
Central League 51–53
Chadwick, Sir Edwin 73
Chadwick, Henry 31, 71–72, 125
Chance, Frank 209–10
Chandler, "Line" 100, 115n8
Chapman, Dr. George W. 5, 17n24
Chapman, John 42
Charter Oak Base Ball Club of Brooklyn 32–33, 35
Chase, Hal 1–2, 11, 13–14, 16n6
Chicago Orphans 50
Chicago Tribune 15
Cincinnati Commercial Gazette 61, 63
Cincinnati Enquirer 50, 61, 63
Cincinnati Post 50, 63
Cincinnati Reds 46, 50, 59–60, 63
Clarke, Nig 55
Cleveland Naps 1–7, **_10_**–13
Cleveland Plain Dealer 10
Cobb, Ty 1–4, 7, 9–14, 17n19, 19n66, 20n76
Cocash, Joseph 54–55
College baseball 101
College of Physicians and Surgeons (CPS) 71–72, 77
Collins, Eddie 1, 10–14

Index

Columbus Browns 60
Comiskey, Charles 9
Commercialism 89
Concord (NH) Marine 51
Corkhill, Pop 63–64
Cove, Edward 77
Crampton, Rufus 102–103
Crawford, Sam 2, 10–14, 17n19, 55
Creighton, Jim 21, *23*, *24*, 26, *27*–28, 31–35, 38, 40, 43–45, *81*
Crosby Street Gymnasium 75
Cuppy, Nig 63
Currier & Ives 21, 24, 26, 29

Daily, One Arm 63
Dalbey, James William 117n44
Davis, James Whyte 78
Dayton (Ohio) *News* 52–53
Dayton (Ohio) Veterans 52–53
Decatur (Illinois) Commodores 51
Demilt, Samuel 74
Demilt, William W. 74
Demorest's New-York Illustrated News *22*
Detroit All Professional (baseball club) 55
Detroit Athletics 47–48, 51–52
Detroit Free Press 47, 52, 54–55
Detroit Independents (baseball club) 51
Detroit Wheelman (baseball club) 51
Dockney, Patsy 86
Dodge, Dr. Daniel Albert 78
Donovan, Wild Bill 55
Drainage 93
Drebinger, John 20n84
Dunaway, Allen Gilbert 106, 108, 118n48

Eager, Dr. William B. 72
Eagle Base Ball Club (New York) 33
Easterly, Ted 13–14
Eastern League 53
Ebbets, Charles 138
Eckford Base Ball Club of Brooklyn (Eckfords) 24, *25*, 31–33, 35–38, 40–44, 79, 81–83
Eckfords (Brooklyn amateur club) 160, 1653n2
Eloise Hospital 57
Elysian Fields 21, 29
Empire Base Ball Club of New York 32, 34–35
English, Nathaniel 119n73
Enterprise Base Ball Club (NY) 37
Equity Base Ball Club (NJ) 35
Esculpians (Brooklyn amateur club) 77
Excelsior Base Ball Club of Brooklyn (Excelsiors) 21, 23, 28, *29*, 30, 32–33, 35–38, 40–44, 79, 81, 121, 123
Excelsior Club (Baltimore) 34–35
Exercise Base Ball Club (Brooklyn) 36–38

Famous Krause Juniors 54
Fashion Course games (1858) 87, 90
Fences 87–88
Fitzgerald, Thomas 86–87
Ford, Russ 1, 13–14
Fox, Bill 50
Frank Leslie's Illustrated Newspaper 23–24, *30*
Frazee, Harry 213
Fuller, William 75

Galbreth, Rush Denny 119n68
Galvin, Pud 66
Ganley, Bob 132, 136
Gardner's Saloon 66
Garvey, J.P. 10–11, 13, 15
Gibson, Preston 133, 135–137
The Glory of Their Times 4, 17n17
Gorman, Arthur P. 122–123
Gotham Base Ball Club (NY) 33, 35, 75
Grand Rapids (Michigan) Orphans 52–53
Grand Rapids (Michigan) *Press* 52, 55–56
Graney, Jack *10*–14
Grant, Eddie 2014
Green, Paul 16n3
Gregg, Vean 6
Griffith, Clark 134, 215
Griggs, Art 12
Grounds 88–89, 92–93
gymnastics 70, 74–75, 77

Hamilton Base Ball Club (Brooklyn) 37
Hand, Henry William 106, 118n48
Hannegan, Bernard 35
Harlem Base Ball Club (NY) 32
Hart, Jim 50
Hassett (umpire) 51
Hawley, Madame Beaujeu 77
Helf, Hank 139
Henderson, Hardie 64
Hickman, Piano Legs 63
Hill Cemetery 67
Hines, Paul 133–135
Hollington, Rev. Richard D. 18n42
Home Run Polka 129
Hudson River Base Ball Club (Newburgh, NY) 37
Hulswitt, Rudy 4
Husman, John 4, 15, 17n19
Hustonm Col.T.L. 213

Illinois College 100, 102–108, 113–114
Independent Base Ball Club 35

Jackson, Joe 6, 11–13
Jacobi, A. 27
James, Bill 16n18
Jennings, Hughie 10, 18n36

INDEX

Johnson, Ban 7, 18*n*35/36
Johnson, Walter 1, 3, 12–13, **14**, ***135–136***
Johnston, Dr. Francis Upton, Sr. 72, 74
Johnston, Harold W. 102–103, 105, 112, 116*n*22
Jones, Col. Frank 122–123
Jones, Dr. Joseph B. 71, 73, 77–82
Jones, Samuel "Golden Rule" 7
Joss, Addie 1–4, **5**, 6–9, 15, 16*n*8/9, 17*n*17/20; baseball columnist 2; death 4–6; funeral 6–8; pitching style 3, stature in game 2–5
Joss, Lillian (widow) 1, 5, 18*n*42
Joss, Norman (son) 1, 18*n*38
Joss, Ruth (daughter) 1, 18*n*38
Joss, Theresa (mother) 5, 18*n*38
Joss, William (father) 1, 18*n*42
journalism 99–100, 102

Kahler, George 12–13
Kalamazoo (Michigan) *Gazette* 47
Keefe, Tim 37
Kiel, John 56
Kisson, Sam 78
Knickerbocker Base Ball Club of New York 32, 35, 71–72, 74–75, **76**–79, 83, 161
Knox College 113
Kono, Atsushi 154–155
Koufax, Sandy 16*n*8
Krause, August 47
Krause, Augusta (nee Grubba) 47
Krause, Charles "Famous" 46–53, ***54***–57; alias Charles McGau 52–**53**; game-fixing by 54–55; post-baseball life 57

Lajoie, Nap 2, 4, 6–7, 13–14, 17*n*19
Lange, Bill 155–156
Larsen, Don 17*n*12
Law, Ruth 138
Lawrence (Massachusetts) Colts 51
Lenhart, E.B. 149
Leever, Sam 3
Leggett, Joe 22, 26–27, 29–30, 33, **76**, 81
Lieb, Frederick G. 3
Lincoln, Abraham 83
Livingston, Paddy 2, 13–14, 20*n*73
Loftus, Tom 50
Longert, Scott H. 2, 5, 17*n*20/24/26/36

Mack, Connie 209–11
Magnolia Club 161
Major League Players: 1871–1900, Volume 2 63, 67
Marion (Ohio) Oilworkers 51
Mason Citys (WVa semipro club) 66–67
Mathewson, Christy 6
McAleer, Jimmy 2, 8, 19*n*51
McBride, Dick 86

McBridge, George 132, 136
McGraw, John 218
McGuire, Jim "Deacon" 7
McPhee, Bid 50
Merkle, Fred 2
Merrifield, Fred 143
Meyers, John Tortes (Chief) 153
Michigan Athletic Association 47
Michigan League 47
Middleport, Ohio 60, 62, 65–67
Midwest baseball 100
Miklich, Eric ***38***
Milan, Clyde 1, 12–14
Miller, Dr. John 72
Montauk Base Ball Club of Bedford (NY) 32
Montgomery, James 77
Morris, Peter 124
Morse, C.L. 103
Mott, Dr. Valentine 73, 77
Mullane, Tony 60, 63
Mutual Base Ball Club of New York (Mutuals) 21, 32–33, 41, 43–44

National Association of Professional Base Ball Players (NAPBB) 71–72, 77, 80, 82
National Base Ball Club (Brooklyn) 32
National Base Ball Club (Washington, D.C) 121–122, 124–125, 128; constitution 128; fight song 127
Navin, Frank 18*n*36
Nemec, David 63, 68*n*24
New Atlantic Nine 42
New England League 51
New York Base Ball Club 71–72
New York Clipper 28, 36–37, 39
The New York Dispensary ***74***
New York Giants 37
New York State tour 121
New York Sunday Mercury 29, 39–40
New York Times 78
New York Tribune 2
Niagara Base Ball Club (Brooklyn) 33
Nicol, Hugh 49, 51
Norton, Frank 124

O'Brien, Peter 24, 34
Ohio and Pennsylvania League 56
Ohio Gas Meter Company 9
Okuma, Shigenobu 143–144
Old Atlantic Nine 42
Olson, Ivy 10–14, 20*n*76
Olympic Club (Philadelphia) 89
Oriental Base Ball Club of Greenpoint (Brooklyn) 36
Otterson, William 78
Ottignon, Charles 77

Base Ball 10

Index

Pabor, Charlie (The Old Woman in the Red Cap) 68n18
Parr, Samuel W. 111, 112, 119n71
Patchen, Sam 34
Patriotism 90
Pearsall, Dr. A.T. 28, 76, 81–83
Pennsylvania Base Ball Club 160–66
Philadelphia Academy of Fine Arts 168
Philadelphia Athletics 64
Phillippe, Deacon 3
Picked Nine (Philadelphia) 34–35
Pike, Lipman 86
Pittsburgh Alleghenies 66
player compensation 84
Players League 204–07
playing rules (1858) 26
Pomeroy, Ohio 66
Popkay, Fred 47, 51
popularity 121
Powers, Mike "Doc" 2
Powers, Phil (grandmother) 62
Powers benefit game 2, 8
Pratt, Tom 42
Professionalism 84–85, 87, 94–96, 120
public health 71–73, 75, 82–83
Putnam Base Ball Club of Brooklyn 32, 35
Pytlak, Frankie 139

Rambler 100, 102–111
Reach, Al 86
Resolute Base Ball Club (Brooklyn) 41
Revenue 85, 91
Reynolds, Charlie 106, 108, 117n42
Reynolds, Tommy **28**
Robinson, Wilbert 138–139
Rockford (Illinois) Red Sox 49, 56
Russell, Ed 34
Ruth, Babe 139

St. George's Cricket Club 35
St. Louis Browns 60–61, 66
San Francisco Examiner 71
Sandusky (Ohio) *Register* 61, 63
Saulspaugh, C.H. 49
Schaefer, Germany 1–2, 9–10, 17n17
Schalk, Ray 139
Schmelz, Gus 61, 63
Schreiner, Louis 66–67, 69n44
Schriver, Pop 134–35
Scott (coroner, Meigs County, Ohio) 67
Sentinel Review (Woodstock, Ontario) 54
Serad, Billy 63
Shea, Mike 63
Shibe Park 2
Sisler, George 9
Smith, Elmer 63
Smith, Syd 12
Smith, Thomas William 118n67

Snyder, Charles "Pop" 134, 135
Somers, Charles (C.W.) 8, 18n36, 19n48
Southern Michigan League 56
Spalding, Albert 127, 165n1
Speaker, Tris 2, 8, 10–11
Sporting Life 49, 61, 65
Sprague, Joe 35, **36**, 37–45
Star Base Ball Club (Brooklyn) 33–35
Steele, Frank 23
Steele, Peggy 23
Stevens, Richard 35
Stovall, George 7, 10–11, 13, 17n12
Street, Charles E. (Gabby) 2, 11–**14**, 131–132, 133, 135–136, 137–139
Street, Gabby *see* Street, Charles E. (Gabby)
Sullivan, Billy 138
Sunday, Billy 7, 9, 18n42
Swalm, Dr. William 78
syndicate baseball 218
Syracuse Stars 60

Terre Haute (Indiana) Hottentots 49, 53, 55
Thirteenth Regiment, New York State Militia 39
Tholkes, Bob 21, 29
Thompson, Sam 56
Thorn, John 126
Thorn, Richard H. 23, 76
Three-I League 49, 51
touring 121
Tremont Grounds (Union of Morrisania Club) 93
Triplett, Norman 119n69
Turner, Terry 11–14
Typographical Cricket Club 162–63

uniforms 125
Union Base Ball Grounds 24, **25**
Union Grounds (Cincinnati) 124
Union of Morrisania Base Ball Club (Bronx) 33, 35, 41, 44

Vanderhoef, T. 33

Waff, Craig 29
Wagner, Honus 3
Walker, George R. ("Tut") 103, 116n24
Wallace, Bobby 1, 11–14
Walsh, Ed 3, 8, 138
Wanstall, Teddy 9
Ward, Arch 15, 20n82
Ward, John Montgomery 204–06
Washington Monument 131, 133–135, 138
Watson, Art 69n32
Watson, Elisha 60
Watson, Martha Jane (née Cotsman) 60
Watson, Mother (Mrs. H.A.) 63
Watson, Mother (Walter L.) 59–60, 61, 63–64,

INDEX

65, 67–69; death 66–67; early life 60–61; major league stats 64–65; nickname 61–63; post-baseball life 66–67
Weigand, Jim 10
Weight, Sam 123
Western Ontario League 54
Wheaton, William 71
Whipple Academy 105, 110
White, Doc 138
Whitney, John 28
Widmer, Bill 64
Williams, Rev. 67
Williamson, Charles H. 24–25
Winchester (Kentucky) Hustlers 56

Wisconsin-Illinois League 56
Wood, Joe 1, 8, 11–12, 14
Woodlawn Base Ball Club (Bronx) 37–38
Woodstock (Ontario) Maroons 54
World Series (1887) 92
Wright, George 123
Wright, Harry 90, 123, 125
Wycoff, Van Brunt 78

Young, Cy 1–2, 6–7, 9, 11–12, 18n38
Young, Nick 191, 201n2
Youngstown (Ohio) Oil Works 56

Zanesville (Ohio) Kickapoos 60–61, 65–66

www.ingramcontent.com/pod-product-compliance
Lightning Source LLC
Chambersburg PA
CBHW032049300426
44116CB00007B/662